PRAISE FOR *THE SCIENCE OF THE GOOD SAMARITAN*

In an era when the proliferation of social media gives greater awareness of and access to the needs of the people we get to do life with, it is stunning to watch us descend into cyber shouting matches. But this is why I cannot think of a timelier book than *The Science of the Good Samaritan*, which lovingly reminds us of the biblical call to love our neighbors tangibly and to right the wrongs that are within our power to rectify.

Nona Jones, tech executive, speaker, and author of *Killing Comparison*

When Jesus wanted to introduce folks to his way of life through neighbor love, he told a story that reflected his own time and place—the parable of the Good Samaritan. Emily Smith is a gifted storyteller who has found a compelling way to capture the heart of this story for our day. This book is a gift.

Jonathan Wilson-Hartgrove, author of *Reconstructing the Gospel* and assistant director for partnerships and fellowships at Yale University's Center for Public Theology and Public Policy

A courageous Christian and brilliant scientist, Dr. Emily Smith is willing to tell us the truth, no matter the cost. She takes the reader on a powerful journey of Christian witness during a global pandemic that compels us toward solidarity with the poor, the hungry, and the sick as an expression of love for our neighbors. She is an expert on mercy and inspires us to be the same.

Jeremy K. Everett, executive director, Baylor Collaborative on Hunger and Poverty, and author of *I Was Hungry*

A timely and absolutely crucial work that defines, refocuses, and humanizes what it means to be a good neighbor—a goal we all need to strive for in our increasingly challenging landscape. It's the only way to move toward a healthier, more resilient society.

Katelyn Jetelina, MPH, PhD, epidemiologist and publisher, Your Local Epidemiologist

An excellent and much-needed exploration of the moral imperative of facing up to the realities of widespread inequalities and our shared histories as a way of being devoted to service to our neighbors and communities. In this book, Dr. Emily Smith makes a passionate and persuasive case for dismantling inequality.

Dipo Faloyin, author of *Africa Is Not a Country*

When Jesus was asked, "Who is my neighbor?" he responded with one of his most famous parables. In her inspiring first book, Dr. Emily Smith reflects on what the parable of the good Samaritan means in the twenty-first century. Using science and stories, epidemiology and exposition, she explores what it means to center our neighbor, what that centering can cost, and the courage it takes to do it. This compelling book asks all of us to examine how we can be better neighbors.

Dr. Mark G. Shrime, author of *Solving for Why*

Addressing global health inequities lives in a fragile space between understanding the science and history that drive health inequities and the faith that can support us to help make a more equitable world. It is from this place that Dr. Emily Smith writes a fascinating account of her own journey. She shares what "thinking bigger" about loving your neighbor really means through both epidemiology and faith lenses. She writes with a voice that is her own—authentic, friendly, insightful, courageous, and full of lessons learned from her own life experiences. Dr. Smith's journey from her own kitchen table to some of the most challenging areas of the world will inspire your own path to add meaning to your life through loving your neighbors.

Henry E. Rice, MD, co-director, Duke Center for Global Surgery and Health Equity; professor of surgery, pediatrics, and global health, Duke University School of Medicine, Duke Global Health Institute

The Covid-19 pandemic taught us many lessons applicable to future global health threats, but perhaps the overwhelming one was the harm caused by inequities in access to healthcare, non-pharmaceutical interventions, and, of course, vaccines and essential medicines. There were no shortages of inequalities based on income, race, or even political affiliations that produced devastating health outcomes. Dr. Emily Smith reminds us of the importance of kindness and compassion in addressing health inequities, as well as of the vital but often underappreciated role of religion as a healing force. She provides important guidance for facing future pandemic and other health threats.

Peter Hotez, MD, PhD, DSc (hon), FASTMH, FAAP, dean, National School of Tropical Medicine, Baylor College of Medicine; co-director, Texas Children's Hospital Center for Vaccine Development

Why do well-meaning people look away when they could be Good Samaritans? If we continue to walk by and ignore the plight of our fellow humans, can we survive as humankind? Dr. Emily Smith tackles these urgent questions in this timely book. She gets at the heart of what it means to be a good neighbor and what it will take to walk the path of solidarity and allyship. The book is a powerful reminder that we all sink or swim together. As Dr Smith eloquently declares, we need a world of people who will not walk by. Our collective future depends on it.

Professor Madhukar Pai, Canada research chair in epidemiology and global health, McGill University, Montreal

Dr. Emily Smith reminds us that most people in our global community live on the margins—they are poor and overlooked and have limited access to healthcare and basic human rights. She uses her own faith journey to explore the complex, underlying issues contributing to this problem. She challenges our thinking and encourages us to use our unique gifts to make a positive difference. As a missionary surgeon working among marginalized populations, I can say confidently that Dr. Smith gets it. This is a must-read for those asking how they can use their skills to make a difference.

Dr. Paul (MD) and Jennifer (RN) Osteen, associate pastor, Lakewood Church, and missionary surgeon

Emily Smith offers a fresh hermeneutic for understanding what is perhaps the most important story of the Bible—the parable of the Good Samaritan. With a new vocabulary for rethinking how to love our neighbor, she challenges us to live fully into the parable for a better, safer world for all.

Jenny Dyer, PhD, founder, The 2030 Collaborative

We desperately need more conversations about faith and public life, and about what it truly means to be a neighbor. Dr. Emily Smith has given us a gift toward that end. She blends her captivating personal story with informative analysis of public health challenges and practical steps for the average person. A crucial and helpful book for anyone genuinely asking the question, "Who is my neighbor?"

Kaitlyn Schiess, author of *The Liturgy of Politics* and *The Ballot and the Bible*

The SCIENCE of the GOOD SAMARITAN

The SCIENCE of the GOOD SAMARITAN

THINKING BIGGER
ABOUT LOVING
OUR NEIGHBORS

DR. EMILY SMITH

ZONDERVAN
BOOKS

ZONDERVAN BOOKS

The Science of the Good Samaritan
Copyright © 2023 by Dr. Emily Smith

Requests for information should be addressed to:
Zondervan, *3900 Sparks Dr. SE, Grand Rapids, Michigan 49546*

Zondervan titles may be purchased in bulk for educational, business, fundraising, or sales promotional use. For information, please email SpecialMarkets@Zondervan.com.

ISBN 978-0-310-36669-0 (softcover)
ISBN 978-0-310-36673-7 (audio)
ISBN 978-0-310-36672-0 (ebook)

Published in association with The Bindery Agency, www.TheBinderyAgency.com.

Cover design: Curt Diepenhorst
Cover illustrations: Yifei Fang / Getty Images; Galyna_P / Shutterstock
Interior photos: Author's personal collection unless otherwise indicated
Interior design: Sara Colley

Printed in the United States of America

23 24 25 26 27 LBC 5 4 3 2 1

In solidarity . . .
To Paul for teaching me the phrase
To Henry for anchoring it
To Edna for empowering it
To my children for embodying it
To my husband for living it

Thou shalt love thy neighbour as thyself.
JESUS (CHRISTIANITY), MARK 12:31 KJV

Health is the greatest of gifts.
THE BUDDHA (BUDDHISM), DHAMMAPADA XV.204

Perform all work carefully, guided by compassion.
LORD KRISHNA (HINDUISM), BHAGAVAD GITA

*Whoever saves the life of a person is as if he has
saved the life of the whole of humankind.*
QURAN 5:32 (ISLAM)

*Whoever saves a life, it is considered
as if he saved an entire world.*
MISHNAH SANHEDRIN 4:9 (JUDAISM)

Love your neighbor. That's just being a good human.
MY KID, AGE NINE

CONTENTS

PART 3: COURAGE

AUTHOR'S NOTE

I am a straight, White, Christian cis woman (pronouns she/her/hers) from the United States of America who graduated from and works in universities in high-income settings. Those descriptors have granted me privileges and advantages, and it is important for me to acknowledge my own social location as we begin this book.

I acknowledge that the land I live on and work in today is the "traditional and ancestral homelands of the Eno, Shakori, Sissipahaw, Occaneechi, other people of Siouan descent, and their descendants, the Occaneechi Band of the Saponi Nation. Although they lived in separate villages and developed distinct identities, they spoke a common Tutelo-Saponi language. In this language, their descendants call them Yésah, which means 'the people.'"[1]

I also acknowledge that I grew up in New Mexico, the traditional lands of the Tiwa Indians (Tigua), Pueblo (Pueblos of Acoma, Cochiti, Isleta, Jemez, Kewa, Laguna, Nambé, Ohkay Owingeh, Picuris, Pojoaque, Sandia, San Felipe, San Ildefonso, Santa Ana, Santa Clara, Taos, Tesuque, Zuni, and Zia), Apache (Fort Sill Apache Tribe, the Jicarilla Apache Nation, the Mescalero Apache Tribe), and Navajo nations, and I honor with gratitude the land itself and the first communities that lived here.

Although I have worked hard to decolonize my work and heart, it is a work in progress.

INTRODUCTION

I'm beginning this introduction as I sit at my kitchen table—the plain, "Anne with an e" kitchen farm table I bought used and then refinished over a few weeks—with freshly picked flowers from my garden in a vase next to me. My table has scratches on it from when my son learned to write his alphabet with his granddad's (my dad's) help, pushing through the paper a little too hard with his fingers as he tried to figure out how to hold his pencil. I love those scratches.

My table isn't fancy or Instagrammable, but it's mine, and it has held conversations, dreams, hearts, and tears. It's also where acquaintances become neighbors, and this is where I'm starting this introduction over. Again. I've written it twice before, and now here I am with a blinking cursor and a blank page.

Aren't you supposed to start a book with a story of triumph or trauma? With something that makes the reader want more? Since I've never written a book before, I don't know. But I thought that's what you were supposed to do. So I wrote an introduction with trauma and drama. Then I wrote one with triumph and restoration. And then I made them each a chapter tucked in between the other stories of triumph and trauma and real life. And I started over again. Because how would I start a conversation if you were sitting here with me at my table?

Certainly not with triumph or trauma. I'd probably start by

serving you coffee in one of my mismatched cups and telling you about this book.

Despite its title, it's not a science book, so I promise not to bore you with, for instance, the Krebs cycle. Besides, I promptly forgot all about it approximately 0.4 seconds after taking the MCAT required for medical school (although I ended up getting a PhD instead, which I'll tell you about later in the book). And it's not really a faith book either, so I promise not to give you the meaning of Hebrew words from the book of Leviticus. It's also not necessarily about how to love our neighbors practically. Sure, you'll find a little bit of that, but some incredible books are already out there helping us do that.

This book will show you that truly being a neighbor goes way beyond simply donating food or money. It's the "and also" way of neighboring. (You'll notice the phrase *and also* a lot in this book, along with my love for nachos, Beyoncé, and *Anne of Green Gables*.) It's about doing the good things like donating food or money *and also* changing our hearts and posture to match those deeds. It's about shifting our perspectives away from just being good enough to living into a life of neighboring that comes as naturally to us as thirst. Not as a to-do list but just being who we are. It's a radical shift in our thinking and worldview that will transform us into being different people.

That brings me to Jesus' parable of the Good Samaritan, found in Luke 10:25–37. And because I believe that story's three themes— *centering*, *cost*, and *courage*—have taught me this life of neighboring, that's how I've organized this book.

Part 1, "Centering," is mainly about changing our mindsets to think like a neighbor. We do this by challenging our current worldview or refocusing our attention and then centering our hearts and minds on what Jesus centered on.

Part 2, "Cost," follows centering, because it will cost us something to center on our neighbors. Think of this as the in-between time. The time between when we center our actions, attention, and heart correctly and then need courage to fully live out that change.

This brings me to part 3—"Courage." This final section is about how we can live as neighbors in word and deed. It will take bravery to do so, but the result is being who I think we were always meant to be—neighbors. I truly believe that the better we center on the right things, the more courage we'll have to be neighbors, despite the cost.

As I mentioned, this isn't just a faith book any more than it's just a science book, but I've written it from my perspective as a Christian as well as an epidemiologist. For those of you from another faith tradition or not of one at all, I sincerely hope you won't feel like I'm preachy or trying to convert anybody—neither of these is my intent. I also don't want to position the Christian faith as the best or only faith. My personal faith has been my starting point, but it doesn't have to be everyone's. I hope you'll see that's the case through the stories of several friends of different faith traditions or none at all. As the quotes in the front of this book reveal, loving our neighbors is universal among the faith traditions. It's just being a good human, as my kid says.

Last, this isn't a book about traveling across an ocean to a different country. In fact, you don't have to go anywhere. Although I can't remember who said it first, I heard this saying at my work: "Local is global, and global is local." To me, that means we're all connected. We saw that in bright bold colors during the COVID-19 pandemic, didn't we? When a virus swept the globe across every continent. This phrase also means you can go all over the world or go nowhere at all to be a neighbor.

I guess I'm trying to say that being a neighbor can be done anywhere by anyone. Some of you are bright-eyed students with dreams of traveling to distant countries for your career. Others of you are reading this book at 3:00 a.m., tending to a sweet baby who won't sleep for more than three and a half minutes. To each of you I say, "Solidarity!" And that each of you is a neighbor by simply being one to people around the world or to your own children, elderly parents, or friends. Being a neighbor happens where we are and with the people around us.

We've all lived through those few years of a deadly and scary pandemic and everything that has meant to our individual lives. So here at the beginning, dear reader, I'm thinking of you, about how we each have a story full of the trauma we've collectively experienced—and likely some triumph too. But now we're questioning what's next.

I think the answer lies in a life of neighboring around a table like the one in my kitchen, but also around another table. A much bigger one. We'll get to that one by the end of the book, I promise. But first pull up a chair and let me get you a cup of coffee. I'm so glad you're here.

Emily

PART I

CENTERING

CHAPTER I

TWO QUESTIONS ASKED

Who is my neighbor?
AN EXPERT IN THE LAW

Who was the neighbor?
JESUS

I know the title of this book has the word *science* in it. And we'll get there, I promise. But I need to start with musical instruments, specifically the cello. You see, I've always loved art and music. I played the piano—still do at times—and I was also part of the percussion section in my high school band, mainly playing the marimba and sometimes the cymbals when I was feeling spicy.

But I've always loved the sound of a cello and how a person can sway back and forth while playing the notes that seem inside them and need to come out. So as a premed student at Wayland Baptist University in the panhandle of Texas, I decided to become a cellist.

Well, kind of. Cellos were expensive to rent, so I figured I would start with a cheaper string instrument and rented a violin.

I took lessons from a great teacher in the university's music department and had grand ambitions of becoming one of those women playing in an orchestra wearing a flowy dress. I think to help inspire me, or maybe to persuade me to switch to a cello because she was also hearing me try to play the horrid "Hot Cross Buns" weekly (and failing miserably), my teacher gave me a CD recording by one of the best cellists in the world—Yo-Yo Ma. I had never heard of him, but I played that CD on repeat at full blast in my dorm room for weeks.

Fast-forward with me. Still in college, I was spending a summer in Saratoga Springs in upstate New York to work as an assistant at a camp for high school kids through Johns Hopkins University.

One weekend, we went to an outdoor symphony concert where you brought your own blanket and dinner and picked a spot to sit on a giant grassy knoll. The symphony played several compositions over an hour or so, and the evening ended with a standing ovation and whistling from the crowd. Then the magic happened, and I need to paint a scene in your mind for the fairy dust to land on you too.

The entire symphony left, and after packing up their dinners and blankets, just about everyone on the grass had left too. I'm not sure why I stayed, but it was probably because it was a gorgeous summer evening with dusk just settling in, and I didn't want to miss the moment and how beautiful it all felt. A friend sat beside me.

Then without any fanfare or introduction, a man walked onto the stage with a cello and started to play the prelude to the Cello Suite No. 1 in G Major by Bach. It was like someone froze all of us with fairy dust, because for the next few minutes, no one—especially me—moved. We were all enamored by the beautiful music. The musician played effortlessly, masterfully, emotionally, perfectly. Then as silently as he appeared on stage, he walked off to thunderous applause from those of us still there.

I looked at my friend with tears in my eyes and asked, "Who was that?"

Her response? "Yo-Yo Ma."

I had found myself at a free concert with the greatest cellist in the world. That night was magical, and I learned there's a difference between *wanting* to be a cellist and *being* one. A difference between being proficient enough to say, "I play the cello," and mastering the instrument. I was so struck by Yo-Yo Ma's effortless playing, which seemed entirely natural to him, like he was doing exactly what he was made to do—creating life with the cello's strings.

I wanted to be a cellist, but I was practicing minimally, only enough to show the practice log to the teacher. I was living, *How much is good enough to be a cellist?* while Yo-Yo Ma was living *being* one. And he'd been living it for years. Wholly, fully, naturally in a way that he could jump onto a stage and play without any sheet music because the notes were in him, completely captivating whoever was listening.

When people ask who's the finest cellist around today, many answer with his name.

———

I start with this experience because I think it illustrates the central point of this book. Lots of us are familiar with Jesus' Good Samaritan story in the tenth chapter of Luke. It's about an injured man who needed help on the side of the road and how two people merely walked by him before a Samaritan man finally stopped to help.

Tucked around this story like two pieces of bread around a

cheese and turkey sandwich are two questions whose distinctions we can miss at first glance. They seem the same on the surface, but they're different in *how* they were asked and *who* asked them. First, an expert in rabbinical law who had just asked Jesus how to live forever and was told to love his neighbor said, "Who *is* my neighbor?" That's the first question, and Jesus responded with the Good Samaritan story before even asking the second question, "Who *was* the neighbor?"

I imagine the first question was asked with a posture of challenge, the speaker sitting back in a comfy chair, arms crossed. It's almost a non-question question. You know, the rhetorical *gotcha* type of question. It was asked by a man who might have been trying to get out of being empathetic. Or compassionate. Or perhaps to preserve his comfortable way of life by asking how much is just enough to be *enough* of a neighbor.

Jesus, however, asked the second question after he told a story about *doing* something, after someone had *been* a neighbor. "Who *was* the neighbor?" is in the past tense, asked *after* something was acted on. This is a question not of a posture but of a lived experience. If the expert in the law was trying to wrangle out of neighboring more than just enough, Jesus was showing us what it looked like to be a neighbor wholly. With compassion and abundance. With a *withness* toward the man needing help.

Do you see the difference in postures? Worldviews? Starting places and actions? If you look closer at the passage, the most important difference is one of centering. At the *center* of both questions is a person in need on the side of the road. In other words, the centering is around someone on the margins. The differentiation between who neighbored and who didn't is around, is centering on, that man. And a Levite and a priest, both of whom symbolized positions of power and privilege at the time, ignored him.

Let's focus on the centering in the story, because I think that holds the key to changing us into *being* a neighbor rather than our simply trying to be good enough.

———

We don't often use the word *centering*. The first time that word made sense to me in an understanding that seeped deep into my bones was the result of a dream I had in high school. I didn't and still don't often have these types of dreams, but this one has stuck with me.

In my dream, a large crowd of religious people in long robes had formed a circle and were looking inward at one another, shouting and raising their hands in frustration. Although I don't remember what the argument was about, I do remember it was about something religious, like debating Scripture or doctrine. Not far from them sat a woman with messy, filthy hair, wearing dirty clothes. She looked poor or sick and was perhaps both. Then Jesus walked into the scene. He looked at the crowd, then immediately moved to sit next to the woman, putting his arm around her. Jesus centered her, not the crowd.

It would be years before I told anyone—my husband—about that dream. And now I'm telling you. That was my first understanding of what *centering* looks like, and it's been in my bones ever since.

Centering is what we give our attention to, what we focus on, what compels us. The Good Samaritan story shows us that centering on our neighbors requires us to shift our attention and focus toward our neighbors. It's a way of *being* rather than *doing*, and Jesus used the question of who was being a neighbor to illustrate this to us.

In practical terms, being a neighbor is going beyond simply doing good acts like giving food to the local food pantry a few times a year or making a monthly donation to an organization that serves orphaned children in countries we never visit. Neighboring means we go beyond those acts of doing to becoming people of being. That means we donate the food and give the money—*and also.*

We take a hard look at how we're spending the rest of our money. We examine what we're giving our attention to on social media or the news to determine if we're centered too much on the loud voices there and miss the voice of Jesus. We choose the people we spend time with wisely, knowing that sometimes racist remarks can seep in to become a part of us too. In other words, we become people of neighboring.

What and who we surround ourselves with and give our attention to highlights what we center around. Is it our neighbors?

————

Telling the Good Samaritan story wasn't the first time Jesus redefined who was supposed to be in the center. In many of his teachings, he centered around and on the typically ignored or overlooked. When his disciples asked him who is the greatest in heaven, Jesus put a child in the middle of them and said faith like a child is the goal.[1]

In another story, Jesus was walking among a huge crowd when he suddenly stopped and asked who had touched him.[2] A woman who was so ill that she'd spent all her money on health care, marking her medically impoverished, stepped forward and said she touched the hem of his garment to try to become healed. She—a woman, and a sick one at that—lived on the margins of society and tried to sneak in, perhaps from shame or embarrassment. But Jesus centered her, stopping the entire crowd around him to find her.

Jesus even showed us neighboring when he preached his first sermon ever in the temple before formally entering his ministry.[3] He could have used the breakout moment to say anything, maybe something to show off his deity. But he used that crucial moment to take the scroll handed to him and harken back to the book of Isaiah, sharing that he had come with good news for the oppressed, the imprisoned, the poor. Choosing in his first sermon to teach about liberation for the captives rather than about military might and political conquest. Even choosing to come into the world as a baby born in a lowly manger to an unmarried woman—a peasant Palestinian—and a carpenter. And the shepherds, one of the most marginalized groups in society at the time, were *the first* to hear about the baby's birth from an explosion of song.[4]

He centered on those in the margins. Other times, he centered lepers, blind people, sick people, untouchable people, distressed people, unreachable people, and women who were ashamed.[5] In what was probably the largest crowd he taught, the huge one up on a hill, he centered the searchers, the end-of-the-ropers, the hungry, the caring—and he called them all "blessed."[6] And in another one of my favorite scenes, Jesus centered the strangers, the refugees, the migrants, those needing a meal and a bed, and he called them those who represented him.[7] The writer of Hebrews called them angels.[8] Even in his last request as he was dying on the cross, Jesus centered his mother and her practical needs to ensure she was going to be taken care of.[9]

Jesus centered the people on the margins with his focus, his attention, and his life. Stopping entire crowds for impoverished women and little children. Even at his death, Jesus chose not to enter Jerusalem the traditional way kings or rulers came into town at the time—through the main gate.[10] Instead, he went through a different gate, and on a donkey. His posture from the beginning was humility, which is why in the book of Philippians the apostle Paul talks about that posture being an example for us.[11] Which brings me once more to the question Jesus asked after telling the Good Samaritan story: Who *was* the neighbor?

———

After two religious leaders walked by the needy person on the side of the road, a Samaritan man stopped, took care of the injured man's medical needs, and then paid for him to stay at a hotel to recuperate. We can see that the *centering* happens around the person in need. In other words, the underlying command to *love thy neighbor* was the central point of Jesus' story, displayed by action and deed, not simply by words.

From the get-go, the command *love thy neighbor* has been like a verb, an action. Not a suggestion, a hashtag, or a bumper sticker. Again, asking who the neighbor was indicates someone in the story had acted like one, and I think Jesus himself was centering the story around the *act* of neighboring.

Have you ever heard the saying that people will know us by our fruit? How we live, how we spend, to whom we listen, how we talk are all the fruit of whatever we've chosen to center on. For the Good Samaritan, caring for the man by bandaging his wounds and paying for his food and lodging was the outward display— the fruit—of his inward centering. His centering on the neighbor showed his heart and his faith. Maybe that's what James meant when he wrote, "Faith by itself, if it is not accompanied by action, is dead."[12]

Many of us who ascribe to the Christian faith heard the Good Samaritan story at Vacation Bible School or Sunday school as little kids. But this mantra of *love thy neighbor* can also be found in the Torah (check out the book of Leviticus), in the Quran, and as the Golden Rule many learn in non-faith settings (I've noted several of these at the beginning of this book). It seems to transcend cultures, borders, and beliefs. But what does it mean *now* to love our neighbor?

So what does it mean to be a modern-day Good Samaritan? To me, it's recognizing who is on the side of the proverbial road in the margins of poverty, health care access, or anything else that *others* people, and then centering on them to do something about it. This also means examining ideas like privilege, power, politics, and people. Ideologies and identities. With humility and courage.

———

No one has shown me what centering looks like more than my friend and colleague, Dr. Edna Adan Ismail. I first learned about Edna when I watched the PBS documentary *Half the Sky* and read the book of the same name as a graduate student in epidemiology. The book, written by Pulitzer Prize–winning journalists Nicholas Kristof and Sheryl WuDunn, told about women around the world "holding up half the sky" with their courageous work. Edna was one of those featured women, and as I watched the documentary, I was inspired by the stories.

Edna was Somaliland's first official midwife, a prime minister's wife, the country's first female cabinet member, and a World Health Organization diplomat for two decades. She's been dubbed the Muslim Mother Teresa, but I would switch that around to say Mother Teresa was the Christian Edna Adan Ismail. Her efforts included working with presidents, the United Nations (UN), the World Health Organization, and becoming part of a UN task force that coined the term *female genital mutilation* in her campaign to stop the practice in the world, including in her own country of Somaliland.

Edna has legendary stories like when she built a hospital in Mogadishu, the capital of Somalia at the time, in the 1970s during the brutal dictatorship years. She was given a plot to build her hospital on, but the land was lower than the surrounding area and needed to be filled in. Lacking money to fund this effort and without help from the government, she followed construction trucks and tractors full of dirt from other projects in her Volkswagen Beetle, honking at the drivers and then leading them to dump their loads onto her site. When Edna retired from the World Health Organization, she took her full pension and used it to build another hospital she'd been dreaming about since she was twelve in Somaliland, her home country that was decimated during the horrendous civil war with Somalia in 1991.

Me with Edna Adan Ismail at the Washington, D.C., conference where I first met her

After earning my master's degree followed by a PhD in epidemiology, with five gap years in between and the birth of two babies, I landed my first job—a dream—at the Duke Global Health Institute. There I began working on research projects related to children needing surgical care, mostly in low-income countries.

At one point, with my mentor, Dr. Henry Rice, I attended a national surgical conference that included a side event focused on global surgery. Toward the middle of the day, a woman with incredible passion in her words took the podium. It had been ten years since I'd learned Edna's story, but I immediately recognized her.

Before I go on, I need to tell you I often feel awkward in social situations. I'm an introvert who giggles when she's nervous, which is often, and I'm definitely an overthinker when it comes to confidently walking up to a legend like Edna. When I'm nervous, my head and voice shake, or I take a photo to have something to do with my hands. So it took a while to persuade my feet they should agree with my heart and go say hi to Edna.

Fumbling my words, I told her how much I admired her work and that I'd followed her story since my early twenties. And because I was nervous, I did what anyone in those situations does—I asked for a selfie, to which she graciously agreed. I still have that photo in my office, along with photos of my other two heroes you'll hear about in this book, and my wide eyes and huge grin still make me laugh.

After returning to my seat and probably overthinking everything I should have said, I got up the courage to talk to her again. Only this time I told her I was an epidemiologist and asked if there was anything I could do to help her. We've been working together ever since.

At age sixty, when she could have simply retired, Edna spent all her money to center on her neighbors in her country. She built that beautiful hospital, complete with solar panels, running water, a laboratory, a maternity ward, and operating theaters along with inpatient and outpatient units. What struck me, though, is *where* she built it.

Do you remember when I told you earlier about the plot of land Edna asked the country's president for to accommodate her hospital? He responded that she could have "that place." *That place* was on the outskirts of town where the Somalia military rounded up dissidents and punished or killed them, a place that's now the communal dump near a camp for more than ten thousand displaced people. Edna called it "dirty, smelly, neglected, and despised," and everyone in town knew what *that place* was.[13]

And also.

It was a place in a very poor area on the outskirts of town where the gruesome statistics of maternal mortality, like hemorrhaging and eclampsia, were lived out with no hospital in sight. In fact, women living in this area would have to walk 2.5 miles to the nearest hospital to get care during labor—over a bridge that often flooded. *That place* was the margins. But *that place* is where Edna built her hospital, one of the best in East Africa. *That place* is where she centered on the margins.

Edna has taught me so much, but the greatest is this lesson of centering. She could have retired comfortably anywhere, but she chose to go where the need was greatest, on the margins, and start there. She centered her money, her time, and even her home as she lives in an apartment on the hospital grounds. She reminds me a lot of the Good Samaritan. She stopped, she acted, and thousands of women's lives have been saved because she did.

And also.

A gal from a small New Mexico town thousands of miles away was inspired to try to do the same with her life.

———

Centering around our neighbors takes the hard work of leaving the large crowds, like those in my dream, and noticing how Jesus centered and who he centered around. It's challenging, because it's about inner heart work that requires us to ask hard questions and allow that way of being to become a part of us. And it requires courage and means that our lives might look different from how we thought they would. But trust me, friends. If we center on the wrong things to just be good enough–type people, we may be satisfied for a time, but I don't think we'll ever be who we were meant to be—neighbors. Centering does that for us.

We can't redo the past, but we can reimagine the future. To do this, however, we must ask the right question. We have to recognize that asking *Who is my neighbor?* is the wrong one—it's the one about being just good enough. The right one is *Am I a neighbor?*

That will determine who we become and help us imagine a future where we no longer avert our eyes and walk by people in need. We stop and we act—and we'll talk in depth about how to do that in the pages to come. But I think that, over time, stopping and acting centers us around our neighbors, and one day this will just be who we are. Asking the right question with the right posture changes us. It did me.

My hope is that at the end of our lives, each of us can answer the question *Who was the neighbor?* with a resounding "I am!"

CHAPTER 2

THE BEGINNING FOR ME

I don't preach a social gospel; I preach the gospel,
period. . . . When people were hungry, Jesus didn't say,
"Now is that political or social?" He said, "I feed you."
Because the good news to a hungry person is bread.
DESMOND TUTU

When I grew up in Lovington, New Mexico, a tiny town in the far southeastern part of the state and eighteen miles from the Texas border, the culture was more like the West Texas culture of rodeos and Southern hospitality and flatlands and dust storms than the pretty landscape and art scene in Taos or Santa Fe. It was oil country, with tumbleweeds as a nuisance, not fancy decor like you see in California.

This was in the 1980s and '90s, and the town had only about nine thousand people. When we got a Sonic Drive-In during my years in our one high school—well, y'all, you would have thought Oprah was giving away cars. Strawberry slushies for the win! Friday nights were for football, school dances at the youth center, and driving slowly down the main drag. And by the main drag, I mean a few blocks, and by driving slowly, I mean *really* slowly, because it was just a few blocks. Not many people know where Lovington is, but to me and lots of my friends, it was everything.

The All About Me book I made in Mrs. Rutledge's class

One of my first memories is from when I was in Mrs. Rutledge's kindergarten class. Imagine six-year-old me, with curly blonde hair I loved to have braided like Jo March's was or up like Anne-with-an-*e* Shirley's was. I was slightly shy, and especially smiley and giggly.

Mrs. Rutledge had asked us to make an art project titled "All About Me," depicting who we were by creating drawings on sheets of construction paper. We drew our families and our hobbies, and what I remember the most is drawing what we wanted to be when we grew up.

And that's where my beginning begins. I drew both a missionary and a singer.

First, I wanted to be the next Sandi Patty. I knew all the words to "Love in Any Language," and I even wrote Sandi a letter when I was eleven-ish. But I also wanted to be a missionary. I was raised in a great home and a great church where my parents led the worship with my mom on the organ, my dad on the piano, and both singing. We often had missionaries speak at the church, and they would stay at our house. Some of my earliest memories are of asking them about their adventures, their lives, their how-I-got-there stories. I was enamored, and from a really early age I knew I wanted to do something like what they were doing in the world.

———

Fast-forward a few years to 1996, the year I started high school. I was still smiley, my hair was still curly-ish, and I still loved learning. I was in Mr. Acosta's science class when one day he started teaching on what I thought was the coolest thing I'd ever heard about. Wait for it . . . DNA. Learning about DNA for the first time was like the Backstreet Boys meeting a Trapper Keeper (the coveted kind with the strong Velcro and double pockets) with a side of slap bracelets. (Remember, we're in the late '90s.) After class, I said to Mr. Acosta something like, "That's the best thing I've ever heard! How can I learn more about it? I love life!"

You get the idea, and the enthusiasm was genuine. Guess what he gave me. Wait for it—a *college* textbook on genetics. Guess what

I did. I read it all. And guess where I read it. On a school bus trip to a football game. Not because I was a cool cheerleader or on the fan bus, but because I was in band. Yes siree, you betcha I was.

I was an overachiever from the beginning. Science or band would be nailing it, but science *and* band? Double nailing it. Nowadays, sitting at Starbucks wearing cute overalls and nerdy glasses from Target—without a prescription—is "in." But being nerdy wasn't nearly as cool in the '90s. Trust me.

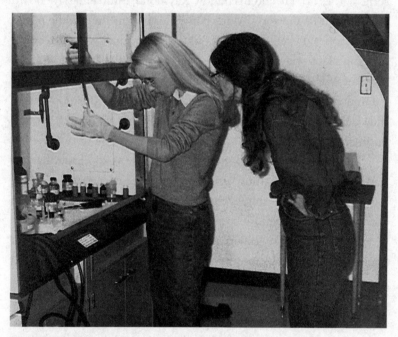

Me with Dr. Strahlendorf at Texas Tech University. I was likely very nervous.

All kidding aside, I was enamored and captivated by all things science, especially the greatest thing ever—DNA. Later that year, probably after I continued to nag him with questions, Mr. Acosta introduced me to his colleague at Texas Tech University, Dr. Jean

Strahlendorf, the first woman scientist I ever met. She had a neuro-physiology lab and asked if I would do my science experiment with her. I felt like I was living a dream with that science experiment.

And can I tell you about my science fair board? I was so proud of it. The previous year I used one of those trifold boards you can buy at Staples. Not this year, fellow science nerds. My dad, who had been a fourth grade and gifted teacher for thirty-plus years, including a year as my own fourth grade teacher, did what awe-some heroes do. He and his buddy, Raymond, built a massive board for me. Out of plywood. With panels hinged in the middle of the trifolds to hold even more data. The final product was six feet tall and four feet wide with plenty of panels to display the glorious pictures of Purkinje neurons I'd hand-laminated in matching back-ground colors to make the scientific method sections pop with a blue border. (Mom, I'm sorry for using all your computer ink and lamination sheets.)

The size and plywood meant the board was so heavy that my dad had to lug that thing around to every science fair I went to. Local, regional, and state competitions. (Dad, thank you, and I'm sorry about your back.) Never once did he complain, though, lug-ging that beauty around while I carried muffins my mom made for the entire team. My parents were awesome in their full support of the science fair—or rather, of me.

My senior year of high school, I—or rather my dad—lugged that behemoth-sized plywood board to the local gym where I was to be judged by a team of administrators and teachers, all of whom I knew since Lovington was a small town. I won the local competi-tion and brought home a huge trophy and a couple of great graphing calculators. Then I went to the regional fair and won there too. Then off went the other participants and I, with one of my favorite teachers, Mrs. Dodd, to the state science fair in Albuquerque, New Mexico.

Patti Hogue

Me with my science board

I knew this was the gateway to my years-long goal of making it to the International Science Fair, which was usually held in another country, and full of kids who loved science and engineering just as much as I did. And I was nervous about it. The year before, I'd barely missed out on the International Science Fair when I didn't failed to make it into the first few spots. So I was on a mission.

Imagine lots of boards of various sizes, some bigger than others like mine, in a huge gym, lined up in several rows on tables and filled with the results of all sorts of experiments. I stood waiting with my great panels displaying microscopic sections of neurons and a huge notebook with all my experiment documentation in case I was asked any questions.

And I waited some more.

Finally, a female judge, of which there were few in the judges group, came up and told me the judges weren't coming to my board because they believed there was no way I could have done this level of work. They also said I looked more like a model than a scientist, probably because I was a girl, five foot ten, and had blonde hair. I'd been disqualified in the judges' minds by my gender and possibly by my height and hair too.

So I ended up losing that year. Again. To boys with not-as-good projects. I was devastated.

The story doesn't end there, though, but I'll spare you the details in the middle. Mrs. Dodd found another science competition I could try instead, and I enrolled a bit apprehensive and a lot insecure. My mom drove me in our blue van to a little town where the first level of the competition was held. And I won. Then we went to the regional competition and the state competition, and I won those too, which took me to the national competition in San Diego, California.

Some of the other competitors had conducted their science experiments at distinguished Ivy League schools like Harvard or with major funding from large pharmaceutical companies, so I felt out of my depth. Eventually, though, I was one of the winners at the Junior National Science and Humanities Symposium, resulting in a huge scholarship, which meant a lot to this gal from a small (and wonderful) town in New Mexico, and a trip to the international competition in London.

By the way, I did end up doing some modeling later in life—modeling statistical multivariate regression models and geospatial analyses to help children in low-income countries.

———

After going to London and then spending a summer at home, I was enrolled as a premed student at Wayland Baptist University. I still deeply wanted to work in the global health field, and I thought the only way I could do that was as a medical doctor. (Also, being a professional singer was no longer in my future.)

I was still smiley, but I was extra smiley after I met my cute, taller-than-me, redheaded, guitar-playing future hubs. We graduated, got married, and moved across the country for his job at a church. I enrolled in a Master of Science in Public Health (MSPH) epidemiology program to increase my chances of getting into medical school. And this is where the story shifts.

I was once again enamored, only not doing something with DNA in medical school or being a missionary like I'd imagined. It was about fully discovering the field of epidemiology.

"Epidemiology" was explained to us graduate school newbies as the distribution and determinants of disease. In other words, what makes a disease spread and who it affects the most. Medicine is about treating individuals, while epidemiology is about treating communities, populations, countries, or groups. And it quickly became clear to me that for nearly every disease, the people most affected by these diseases are those on the margins of society or health care or poverty.

Time after time during the first few classes, I heard about the same theme of margins and poverty and unseen-ness interlaced with poor health and a lack of insurance and food insecurity, all of which were compounded by geography, politics, and systems.

I could tell something was going on in my heart, exactly like what I'd felt in kindergarten, high school, and college. I remember thinking in class that first week, while trying to not cry, *Epidemiology is the story of the Good Samaritan!* It's the science of quantifying a need through data and choosing not to walk by because we can *do something* about it. It's seeing who's on the side of the road. It's noticing. It's stopping. And then it's a reckoning.

Epidemiology might be a lot of data and statistics in spreadsheets others find boring, but to me these data tell a story because they're made up of people. And those people in the margins are the ones Jesus centered on.

I would have been a horrible MD since I cry easily and do not like blood whatsoever. But allowing epidemiology and data and spreadsheets to tell a story of advocacy and justice, love and equity? That was me! I'll tell you more about the rest of my journey in the following chapters, but the reason I needed to start from the beginning, with my missionary dreams and nerdy glasses, is that this book is a fusion of the two things I was initially enamored with— the people of the world and science. And that fusion burst into color when I saw it through the lens of the Good Samaritan story.

Call it equity. Call it faith. I think it's a *both/and* or an *and also*. Like the complementary and enhancing yet opposite sides of a color wheel.

The science of the Good Samaritan.

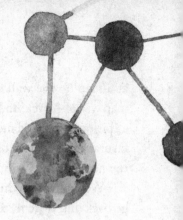

CHAPTER 3

WHAT HISTORY
REVEALS TO US

In the name of God Almighty.

THE GREAT SCRAMBLE, BERLIN, GERMANY, 1885

We can only understand the present by continually
referring to and studying that past . . . when there arise
religious problems, political problems, race problems,
we must always remember that while their solution lies in
the present, their cause and their explanation lie in the past.

W. E. BURGHARDT DUBOIS, "THE BEGINNING

OF SLAVERY," *THE VOICE OF THE NEGRO*, 1905

I n the Name of God Almighty."[1]
There it was, smack-dab in the middle of the page I was
reading. It was a document from 1885 signed by representatives of
fourteen countries who had spent the previous few months looking

at a map on the wall around a large horseshoe-shaped table. The map was of Africa, and the men were partitioning the continent "in a spirit of good and mutual accord, to regulate the conditions most favorable to the development of trade and civilization in Africa." In the name of God Almighty.

We'll return to this table and map a little bit later, but first let's go back in time to trace the historical threads up to this point. Well, before that, let's go to 1980-something, to my childhood in a blue van somewhere on a long stretch of road between New Mexico and California.

When I was a kid, every summer my family traveled from the deserts of eastern New Mexico to California. One of my favorite trips was when we visited the giant sequoia trees. You know, where you all get out of the car and try to hug one of them at the same time. We stood pinky to pinky to see if we could collectively wrap ourselves around the ginormous trunk. We never could, but those pictures remain some of my favorites from that era.

One year, we saw a tree that had fallen over, and you could see its rings in the center. They'd been marked to correspond with certain historical events and years. On the outside of the tree, you really couldn't see its rings, but the tree was a product of each one collectively making the whole.

———

We are also products of "rings" that collectively make a whole. On a superficial level, think of the color of your eyes or the contour of your nose or the arch of your foot. Your eyes and nose and feet are yours, but they likely look a bit like your mom's or grandfather's or cousin's. Have you ever been told you laugh just like your dad or you have your grandmother's eyes? Those physical similarities often extend to personality traits, mannerisms, and behaviors.

We are all products of our history—good and bad, genetic and otherwise.

In the same way, we all live in a world that's a result of our history. Think of where you were born and where you grew up. Then go back in time and think of your parents' lives and upbringing. Go back even further to see where your grandparents came from.

Was your family rich or poor or in between? Were they farmers or politicians or migrants? Did they live in a climate conducive to food production or in a desert where food and water were scarce? Did your family come from "money" or have generational wealth? Did they have proper access to healthy food or did they suffer from malnutrition that affected the in-utero growth of their babies?

When we discover the stories that form the tapestry of our own history, it's not hard to see the threads of individual behaviors and choices mixed in with the threads of societal consequences outside of anyone's control. I guess another way to say all this is that it matters where you were born. Maybe a better way to say it is that it matters *what* you were born *into*. We've all heard the stories about people overcoming dire upbringings with hard work and grit. But in real life those stories are rare. More common are the stories of people who were born into a society and place with poverty or food insecurity or other consequences they could not change.

And they spend a lifetime trying to get out of it.

Or trying to simply survive it.

This is the reality for millions of people in the world. In later chapters, we'll unpack this more to talk about how power, privilege, and poverty are inextricably linked in these stories. But before we peel back those particular onion layers, we need to look at the history of the margins.

First, though, I want to make a quick case for why it's important to look at this history. During the pandemic, when I shared online about systemic racism and structural violence and global health through a historical lens, I received mounds of comments, emails or, ahem, thoughts. Most were to the effect of wanting to move past the past. *Why bring up something you can't change or wasn't your fault?* or *It's not my fault, and we just need to move on.*

If you find yourself asking those questions or becoming frustrated with so much emphasis on the past, that's probably an indication that you haven't seen the tree rings inside. And I'm not throwing shade at you if that's the case. I learned much of this history outside of school, when I was well into my late twenties and early thirties. So come with me as I make a transverse cut through the rings of history to see how the tree of marginalization was formed.

There's a long and fraught history of how empire, religion, and health are linked. Notions of colonial and imperial ambitions from power players, mainly from European descent, have influenced religious ambitions. But the more truthful way to say it is that White privilege—or Western privilege—has been used for religious conquest and land and power grabbing, and sometimes both, in the name of God. The results often carried health consequences—not for the ones in power but for the oppressed and conquered.

If you trace this power play forward through decades, the result is deeper poverty and increased poor health that has become embedded not only in individual genealogies but now in systems. The phrase *the system isn't fair* summarizes how this thread of conquest and power from hundreds of years ago affects people's real lives today, including where, how, and if they live.

To better understand this, let's first go to Rome, one of history's largest, most formidable empires, where attempts to improve health through a global viewpoint—that is, one that defines a health problem that extends beyond national borders—was sadly not really predicated on empathy or compassion. It was motivated by commerce, the market, and trade routes.[2]

Back when Rome was the center of the world's empire, people believed prevention was more important than a cure and recognized the causal link between cleanliness, or not, and good health, or not. In other words, while they believed the gods played a major role in how long people lived, they also understood that preventative measures, such as improving water systems, removing sewage and trash, and overall personal cleanliness improves health.

Remember the cool pictures of Roman aqueducts in your fifth-grade history book? Those were among the first documented public health interventions. One of the aspects I love about the aqueducts is their leveling nature. High-society families with lots of grapes and servants and togas (that's what we saw in those textbooks, right?) could have their homes connected to the water, while the poorer families could still get water from a cistern or well. So clean water was available to all. For free. True equity would have meant that everyone could get it quickly and conveniently when they needed it, but at least it was available to everyone.

Sadly, if we fast-forward through history, at the end of the first century AD, Rome was allocating 30 percent of their massive water supply to farms, gardens, and to privileged class families with villas. But the sewage systems were not linked to the poorest communities.

Now, stay with me here. Yes, Rome improved water systems because they thought it would help improve their citizens' lives. Sounds good, right? But the next part of the story is where it gets a bit wonky. In 272 BC, water transportation was moved underground. Why? Because it would improve public health even more through some special elements found only underground? Maybe in part, but the main motivator was to save time and money, thereby improving efficiency, commerce, and profits.

Do you see the both/and aspect of this development? What *looked* like empathy was actually fraught with overtones of money (greed?), power, and commerce. It reminds me of the first question about the neighbor in the Good Samaritan story—the question about who my neighbor is. It *sounds* like empathy, but it's a cop-out to real caring.

Now, I'm all for efficiency—just ask my kids about my getting-ready-for-school system of lunch packing and bookbag finding. It's a system, semi well oiled, but efficient-ish. What I'm not all for is the *so that* coming next. What I'm not for is efficiency *so that* nations can be powerful, *so that* systems can be accessed only by the privileged few, and *so that* those on the margins are left out. On the flip side, efficiency *so that* all people can have access to clean water, access to an adequate sewage system, and the ability to seek good health? That's an empire I can be a part of. That's a kingdom that sounds a lot like Jesus, doesn't it?

———

Fast-forward to the fifteenth century, when imperial medicine came barreling in. I'm differentiating imperial medicine from medicine in general to denote that this type of medicine was conditioned on conquest or *othering*. I'm also bringing faith into the story—namely, Christianity—since the interplay of empire, conquest, health, and faith overlap in devastating ways.

First, let's talk about Christopher Columbus. The conquest of land led by Columbus was in part motivated by faith. King Ferdinand of Spain was bestowed responsibility from Pope Alexander VI "to bring up Christian faith the peoples who inhabit these islands and the mainland . . . and to send . . . wise, upright, God-fearing [Christian God], and virtuous men who will be capable of instructing the indigenous peoples in good morals and in the Catholic faith,"[3] mixing missions alongside colonial expansion. Perhaps a better way to say it is that now missions and conquest were intertwined, each motivating and empowering the other.

Before 1492, more than one hundred thousand Taino Indians lived on the island of Hispaniola in Haiti. They were a powerful and resourceful people living in largely agrarian communities, and they were preeminent in the development of West Indian culture during this time. After their land was taken by France and Spain during the next hundred years, novel organisms and pathogens were brought to the island, demolishing the health of the Indians and resulting in a complete overtake of this society.[4]

To illustrate the enormity of the loss, let me show you the numbers as an epidemiologist. Although numbers are hard to find, historical accounts estimate that half a million up to a few million Taino Indians lived in Hispaniola before Columbus first landed there in 1492. By 1508, sixteen years later, the numbers had dipped to 60,000, and by 1514, only 32,000 were left.[5] After a smallpox outbreak in 1518 and 1519, the population was reduced to 2,500,[6] declining dramatically thereafter.

Just as we saw in Rome, the desire for wealth or power also contributed to the loss of life and, sadly, was justified through a warped lens of faith. Tzvetan Todorov, a French writer and historical critic, wrote, "To propagate the faith presupposes that the Indians are considered . . . equals (before God). But what if they are unwilling to give their wealth? Then they must be subdued . . . so that it may be taken from them by force; in other words, they are to be placed, from the human perspective this time, in a position of inequality (inferiority)."[7] Nowadays, this would be recognized as taking away a person's agency, personhood, and value and placing an inferior status on them because of it.

———

Now let's fast-forward about one hundred years. If our former example showed us that empire results in othering, the next example shows us how this othering can be weaponized into racism. In the 1600s and 1700s, early European colonizers in West Africa attributed the extremely high death rates they observed from infectious diseases among indigenous populations to the indigenous people having "savage bodies" compared to their own White ones.[8] We can trace this thinking back even further to a Benedictine Monk, Ranulf Higden, who had mapped the world and claimed Africa contained "one-eyed people who used their feet to cover their heads."[9]

From there, we can trace this racism forward over time to people viewing health disparities as the fault of unalterable biology, not due to risk factors outside of biology, such as colonialism or slavery.[10]

Contributing to the defense of slavery was the absurd belief that Black bodies were better suited for tropical climates than White bodies. This belief was, in part, due to poorly designed and racist epidemiological studies. In 1835, the British Empire compared mortality rates of European soldiers stationed either in West Africa or in the United Kingdom.[11] The differences in death rates ranged from eleven in the United Kingdom group to nearly five hundred per one thousand in the West Africa group. The same mortality difference, however, was not observed for soldiers of African descent. After widely distributing these results, it was concluded that persons of African descent had hardier bodies ideally suited for tropical climates and were therefore more "suited for labor" than White bodies—"evidence" that was used to justify the transatlantic slave trade.

In another horrific turn of events the United Nations would describe as one of the worst genocides in history, in southwest Africa or part of Namibia today, 80 percent of the population known as the

Herero were killed by German colonial forces between 1904 and 1908.[12] The people not killed were sent to prisoner camps and often subjected to scientific experiments. The women were forced to collect the skulls of those who had died, and the skulls were then sent back to Germany, where subsequent science experiments were performed to justify the idea that Black people were biologically inferior.[13]

This belief that you could determine a person's intellectual ability by the shape of their skull was termed phrenological research, and thankfully, it's been discredited. Many historians believe that before the discrediting, however, these experiments set the stage for Nazi ideology of the purity of the White race.[14] To date, 80 percent of the remains of the Herero people, others killed in Africa during similar colonial conquests, and thousands of rich African heritage items, such as the beautiful Benin bronze structures or sacred Ethiopian tabots believed to represent the ark of the covenant, have yet to be returned to their home country.[15] The heritage items remain in the country of the colonizers in museums such as the British Museum in London, New York City's Metropolitan Museum of Art, and the Quai Branly in Paris without significant restitution or reparations.[16]

This ring of the marginalization history tree through conquests continued through the 1800s and also included the exchange of foreign pathogens from the colonizers to indigenous communities. In historical terms, the exchange of organisms triggered by conquest was coined "ecological imperialism" by famed historian Alfred Crosby.[17] Millions of indigenous peoples across the Americas were killed by ecological imperialism. The same story played out throughout the Americas due to European conquest and explorations, with the same consequences from pathogens such as tuberculosis, smallpox, and measles.[18]

Most often, millions dying from foreign pathogens that could not be fought off by their immune systems was unintended. Yet that doesn't negate the fact that millions died. The reason? Conquest, power, gold . . . faith. You can trace this throughout the slave trade from West Africa and the blood diamonds mined along similar routes.[19]

I read Adam Hochschild's book *King Leopold's Ghost* at the same time I was taking a class on the history of how HIV and AIDS spread throughout the world and working on my dissertation proposal on HIV among pregnant and breastfeeding women in the Democratic Republic of the Congo.[20] The book had a map summarizing the colonial conquest and enslavement of Africans in the Congo by King Leopold II of Belgium, including the brutal killings and plundering of ten million people. In horrific irony, the king was considered a great humanitarian and a philanthropic monarch by many because he welcomed Christian missionaries to his new colony. But he was also challenged by brave rebel leaders and a few missionaries who fought back.

I was struck by not only the history but also the map, and I saw a similar map in my history class on the spread and distribution of HIV in the early days of the epidemic in the Congo. The trade routes of commerce and conquest from the late 1800s mirrored almost exactly the spread of poverty, HIV, and women's rights issues one hundred years later. It's like I had one of those transparencies we used in math class and laid the map of conquest directly on top of the map of poor health and poverty. It fit—too perfectly. This area of the world was where many slave ships to the Americas ported in the "great river's mouth . . . from the Kingdom of the Kongo."[21]

———

Let's go back to that horseshoe-shaped table and large map on the wall in 1884.

The table was in the Berlin home of the German chancellor, Otto von Bismarck, who feared Germany would be left out of the other countries' plans to parcel out the African continent between themselves. The map was largely inaccurate, drawn by people who had never visited the continent or had seen only the western parts of it used during the slave trade. Nonetheless, the map was large, measuring sixteen feet.

The chancellor had invited men representing fourteen other countries—Britain, France, Germany, Austria, Belgium, Denmark, Spain, the United States, Italy, the Netherlands, Portugal, Russia, Sweden-Norway, and Turkey (also known as the Ottoman Empire). No one from Africa was invited to the meeting, although the Sultan of Zanzibar requested to attend and was denied.

This gathering would be named the Berlin Conference, but it's also more appropriately known as the Great Scramble. In the best account I've read about this meeting, in the book *Africa Is Not a Country*, Dipo Faloyin wrote, "Eighty per cent of Africa was still free when Bismarck rose to stand in front of that map at around 2 p.m. on the first day of the conference. (Within thirty years of that moment, 90 per cent of Africa would be controlled by Europe.)"[22] Although many African countries gained independence in the 1960s, the effects of the haphazard colonial scramble last to this day.

Let me give you an example of how this scramble played out from my own work in Somaliland with Edna Adan Ismail, the woman I first mentioned in chapter 1.

Edna was born in 1937 in Hargeisa, Somaliland. At the Great Scramble fifty-ish years earlier, Somalia was separated into two areas. The northwestern area would be colonized by Britain, known as the British Protectorate, and the southern area containing the current capital of Mogadishu would be colonized by Italy.[23] I will refer to these areas as Somaliland, indicating the northwestern part colonized by Britain, and Somalia, indicating the southern part colonized by Italy and containing Mogadishu. If you've seen the movie *Black Hawk Down*, that's Mogadishu.

Looking at a map of Somalia, you'll likely not see Somaliland indicated since it's not recognized as an independent country. But let me show you where it is. Find Yemen, then go south a bit across the Gulf of Aden, a gorgeous clear-water port used for the majority of imports and exports in that part of the world. The beaches look just like the beaches in Northern California, but they're dotted with colorful fishing boats and women wearing bright hijabs and clothing.

Now go to the area of Somalia between the Gulf of Aden and neighboring Ethiopia. That's Somaliland with the capital city of Hargeisa in the western portion and most of the eastern portion being rural, with nomadic clans and families and acacia trees dotting the landscape. Somaliland is a country rich in heritage, including artifacts from the Silk Road trade, the Ming dynasty in China, and ancient Egypt to name a few, and a gorgeous tapestry of landscapes ranging from red deserts to the majestic Golis Mountains.

In Somaliland, the British rule before 1960 involved building new schools and hospitals and providing military protection while working with the indigenous communities to trade livestock. Edna's grandfather was a successful camel merchant in the country and served with the British in both world wars, and her father, famed and revered in Somaliland, was a doctor. In 1961, Somaliland gained independence when the British left, and most of the qualified health professionals, who were British, also left.

In Somalia, however, the Italians worked to establish a plantation colony through violent measures and would later be aided by the Soviet Union in military efforts during the Cold War.[24] And in 1969, Somalia became intertwined with the Soviet Union and mounted a brutal dictatorship of its people, including in

Somaliland, under a new president, Siad Barre. For nearly twenty years, Somalia committed horrendous human rights atrocities, such as mass executions, bombings, planting land mines, and displacing millions of people, ending in a civil war between 1988 and 1991.[25] During this time, Edna was imprisoned, and several of her family members living in Somaliland were killed in the war.

Today, Somalia continues to experience chronic instability, war, and terrorist activity, while Somaliland has a functioning government and has not had a terrorist attack in fifteen years. The modern-day trajectories of Somalia and Somaliland can be traced back to the colonial era—to the colonizing countries' motivations and ensuing actions. In the case of Britain's approach to Somaliland, it was largely supportive, while Italy's approach to Somalia was that of war and greed. The Great Scramble of 1885, discussed over a large map on the wall and a large table by non-Somali men, continues to impact the countries to this day, including the beautiful people of both Somaliland and Somalia.

———

Let's go back to that horseshoe-shaped table and giant map one more time. In German chancellor Bismarck's opening speech, he reminded the men that Africa would benefit from civilization and Christianity and harkened to the writings of the famed missionary at the time, David Livingstone, which many of the men would surely have known about. The continent was then partitioned with somewhat arbitrary lines, cutting through lands without acknowledging existing tribal territories, clans, or kingdoms.

Dr. Olayemi Akinwumi from Nasarawa State University in Nigeria notes that this conference was the originator of current conflicts in the continent: "In African studies, many of us believe that the foundation for present day crises in Africa was actually laid by the 1884/85 Berlin Conference."[26] These arbitrary borders interrupted existing trade routes and established new colonies that would later become the countries suffering the most from civil war or poverty.[27] It's estimated that one-tenth of all ethnic groups in the continent had their territories split up by the new borders drawn haphazardly at the conference, and civil conflict is 25 percent higher in these areas compared to areas not split.[28]

The final day of the conference—February 26, 1885—was codified by the representatives signing the General Act, with the exception of the delegate from the United States. Over the coming years, nearly every country in present-day Africa was colonized by the European powers, often with military force and horrific atrocities to the indigenous people, in the name of empire and god.[29]

———

This brings me back to how we started this chapter: "In the Name of God Almighty." We are all products of history and of systems, populations, and the communities we live in. When I first started reading these stories that had never been taught to me in school, I noticed it felt uncomfortable to have so many of my thoughts and preconceived ideas challenged. What do we do when we realize there is more to the story than the history we were taught—and that this reality has affected generations of people unequally? What do I do?

I think we have a choice to make on how to respond at that crossroads. We can either listen and learn or remain stuck in a false sense of reality. To me, the latter choice is equivalent to a modern-day "walking by" in our Good Samaritan story. Hearing the history of Edna's life *and* her country's history is when my heart changed, which also changed where my actions were centered. Proximity to others' stories does that to you, doesn't it? It changes us, for the better, because the reality becomes . . . real. We may not be able to right all wrongs throughout history, but we can do our part to right the wrongs of our heart by thinking correctly and then acting accordingly. Good Samaritan–type thinking. In the name of God Almighty.

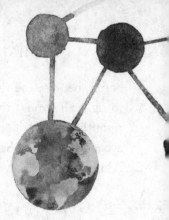

CHAPTER 4

SYSTEMIC RACISM AND LUCY

The poor person does not exist as an inescapable fact of destiny. His or her existence is not politically neutral, and it is not ethically innocent. The poor are a by-product of the system in which we live and for which we are responsible. They are marginalized by our social and cultural world.

FATHER GUSTAVO GUTIÉRREZ

I should have known I would be a researcher when I was in Mrs. Hess's fifth-grade class. One of our assignments was to write a book report using at least five references. Well, sign me up. I loved books, and writing about books was even better. I chose one about Frederick Douglass, and off I went to the library.[1]

I checked out every book I could find on Frederick Douglass and stuffed all of them into my bag. All of them. And then I grabbed my next favorite items in the world: sticky notes and highlighters.

Anyone with me here? Give ya girl some school supplies, and she can go to the moon. I read each book with enthusiasm, marked up sticky notes with quotes to use, and then did it all again.

The assignment needed to be about five pages with, again, at least five references. But your overachiever girl here was not messing around. My final project was fifteen pages long with at least fifteen references. Ahem, that's what I call research. Or nerdy.

Maybe more than research started that day for me, though. Yes, I was learning that my natural inclination, my enjoyment, was for nerd stuff like research. Why did I choose Frederick Douglass, though? I don't remember, but I do remember what I learned.

In 1838, a few years after being caught trying to flee slavery in a canoe and being returned to the Wye House, the plantation where he lived, Mr. Douglass escaped on the Underground Railroad. He rose to be a central figure in the abolition movement, including advising President Abraham Lincoln, and he was a mentor to the formidable journalist, activist, and educator Ida B. Wells.[2]

In his landmark speech in 1852, "What to the Slave Is the Fourth of July?," he strongly wrote about the hypocrisy of White American colonists constructing a new country through slavery after reminding them they'd been colonized themselves under British rule. Toward the end of the speech, which I encourage you to read in its entirety if you haven't, Mr. Douglass says,

> What, to the American slave, is your 4th of July? I answer; a day that reveals to him, more than all other days in the year, the gross injustice and cruelty to which he is the constant victim. To him, your celebration is a sham; your boasted liberty, an unholy license . . . your prayers and hymns, your sermons and thanksgivings, with all your religious parade and solemnity, are, to Him, mere bombast, fraud, deception, impiety, and hypocrisy. . . . There is not a nation on the earth guilty of

practices more shocking and bloody than are the people of the United States, at this very hour.[3]

Those practices he alluded to were referenced earlier in his speech and included the inability to vote or obtain a proper education. And the vast difference in laws against Black men in Virginia subjecting him to death, of which there were seventy-two, versus White men for the same crimes, of which there were two. The examples of racism Mr. Douglass shows us are examples embedded within or by systems. Education, laws, voting systems.

In other words, the racism was structural.

———

The last chapter took us on a historical crash course through modern-ish-day examples of "walking by" in the Good Samaritan story, and those individual walking-bys have collectively coalesced into something bigger. The whole is the sum of those parts. History begets the next, which impacts the next, which is molded into the next. If we don't root out racism and othering and walking-by, they won't root themselves out on their own. They'll be molded into more—like a wound that never heals but spreads sepsis throughout the whole body. It will also start spreading to others. And then to what surrounds the individuals—systems, institutions—embedding racism, othering, and other forms of walking by into them.

When the past predicts the future, when the past impacts the future, when our present systems (social structures, health care, colleges and universities, agencies, government organizations) have built-in symptoms of inequity, these are the fruit of rotten roots. Of racism. Of othering.

This is called *systemic racism*.

Let me explain why it matters and how it plays out in the Good

Samaritan story. The definition of systemic racism found in the *Oxford English Dictionary* is "discrimination or unequal treatment on the basis of membership of a particular racial or ethnic group (typically one that is a minority or *marginalized*), arising from *systems, structures,* or *expectations* that have become *established within* society or an institution" (emphasis mine). Notice that what we're talking about is racism embedded *within* structures. It's when past policies, beliefs, and individuals' actions have taken root in today's societies, social structures, and institutions such as schools, government organizations and agencies, and churches.

———

Let me stop here for a breather. It's really easy at this point in any historical account to say, *Well, it's not like that anymore.* It's easy to acknowledge that what happened in the past was wrong, especially isolated individual acts. It's an entirely different thing to acknowledge that those individual acts became collective and still permeate our world today. So let me give you two examples you may be familiar with, especially after the pandemic, of how individual walking-bys still impact people today and, in fact, have even deepened in their impact—X-rays and oxygen monitors.

X-rays were discovered in 1895 by Wilhelm Conrad Röntgen, a professor of physics in Bavaria who later won a Nobel Prize for the discovery.[4] The innovation of the X-ray machine, which would later be used in hundreds of diagnostic procedures such as mammography and the diagnosis of a broken bone, was largely based on skin and bone thickness.

Do you remember when we talked about the false belief that Black bodies were hardier than White bodies and how that false belief was used to justify slavery? This same belief translated into medical textbooks, such as the 1863 *Introduction to Anthropology,* which read, "The skeleton of the Negro is heavier, the bones thicker and larger in proportion to the muscles than in the European."[5] Radiologists and technicians then used higher radiation exposure during procedures, sometimes nearly double the amount, thinking that darker skin would have some resistance to the X-rays. And those beliefs persisted even deeper into other medical textbooks nearly one hundred years later.[6] In 1959 . . .

Hold up! Read that date again and slowly let it sink in.

In 1959, *An Atlas of Normal Radiographic Anatomy* described the bones of Black people—specifically the skull bones—as "thicker and denser" compared to those of White people.[7] Differences in bone density reporting can be found as late as 1997 in medical literature. Hold up again . . . *1997?* Not until 1968 did the United States Public Health Service's National Center for Radiological Health raise a red flag about these claims.[8]

As epidemiologists, we're trained and then trained some more to measure the primary factor we're looking at (like race), the primary outcome we're evaluating (like bone density), and anything else that could affect that relationship (like nutrition and exercise). We're also trained to ask the right question. The question about Black bodies and White bodies was the wrong one because it was steeped in historical racism, regardless of whether the researchers asking the question knew it. The right question was, *What impacts bone density after taking everything into account?* [9]

The first question is biased because it wrongly assumes Black bodies are denser, while the second question takes out the systemic bias to ask the correct, equitable question. In today's terms, one is conspiracy theory and one is good science. One motivation is upholding a racist belief and one is improving public health—for *all* people.

Now let's look at the second example. In 2020, I bought my first $20 pulse oximeter, which monitors oxygen levels. I hadn't really paid attention to them other than when I took my kids to their well-child checkup visits. But when COVID-19 hit, we were encouraged to have a well-stocked kit at home complete with fever-reducing medicines, hand sanitizer, Lysol (if you could find it on the shelves), masks, and a pulse oximeter. I already had most of these things at home, but the pulse oximeter? I placed an online order for one, just in case.

Not until months later, on an epidemiology collaborator-friend's social media post, did I see an article on racial and ethnic bias in pulse oximetry measurement.[10] This inaccuracy had been reported since the 1990s.[11] Wait, *what?* With a pulse oximeter like the one I'd bought just months ago? Here's what I learned.

We all know we need oxygen to breathe. We also need it flowing in our blood and throughout our bodies for the benefit of our cells, veins, and tissues. Without it, damage to nearly every organ can occur with a result of potential death. Like water and blood, oxygen holds us together, so measuring oxygen holds us together too.

Enter the pulse oximeter to the backdrop of a Beyoncé soundtrack. This little device, introduced in the 1980s, measures blood oxygen levels when you place the device around your fingertip. The pulse oximeter was deemed "the most significant technological advance ever made in monitoring the well-being and safety of patients during anesthesia, recovery, and critical care."[12] (I see you, pulse ox, showing off like a boss during some of the most critical times in a person's life.)

A few years later, however, Dr. Amal Jubran, a research fellow at the time, and Dr. Martin Tobin, an associate professor of pulmonary medicine and critical care, both at the University of Texas Health Science Center in Houston, Texas, noted that pulse oximetry was less accurate in Black patients hospitalized with pneumonia, chronic obstructive pulmonary disease, congestive heart failure, and other conditions requiring close oxygen monitoring compared to White patients with the same conditions. In fact, *two and a half times* less accurate. In other words, pulse oximeters can show false oxygen saturation levels for Black patients compared to White patients. And this can result in dire consequences. Low oxygen saturation can be life-threatening if missed.[13] And during the beginning of the COVID-19 pandemic, it was clear that oxygen monitoring played a major role in monitoring the disease's progression to a more severe form, including the decision whether to intubate the patient.

In 2021, Dr. Ashraf Fawzy, a physician from the Division of Pulmonary and Critical Care Medicine at Johns Hopkins University School of Medicine in Baltimore, Maryland, and his colleagues reported higher rates of hypoxemia, a condition where the blood's oxygen levels are below normal, for Black, Hispanic, and Asian patients compared with White patients.[14]

In addition, and perhaps with greater consequences, this delayed treatment for the patients.[15] According to the US Centers for Disease Control and Prevention guidelines for COVID-19 treatment, blood oxygen thresholds were commonly used as markers for who needed swift therapeutic intervention as well as for a triage mechanism.[16] For example, the use of remdesivir, the treatment for hospitalized patients with COVID-19, or the use of supplemental oxygen, was given to people with a blood oxygen threshold of less than 95 percent. Another major treatment, dexamethasone, was frequently prescribed to patients who needed supplemental oxygen and was based on oxygen measurements from pulse oximetry, among other clinical markers.

Last, overestimating oxygen levels could also lead to discharging patients from the hospital prematurely. In the first few years of the COVID-19 pandemic, one in eleven patients hospitalized were readmitted within two months with respiratory distress, a condition that could be forewarned by accurate pulse oximetry.[17] In some hospitals, the readmission rate was over 50 percent, particularly among underserved communities, Black and Hispanic families, and people living in poverty.

Now come with me to one of the most premier and well-equipped health systems in the world, the Johns Hopkins Health System with hospital sites in Maryland and Washington, D.C. In a peer-review analysis of data collected from 2020 to late 2021 at these hospitals, researchers looked at more than seven thousand patients hospitalized with COVID-19, of which 5 percent were Asian, 39 percent were Black, 18 percent were Hispanic, and 38 percent were White.[18] The oxygen levels of all the patients were recorded, along with what treatments they received and delays in their treatments, and the researchers assessed whether all that differed by race/ethnicity.

They found that blood oxygen levels were overestimated for Asian, Black, and non-Black Hispanic patients compared to White patients. And more Black and Hispanic patients received delayed treatment than White patients due to a delayed *recognition* of their need for treatment *because of the inaccurate oxygen values*.

Read this next part slowly to let it sink in, because the numbers are striking. Thirty-five percent of Black patients and 38 percent of non-Black Hispanic patients received delayed treatment compared to only 20 percent of White patients. *Nearly. Double.* Full stop. We know that in-hospital mortality during the height of the pandemic among Black and Hispanic patients was much higher than White patients and that in-hospital mortality is higher in patients with occult (hidden) hypoxia.

Putting two and two together, it's quite possible that these are linked. A simple pulse oximeter device, created and calibrated and tested years ago in mainly White patients, impacts today's patients in unequal ways.

In order to make the best clinical decision in an emergency, we need accurate knowledge. For all. That hasn't always been the case, and it's disproportionately affected patients of certain racial and ethnic groups. Like the X-ray example, this highlights the reality that individual decisions from decades ago trickle down into the present in collective ways. Decisions on how pulse oximeters are made and *not* made, how the oximeters are calibrated, and more importantly, *who* they aren't calibrated *to* impact individual lives today.

I highly doubt that all radiologists and X-ray technicians from 1895 to 1968 or beyond would call themselves racists. They were doing what they were trained to do with textbooks written by other people from years before. I also highly doubt that makers or users of pulse oximeters would consider themselves part of an oppressive and unjust system that produced and used possibly inaccurate devices. They're most likely unaware of the inaccuracies in the device and are simply doing their jobs with a tool that's been on the market for a long time, passed down from their medicine professors and engineers. But this is a clear example of how individual beliefs, which clearly are racist, became embedded in textbooks and teachings and medical practitioners likely passed them down to their mentees and the following generations, resulting in systemic racism.

May I give you some hope before we go on? Thousands of people are doing the hard and holy work of dismantling racist systems and structures, in big and small ways. Sometimes we think doing the work of loving our neighbors happens only in individual actions. Sometimes, however, it's done in larger, more systemic ways. Let me show you what I mean.

In the 1840s, in Montgomery, Alabama, Dr. James Marion Sims, a founding father of gynecology, arguably the most famous surgeon of the nineteenth century in America, and president of the American Medical Society in the late 1870s, performed experimental procedures on enslaved women without their consent and often without anesthesia.[19] Dr. Bettina Judd, a professor at the University of Washington, who wrote a book on the history of experimentation on enslaved women, noted, "Sims understood enslaved women not to have the same pain threshold as White women. . . . The belief that Black folks, particularly Black women, are . . . impervious to pain has a history."[20]

The procedure that catapulted Dr. Sims to fame was his successful operation for vesicovaginal fistulas, a childbirth complication where a hole develops between a woman's vagina and bladder. The complication leads to constant urinary leakage, odor, and discomfort, and it's been called one of the worst childbirth complications. Surgery is the only treatment. Dr. Sims would later open the first Woman's Hospital in New York City and perform the same operation on White women, but this time with anesthesia.

Although other surgeons had tried to repair the fistulas, they were met with little success until Dr. Sims's groundbreaking work. Along with the successful procedure for fistulas, Dr. Sims would also be credited with the development of vaginal speculums still used in gynecological exams today and referred to as "Sims." However, there is a growing movement to rename this speculum away from "Sims" to "Lucy." Let me tell you why.

Sims operated on dozens of enslaved women without consent or anesthesia, sometimes up to twenty times on a single patient who would be on all fours. We know only the names of three of those patients: Lucy, Anarcha, and Betsey.

Lucy, an eighteen-year-old girl who was enslaved, nearly died after Sims operated on her for postpartum urinary incontinence, and in his autobiography he recorded it took Lucy two or three months to recover.[21] Anarcha, a seventeen-year-old girl, had thirty operations after a traumatic birth and delivery before Sims finally succeeded in his operating method.[22] It had taken four years of experimentation.

Statues were erected in his honor in the Alabama State Capitol in Montgomery, in Philadelphia outside his medical school, and in New York City's Central Park. In 2018, the statue of Dr. Sims perched on a massive stone platform in Central Park was removed after strong activism and replaced with a plaque. The plaque includes the historical accounting of the monument and then ends with three names: Lucy, Anarcha, and Betsey.

If you go to Montgomery, you'll find the statue in the Alabama State Capitol still stands. But you'll also find a striking monument about a mile away.[23] It's called *Mothers of Gynecology* and was created by Michelle Browder,[24] a Black artist and activist, using colorful scrap metal. It features three statues over nine feet tall, one for Lucy, one for Anarcha, and one for Betsey. Lucy wears a tiara created out of the speculum device Sims invented. Anarcha's abdomen is cut out with her womb full of cut glass, and medical instruments are on the ground nearby. In an interview about the monument, Michelle Browder said, "I feel that if you're going to tell the truth about this history, we need to tell it all."[25]

———

Seventy years prior to Dr. Sims's statue coming down in Central Park, another doctor advocated for its removal. He was Dr. John A. Kenney from the Tuskegee Institute named in honor of the Tuskegee horrors.[26] I had never heard of Tuskegee until I was in my twenties as a master's student in epidemiology. In 1932, the United States Public Health Service began a study on the natural history of syphilis, originally called the "Tuskegee Study of Untreated Syphilis in the Negro Male."[27] The study included 399

Black men with syphilis and 201 Black men without it, all mainly sharecroppers from Macon County, Alabama.

The men, however, weren't told they were participating in what was actually an experiment and were never asked to give informed consent. They were told only that their "bad blood" (a local term including a host of sicknesses) was being treated in exchange for free meals, medical exams, and burial insurance. Fast-forward to 1943, eleven years later, when penicillin was widely available as the treatment of choice for syphilis.[28] Participants in the Tuskegee study, however, were never offered the treatment.

The study lasted another twenty-nine years, even without funding and without informing the men about treatment options. By 1972, when the study finally was terminated, twenty-eight men had died directly from syphilis, one hundred had died from related complications, forty of the men's wives had been infected, and nineteen children had been born with congenital syphilis.[29]

In 1997, President Bill Clinton formally apologized on behalf of the United States for the study, citing it shameful and racist.[30] In attendance at the White House that day were eight survivors or family representatives. The survivors were Mr. Herman Shaw, who was almost ninety-five years old; Mr. Charlie Pollard; Mr. Carter Howard; Mr. Fred Simmons, who was about 110 years old; and Mr. Frederick Moss. Mr. Sam Doner was represented by his daughter; Mr. Ernest Hendon was represented by his brother; and Mr. George Key was represented by his grandson.

───

Let's go back to Frederick Douglass. One hundred sixty-nine years after he made his now-famous speech referenced at the beginning of this chapter, his speech was reread.[31] But this time it wasn't Mr. Douglass who spoke; it was his descendants.

Although we can't fix the past, we can tell the truth of it. This includes telling the truth about systems and structures founded and built on inequities. And then working toward a better future just like Michelle Browder did in Alabama and President Clinton did for the men in the Tuskegee trials. For Anarcha, Betsey, Herman, Charlie, Carter, Fred, Frederick, Sam, Ernest, and George. For those unnamed.

And for Lucy.

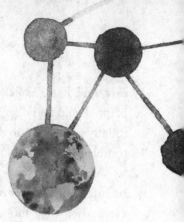

CHAPTER 5

GETTING ALONG ISN'T THE GOAL

They have treated the wound of my people carelessly,
saying, "Peace, Peace,"
when there is no peace.
JEREMIAH 6:14 NRSVUE

I grew up with cotton fields, oil pumpjacks, and John Deere tractors. Banjos, fiddles, cardinals, and trains. A strong lineage of Baptist and Methodist deacons and church attenders on both sides. One set of grandparents grew up in dirt-floored homes near Lubbock, Texas, in the panhandle of the state. Originally known as the Llano Estacado, this was the land of the Teya people before their conquest by the Spaniards in 1541. Later, this indigenous group would be called the Apaches, who moved into New Mexico and Oklahoma after being pushed out of their territory.

This part of West Texas has tumbleweeds the size of small

cars, and I still chuckle when I see a massive tumbleweed spray-painted gold and displayed as a fancy schmancy art piece in a store, usually with a hundred-dollar price tag. I should have gone into the tumbleweed business instead of science!

My grandparents told stories of growing up with dirt storms so intense that everything in the house was covered with dust even when they hung bedsheets doused in water or stuffed wet towels or rags in every nook and cranny of windowsills and doors and cracks in the floors. My grandmother told me about the hard work of cleaning after those storms. She also told me about putting eggs at the bottom of the bed so they wouldn't freeze in the cold winters.

This set of grandparents lived on a cotton farm passed down from their parents, and they'd worked extremely hard to build it into a fairly substantial multiacre enterprise. They told stories of working before the sun came up to after the sun went down during harvest season. Of my grandmother taking three solid meals to the fields every day, cleaning up the kitchen after every meal, and doing it all over again the next day. All while raising four children, serving in church, taking meals to others in the community, and when the grandkids came along, loving us to pieces. "A bushel and a peck and a hug around the neck," my grandmother would say to us.

I loved spending summers on the farm. I would usually find a tree in a quiet spot or somewhere equally inviting to read or write. You could "see for days" across the flat cotton fields in that part of Texas. I also learned how to make banana pudding with my grandmother, and I accidently dropped eggs so many times that she cut out a funny poem about dropped eggs from her newspaper and mailed it to me at college. I framed it and still have it hanging in my kitchen.

At Thanksgiving or Christmas, Grandmother would rise really early to start her special dressing recipe. I always loved sneaking into the kitchen before the sun came up without any of the other grandkids or family there to "help" her. She would throw in some sage and say, "Taste that and see if it's ready." I didn't know what I was doing, but my eleven-, thirteen-, or fifteen-year-old self would dip in my spoon, taste it, and say something like, "I think it needs a hint more salt." I asked her to write down the recipe after I was married, and it's full of pinches of that, hints of this. *Eyeball until it looks sloppy but not too wet. Bake until it looks right and doesn't jiggle in the middle too much.* I have that framed too.

I lived with my grandparents for a summer during college, and I visited them often during those years since their farm was only forty-five minutes away from the university. I usually brought several friends with me, and my granddaddy typically took many of them out to walk the land since they'd never seen a cotton field before. Grandmother always made her famous banana pudding, teriyaki chicken, and fried potatoes, okra, and onions for us. And homemade cornbread in her cast-iron skillet. We usually ended the night with a game of chicken foot or regular dominoes.

I lived in the abundance of my grandparents' hard work that resulted in their living in a nice home very different from the one they grew up in. Or even what their own grandparents grew up in.

My other set of grandparents lived in Oklahoma, in the original land of the Cherokee people, and I have just as many sweet memories from visiting them. This side of the family was full of music, art, and, once again, hard work. They also didn't come from wealth, and my grandpa, a tall, thin man who wore too-short pants with too-long socks, worked the railroads for decades before retiring.

Everyone seemed to play a musical instrument, and they even had a Southern gospel band for a while. Grandma led the singing— and goodness, could she sing! My aunts sang and played the fiddle or banjo, my dad played the piano, my uncle played everything, and my grandpa tapped his knee. Some of my favorite memories are when everyone pulled out instruments and sang.

After the jam sessions, some of us would retreat to my grandparents' backyard that was like an oasis—in the middle of Oklahoma—and I would birdwatch with Grandma. She loved cardinals and had tons of birdhouses she'd painted. I have several of those now in my own garden. She was the first person to call me Emi, and she encouraged my love of playing the piano by ear just like some of the other family members did. And my love of art. And of writing. She was the first real author I met, having written and illustrated a joke book I still have.

These grandparents also lived simple lives, in the best of ways, faithfully serving their family and their church. When I was growing up in the '90s, the expressions *carpe diem* and *achieve-achieve-achieve* were everywhere. But my grandma taught me it was okay to live a simple life, quietly watching the birds, appreciating art and music.

And what my tall and thin grandpa taught me was that success sometimes looks like sitting for hours stoking a fire. When I sat with him by that fire, he would often say, "Oooooohhhhh, I love you, Granddaughter." Goodness, I cry just writing that, because I can hear him saying it. He also loved it when I held his hand during a walk around their neighborhood, and I did that even as an adult. My Oklahoma grandparents were some of my first teachers in the beauty of simple love.

All my grandparents meant so much to me. I could write an entire book and then another on my memories with them and the impact they had on my life. I've lost all four at this point, and if I had it, I would give a million dollars to walk the fields or watch the birds with them again.

Here's why I've brought them up, though. None of them came from generational wealth, and they all worked extremely hard to build a life for their kids—and then their grandkids—to build on. I'm entirely thankful for that, recognizing that I don't have to work as hard because of what they—and then my parents—built. I wanted you to hear these stories before I go on to the rest of this chapter. I wanted you to hear me say how proud I am of people who lived through dust bowls and the Great Depression. Who penny-pinched and lived simply. Who weren't influencers or famous but nevertheless were known to a few of us as gold. Who formed me.

None came from privilege.

But our family was *and is* privileged.

Because we're White and we had money.

That last statement contains deeply rooted privilege, passed down through injustices, structural and individual, threaded through generations. To my grandparents. And then to my parents. And then to me. Let's talk about that privilege next.

———

I have never and will never own people, making them enslaved. But there's a good chance that someone in my ancestral past did. Because they were White. Yes, I'm living the fruits of my family's hard work during dust bowls and Great Depressions, but I'm also living the fruits of a world still powered by Whiteness. A world where privilege still anchors around wealth and the color of our skin and where history books have been Whitewashed. It's unfair, yes. But we who are White can either acknowledge that privilege and work toward justice within it or push the realities of our own ancestors under proverbial rugs of power.

You might say, "But my family is not wealthy, and they worked very hard to get where they are." Dear friends, I'm sure that is entirely true, and I get that.

And also.

Just being White in the world today denotes privilege. Add in being an evangelical Christian, male, or any other historically held position of power, and that privilege is multiplied. This is because of how history has played out. If we get defensive at that statement, we've missed the point. It's not about us, although sometimes we've made it about us.

We can acknowledge our own families' hard work, just as I have. And I hope you'll trust that the rest of this chapter holds the calluses of my grandparents' hard work in one of my hands while I also recognize there's privilege in the other. It's not one or the other. It's the *both/and*. The *and also*. That's "Good Samaritan" thinking—taking responsibility for ancestral sins and acknowledging the injustices is holy, sacred work.

Let me show you a bit more why this is the case. Starting with Jesus.

———

"That they may be one."[1]

Those are some of Jesus' final words. In chapter 17 of John's gospel, Jesus had just finished giving the disciples a new commandment to love one another. He'd told them that he is the way, the truth, the life, the true vine. He'd promised the Holy Spirit, that he would leave them with peace, that their joy would be made full. He also said the world would hate them, they'd be kicked out of synagogues, and they'd weep, lament, and experience deep sorrow and tribulation.

And then he lifted his eyes to heaven and prayed. He prayed to the Father about the time that had come. Then he prayed for *us*—those of us who will believe in him through [the disciples'] words—"that they all may be one; just as You, Father, are in Me and I in You" (verse 21 AMP).

It's easy to pray that prayer of unity if you're a White evangelical Christian. It's easy to pray, "How good and pleasant it is when God's people live together in unity," as the psalmist wrote.[2] And when those words are interpreted correctly and alongside other Scriptures, those prayers are good and "Amen!" But not until the past twenty years have I understood why Jesus' final prayer for us is a prayer of *true* unity. I used to think it was simply one of, *Let's just all love one another and be kind. We just need to get along.* But I think there's more to it. Jesus' prayer for unity is *inclusive* of all he was about to die for. He was about to dismantle the walls of hostility.

Ephesians 2 talks about the cross dismantling the dividing walls of hostility and Jesus himself being our peace. Why did the cross need to do that? Why couldn't it simply usher in love and kindness and peace? It certainly did all of that, but it did *more*. It brought down walls of hostility, which certainly feels more abrupt than just being kind, doesn't it? Why? Because walls of hostility were up.

If we bristle at the word *privilege* and if the words *I'm not a racist* roll easily off the tongue, we may need to look at the walls more carefully. Or if we're *not* saying, *I'm an anti-racist*, or if we don't see the difference between the two, there's more work for us to do. It's a low bar to be a Christian who says they're not a racist.

But being an anti-racist means I have to take a harder look at the walls of hostility—including ones I haven't noticed before, presently or historically. And then do something about them once I see them. Simply not being a racist or someone who *others* groups of people doesn't solve anything.

Many of us in the White evangelical spaces hear the word *privilege* and think, *I've worked hard to get where I am. Nothing has been handed to me on a silver platter. So I can't be privileged.* I've worked hard too, and so has my family. But that's not what privilege is about. Understanding privilege doesn't discount our own experiences. It does, however, acknowledge the fact that opportunities and resources, both historical and present day, have not been and still are not equal. There is a history to be reckoned with. And once we acknowledge our privilege, it gives us the opportunity to do something.

For much of the White evangelical church, those walls of hostility have been slowly built over decades of oppression. Let's look at a few examples.

———

Back in 1950, a Dutch missionary thinker named Johannes Hoekendijk made the following observation about calls to evangelism in his day:

> To put it bluntly: the call to evangelism is often little else than a call to restore 'Christendom,' the *Corpus Christianum*, as a solid, well-integrated cultural complex, directed and dominated by the Church. And the sense of urgency is often nothing but a nervous feeling of insecurity, with the established Church endangered, a flurried activity to save the remnants of a time now irrevocably past.[3]

When Hoekendijk speaks of the *Corpus Christianum*, he is referencing a state of affairs where the church and Christianity enjoy a central and powerful place in society. Many Christians saw evangelism as a pathway back to a former time when Christians enjoyed majority opinion and were the primary power brokers in public affairs.

Fast-forward seventy years, and it isn't hard to see the same dynamics at play in American evangelicalism today. Though we may be more prone to speak of mission than evangelism, we evangelicals tend to pine for a time when laws enforced a Christian worldview, state-sponsored prayer was present in public schools, and societal schedules revolved around church meetings on Sunday mornings and Wednesday nights. Often these desires are intermingled with our drive for missions and evangelization, as is heard in the calls to "take America back for God." The goal, it seems, is a return to a Christendom state of affairs.

Over the past few decades, many American evangelicals have been recruited into a culture war in which they view themselves the keepers of American morality in a battle for America's soul. Along the way, we have misremembered our past, oversimplified the present, and allowed our imaginations to be molded more by American politics than by the way of God's kingdom as defined by Jesus. Regarding our pasts, we have failed to recognize our complicity in deeply oppressive structures. When we talk about "taking America back for God," we're talking about a return to an America that was good for White evangelicals but certainly not good for everyone. Christendom, it turns out, wasn't all that Christian.

Moving to the present, we've been fed a line that to be a good Christian, we need to vote Republican. The problem here is that our allegiance to the gospel makes politics more complicated than a simple choice between right and left. It is telling, for instance, that many of the same voices who advocate so vigorously against abortion have nothing substantive or constructive to say about calls for justice from communities of color or important issues of earth care and climate change. Or that nearly 70 percent of White evangelicals agree that "an elected official who commits an immoral act in their personal life can still behave ethically and fulfill their duties."[4]

There's a vast disconnect in practice and theology. Word and deeds. Heart and idolatry. Why do we choose one issue and not the other? Shouldn't our allegiance to God drive us to care about all of them? I suspect Jesus would level full-throated critiques at both political parties were he to walk the streets of the US today. Yet we oversimplify the system and make ourselves complicit.

Take a look at how Christians comport themselves on social media. The vitriol and outrage look a lot like the American political machine—and very little like Jesus. Somehow we've allowed the way of the world to overshadow the way of Jesus. Like Peter when he drew his sword in Gethsemane, we abandon the way of Jesus in the very moment we think we're standing for him.

When we take the kingdom as our starting point instead of power grabs, we view ourselves as ambassadors (to borrow a term from the apostle Paul in 2 Corinthians 5:20) rather than culture warriors. As such, our allegiance is to the kingdom come rather than our idea of the America past. Moreover, our action for the kingdom is always held to the standard of King Jesus—we must care about what he cares about and act in agreement with his example and teaching. This is not to say that we should retreat from the public sphere. Especially when it comes to advocacy for those on the margins, Jesus may indeed call us into the fray. It *is* to say, however, that our actions should all flow from our allegiance to Jesus rather than a political party, which has huge ramifications for the way we move through the world.

This means we evangelicals must untangle our allegiance to "Christian" America from our allegiance to the kingdom of God. They may overlap, but they aren't the same thing. Besides, history has shown that allegiance to Christian America hasn't served us well when it comes to faithfulness to Christ. Christendom itself was deeply flawed, and our pursuit of it in the present takes our eyes off Jesus, who rather than seeking power came to serve and poured himself out for the sake of many. What would it look like to allow him to truly mold our presence in the world? When it comes to re-constructing evangelical theology, this is the place to start.

We can be ambassadors or culture warriors, but we can't be both.

As shown by the examples above, some of the wall building happened overtly and is easy to call out. But a lot of it happened covertly, making it hard to call out and easy to normalize, even in church settings. Consider reading Dr. Jemar Tisby's work *The Color of Compromise* on the church's complicity in racism in America. Then read his next book, *How to Fight Racism*. Join a Be the Bridge group and listen, White church. Truly listen.[5]

Our systems have built the "good old days" for a privileged few that many in the White evangelical church are yearning to return to. The problem is that this yearning can also make room for unconsciously blatant jokes with your buddies about the "China flu," complicit silence when the vulnerable aren't being protected, blame-shifting the pandemic to migrants, saying "White lives matter" without recognizing what that really means underneath, or getting mad when people speak in broken English or in a different language than you do.

There is a way to break down those walls, though. Jesus ushered in a true form of peace, because like Ephesians 2 says and as he told his disciples in his final thoughts, *he himself is our peace*. True peace, not cheap peace. Saying you're for peace without standing against these forms of non-peace is cheap. It may be a feel-good peace for a few, but it's not an equal peace for all. Real peace leads beyond being kind to being just. Real peace opens up good old days for everyone's future, not simply recreating the past for a select few.

I know that for many of us, getting along means both sides need to come together—Democrats and Republicans, progressives and conservatives, Whites and Blacks, and a multitude of other sides. The problem is that these sides haven't been weighted equally, historically speaking. So coming together looks more like 70–30 percent instead of a true 50–50. To put it another way, we all know yellow and blue make green. But what if you have too much yellow? Or too much blue? The results will be different. That's what happens when we say, "Let's just all get along and meet in the middle." If there's too much yellow, the middle is not actually the middle. Real peace is making sure there are equal parts yellow and blue to make the true green. When the sides are skewed, that's not real peace; that's privilege.

Dismantling walls of hostility is hard work and might require you to change friends and communities like I did (more about that later). It will definitely require humble soul-searching and empathetic listening, especially if you're White. Real peace also takes a long time. It can involve powerful systems and laws changing to make a fairer, more equitable, and just world. It can also happen in small acts, which is what I think the Good Samaritan story teaches us. It doesn't have to be grand and big. Peace and justice can be found—and made—in the everyday life we find ourselves in.

To me, this also means I recognize that my grandparents could own land or receive grants to purchase farms while others during the same time period were unable do so because of the color of their skin. And that I can recognize my own Whiteness and privilege, and my family's, and work toward building a more just world. Real peace is ushered in when we level the playing field for all.

Getting along is not the goal. Real peace is.

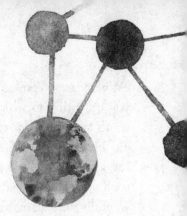

CHAPTER 6

UNKNOWN IS THE NEW FAME

Your desk is your prayer bench.
SAINT DOMINIC

Love only exists among equals.
FATHER GUSTAVO GUTIÉRREZ

At barely twenty years old, I got on a plane for Honduras to spend a month on the Mercy Ships, a medical missions ship providing care to people in some of the poorest countries around the globe. I couldn't speak the language there and had never traveled that far without a family member with me. I'd also sent the application to be a volunteer without telling my parents, so they didn't know until I was accepted. They would have been fully supportive of me going, but with the understandable parental questioning, like

"Where are you going?" "What will you be doing?" and "Who will you be with?" to which I would answer with what every parent wants to hear: "I don't know."

I had signed up as a month-long volunteer, and off I flew carrying a suitcase loaded with my journal, a Bible, and books along with some clothes. I also carried a heart bursting with idealism but woefully unprepared for what I would see. That's okay sometimes, though, isn't it? If we always know what's coming, would we take some of the risks we take?

Upon arrival, I settled into my room on the ship—a tiny space with a bunk bed on either side and just enough room for two of us to stand between them. My feet hung off the too-short bed, but I didn't care one bit. As I said, I was barely twenty, so my back didn't yet hurt after a challenging night's sleep. I was just excited to finally be there.

Until I wasn't.

A few days into the trip, I felt like I'd made a massive mistake. Homesick and lonely and culture shocked, I called my mom from one of the only phones on the ship, which was in a pay-phone-type booth, and with tears told her I was ready to come home. This was in the early 2000s before cell phones and laptops and widespread Wi-Fi, so I wasn't able to book a flight home myself. My mom, who happens to be one of the sweetest people in the world, said she would look into tickets for me and that I should call her back with details later that day.

But something changed over the next few hours. I knew I needed to stay. And I knew I *could* stay. Off I went to the phone booth again to tell my parents, "Never mind. Your girl is cool and can handle this. See you in a month!" Or something like that. And I'm so glad I did.

I spent the next weeks working in the ship's kitchen with an incredible group of people from Africa and Denmark, Canada and

Guatemala. I made hundreds of peanut butter sandwiches for the medical teams to take with them when they traveled to rural areas for health clinics. And the trips I made with them changed me. My goodness, the way poverty stretched its fingers into every aspect of the community's lives was stark.

Me working in the kitchen on the Mercy Ships

As a premed student at the time, I had lots of questions: Why were so many children here sick with tropical diseases or their parents with diabetes? How far away were these families from the adequate medical care they needed? These weren't necessarily individual medical questions, like how to treat a person's sickness, but rather, population-level questions. This was epidemiology; I just didn't know it yet. I was noticing the people and individuals, yes, but my heart was drawn more to the population, the geography, the aggregation of the individuals. The sum of the parts makes up a whole, and those were the questions I was asking.

For the first time, I was seeing what I'd heard or read about. I'd heard about poverty and malnutrition and hunger from the missionaries who had stayed in our home. I'd grown up reading books about the work of Amy Carmichael, Elisabeth Elliot, Hudson Taylor, and Lottie Moon, but I hadn't truly seen what they had written about. Until now. And it wrecked me.

When I returned to the ship after one of those trips, I was supposed to start my shift in the kitchen. But I was having a hard time, and one of the other workers noticed. She was at least forty years older than me and had lived on the Mercy Ships for over a year. And because of her long-term volunteer post, she had her own room. She noticed my tears, and without hesitating, she said she'd take my shift and I could go to her room to rest and regroup without any roommates around.

Her room was the tiniest one I've ever seen, tucked away in the middle of the ship with just enough space for a bed and a desk smaller than you could find at Ikea. And books were stuffed into every nook and cranny possible. I saw a book by Corrie ten Boom and felt teleported back to my own room at home with the same one. I took a nap, enjoyed the quiet, and did regroup a bit.

Here's what I remember most, though, aside from this woman's incredible stash of books: She didn't shame me for my tears or tell me to suck it up. She just let me be sad and confused in the moment. Maybe she'd been through something similar. And maybe because of that, she knew what I needed. I don't know, since I never asked her, but somehow she knew.

After that, I watched this woman when she was serving food or eating meals in the giant dining room and noticed she seemed so happy and peaceful simply being herself. I was an ambitious twenty-year-old, full of dreams of the future—big dreams—believing I could shoot for the stars and go for the gold and be anything and everything if I set my mind to it. All of this translated in my mind to being the best and a leader. Not because I had anything to prove or because I wanted to be the best. I just wanted to be faithful, and I thought that meant being at the top, making the best efforts toward the highest ambitions.

But what if faithfulness looked quieter? What if it was day-in, day-out obedience in small ways too? What if it was never being at the top or the leader or the best? What if it was spending more than a year of your life sleeping in a tiny room in the middle of a ship and making sandwiches for people? Noticing the twenty-year-olds who were struggling with their faith and telling them to go rest? To be who you were in faithful walking, not ambitious hustling?

———

The unseen faithfulness and quiet obedience of the Good Samaritan are part of the strength of the story. He didn't yell, "Behold, look at me, thou-est peasants!" trumpeting that he'd paid for the sick man's food and hotel so he could recover. He didn't post a Twitter thread about how he stopped after the religious leaders didn't (assuming he saw them just walk by). He certainly didn't check to see if his actions had gone viral on TikTok. He simply did what he could where he was, with what he had. And it wasn't just enough but more than enough in that Jesus used this story to illustrate who our neighbors are *and also* who's actually being a neighbor.

The pull of today's Western world is fraught with wealth and capitalism and the pursuit of individualistic code words like *life*, *liberty*, and *happiness*. The way of Jesus in the Good Samaritan story challenges that code and redefines ambition, according to compassion and obedience to a cross, not fame or selfish pursuit or wealth. In pouring out ourselves for one another through humility, we actually find the fulfillment of all ambitions.

I'm paraphrasing here, but it reminds me of when David in the Bible prayed, "This one thing I ask. One thing I want. That I would dwell in the house of the Lord."[1] It also reminds me of when the apostle Paul wrote, "This one thing I know. That I would give up all my ambition and résumé and curriculum vitae for the sake of knowing Jesus my Lord. All of it."[2]

During my last weeks on the Mercy Ships, I continued the normal peanut-butter-and-jelly-sandwich making. I learned to make plantains with a friend from Ghana, who also showed me how to make caramel popcorn for weekly movie nights. (Y'all, that stuff was *good*.) I learned how to make real chai with tea and coffee and steamed milk and cinnamon. I spent hours on the upper deck with my roommates from Denmark, laughing until our bellies hurt and taking silly pictures of our faces in the ship's portholes.

I also visited the hospital in Honduras's capital city to hold babies born too soon and too small or hug toddlers who were recovering from surgery in the children's ward. I continued to see overwhelming poverty and debilitating disease. And slowly, slowly, slowly, I found my heart stopping on the side of those roads.

Near the end of my stay on the ship, I was attending one of our Sunday services. The space was filled with the other hundreds of volunteers or full-time staff from a tapestry of countries, along with several of the people staying on the ship while recovering from their surgeries. During the singing time, the worship leaders asked everyone to pray and sing in their own language.

Friends, that room lit up with an explosion of words. It startled me so much that my eyes shot open, and the first thing I saw were the numerous flags hung around the room representing the nations of the world. Their red, blue, green, orange, and purple seemed to match the tapestry of the songs being sung and prayers being prayed. Then the leader asked everyone to say the Lord's Prayer in their own language.

And I just wept. It felt like what I think heaven will be.

> Our Father in heaven . . .
> Hallowed be your name . . .
> On earth as it is in heaven . . .
> Give us this day our daily bread . . .
> Forever and ever. Amen.

When work becomes our worship and worship becomes our work, this is the faithfulness that changes the world.

The Good Samaritan story teaches us many life lessons, and I hope I always remember one of the main ones it models. It doesn't matter whether we're known, whether people know what we do, whether we're famous. What matters is that we're faithful. Unknown is the new fame.

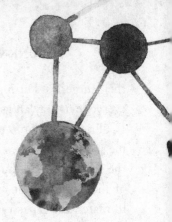

CHAPTER 7

SOLIDARITY AND SNEAKING IN

*The idea that some lives matter less is the root
of all that is wrong with the world.*
DR. PAUL FARMER

It was the early 2000s. I was both a newlywed and a new graduate student at the University of South Carolina earning my Master of Science in Public Health in epidemiology. My days were filled with studying, which I loved, and figuring out how to cook something, which usually meant I called my mom or grandmother for help.

My husband and I were both twenty-two when we got married and then moved across the country to Sumter, South Carolina, where he started a job at a church. We moved into a small home with a tiny front porch. The house was painted white and green and looked like a miniature version of the one in my favorite childhood book, *Anne of Green Gables*.

We were best friends, and the day in and day out of being with each other was a dream I never knew I wanted until I had it. I thought I would get married at forty-five after medical school and never have children. Well, that didn't work out one bit since I got married at half that age, never went to medical school, and had two kids by age thirty. It always surprises people when I tell them my initial plan, because I'm the biggest gush of a mom there is. To this day, my greatest gratitude is that my plan didn't work out.

During this time I was introduced to Dr. Paul Farmer through a book about his life titled *Mountains Beyond Mountains*. He was a medical anthropologist with accolades as long and wide as his compassion and joy. I found myself among the thousands of others inspired by Dr. Farmer, who had started the Partners in Health organization in rural Haiti for the poorest communities without health care access—and in the process redefined what "care" meant in the field of global health and medicine.

Dr. Farmer challenged the idea that the sick should come to us in health care and made a strong case in word and deed that, instead, we should go to the sick. He confronted the colonialistic and patriarchal versions of doing global health care in places where colonial medicine was deeply rooted. And to me, he seemed idealistic and optimistic in the best of ways.

For many of us working in equity-based work, Dr. Farmer is why. He was a once-in-a-lifetime person who was larger than life in ambition but down-to-earth in approach. Humble, deeply tenacious, joyful, and bear-hug kind, he made you want to sit up straight and lean in, and he commanded a room with an effervescent way of making you want to listen to the groans of the earth and the cries from the margins, face on the floor and ear to the earth. Because he lived and worked there. He gave many of us freedom to dream and be who we were meant to become.

Before hearing about Dr. Farmer, I knew only of people in

medical professions—MDs, dentists, nurses—doing what I wanted to do in global health. So I was a little disappointed to not go to med school, instead earning a PhD, because not being an MD felt like I was disqualified from doing any global work. But then I read about Dr. Farmer and who he worked with. Yes, he was an MD, but he was also an anthropologist and worked with people who had PhDs instead of MDs. Perhaps there was a different way to contribute to the good of the world without being a physician?

Dr. Farmer's way of working in our world resonated deeply with me. He was with the people he was treating, hugging them, treating them with dignity and care afforded to dignitaries, and challenging the status quo. I read about his approach to treating people with tuberculosis in rural Haiti. Tuberculosis, especially the drug-resistant kind, needs daily treatment, which is often hard to get to for people living hours and hours away from a medical facility. It's also hard for families who can't afford the daily medication.

At the time, the medical community's concern was that treating patients by going to them in rural, remote areas was too expensive, not cost-effective, and would require too much in the way of personnel resources. But, again, Dr. Farmer and his team flipped that script and went to the people. Daily. Individually. This was the first time I saw someone asking *Why not?* to the statement *It won't work.*

When I heard Dr. Farmer was coming to the University of South Carolina campus, I called everyone I could think of who might be in charge and asked if I could come to the meetings. Mind you, I was twenty-three years old and overly idealistic, but my dad always said you never know 'til you try. So try I did. The worst they could say was no, right? I was turned down by almost everyone, but one assistant told me Dr. Farmer was meeting with a group of undergraduates.

I can't remember if she asked if I was an undergraduate, to

which I probably would have said, "Well, kinda," just to get in. But in any event, I wiggled my way into that meeting, bringing my optimism, idealism, and all five of Dr. Farmer's big, long books. As I mentioned, he was an anthropologist, which means his books are rich with story, agency, and personhood. In other words, they're long with tiny print and footnotes galore. Nonetheless, I devoured them all. In hindsight, I probably should have asked him to sign just one of them, but my googly-eyed self waltzed in with that monster stack of books for him to sign.

This informal gathering for undergraduates and me was full of Dr. Farmer's thoughts on the future of global health and their roles in it. Most of the students were premed, so the questions were focused more on the clinical side of providing care in remote areas. I, however, with nervous laughter asked the smartest question this starstruck woman could muster: "What can an epidemiologist do in global health?"

"Be a great epidemiologist." I don't remember how the meeting ended, but I do remember what came next.

When I returned home, I opened the books I'd taken with me, all of which he had signed, and saw these words I hadn't noticed earlier:

In solidarity

I thought two things about what he wrote. One, how in the world could a leading—if not *the* leading—global health leader possibly think we were in solidarity in our work? I was just a student, and he was, well, Dr. Paul Farmer. Two, I wanted this new term to be central to my own work, as well as how I would read the Bible in the years to come.

What do you think of when you hear the word *solidarity?* I think of someone coming alongside me, holding my hand, walking with me, supporting me, working with me. Solidarity is mutual, respectful, and loving. If we expand that out to the globe, collective solidarity is when we do that together. Can you imagine a world where the church did that together, alongside others like the Good Samaritan? This collective solidarity is important for us in the world and should remind us that our individual actions can become something larger when joined with the actions of others.

In 1971, Father Gustavo Gutiérrez, a well-known Peruvian priest and theologian, published a book titled *A Theology of Liberation.* And as of this writing, at age ninety-four, Father Gutiérrez continues to spend most of his time living among the poor in the slums of Lima, Peru, while also holding the John Cardinal O'Hara Professorship of Theology at the University of Notre Dame. Father Gutiérrez is long heralded as one of the founders of the liberation theology movement with his seminal text in the 1970s, *A Theology of Liberation,* where he advocates for a preferential option for the poor and liberation of those who have been oppressed.[1] He also centered the movement around a specific question: How do we convey to the poor that God loves them?

For Father Gutiérrez, the answer is found only in proximity to the poor themselves. Not just going on a service trip for a few weeks but living among the poor to understand their suffering and see how they live on a typical Tuesday making dinner or a random Saturday evening when their kid gets sick.

In liberation theology, this is called *accompaniment*—a coming beside and with someone. Even just saying the word *accompany* gives us a picture of walking beside someone, doesn't it? Or someone walking beside you. For Father Gutiérrez, though, it means more than just walking beside. It's a sharing of resources, power, privilege, money, and work efforts to ensure everyone is cared for. Equally. It's an amongness or withness.

I love how Pope Francis describes the act of accompaniment. He says it "teaches us to remove our sandals before the sacred ground of the other."[2] *The sacred ground of the other.* For those of you from the Christian faith, this sounds like recognizing the holy in one another as the image of God in which we are all made (see Genesis 1:26–27). Recognizing the sacredness of our neighbors and the ground upon which they stand.

As I told you in the last chapter, my first solo trip outside the United States was to Honduras, working on the Mercy Ships. One day as I traveled with a team deep into the rural part of the country to assist at a medical clinic, we met a woman and those who I perceived to be members of her family on the road. They were crying and started talking to one of our guides whom they knew from other medical visits.

As we followed them to their home, the guide explained that one of the elder family members had been sick with HIV and died a few days earlier. They couldn't afford a coffin and burial expenses, though, so he was lying in the front section of their home, covered with a multicolored cloth. I saw both that and the children of the family running in and out of the home.

I also saw how our group quietly paid for everything they needed for a burial, including a wood coffin. Our leader, whom the woman had recognized, spoke at length with the family. I couldn't understand anything they said since I didn't speak the language, but I do remember the *posture* he took. There was a deep withness with this family. And his compassion stilled the rest of us, almost like time slowed down to honor what was happening. That space seemed so quiet as the burial on hallowed ground was readied. It was a moment of recognizing the sacredness of neighbors experiencing a deep loss and removing our proverbial shoes on the ground upon which they stood, as Pope Francis talked about. *The sacred ground of the other.*

———

We don't always recognize the sacred in the other. At least I don't. Do you know the Scripture that says when we feed the hungry, clothe the needy, tend to the sick, and visit the prisoners and widows, we actually do those things for Jesus?[3] Or the Scripture that talks about entertaining angels without knowing it when we help foreigners or migrants?[4] All these actions are directed toward those dubbed the *others* of society. But to Jesus, they're him. When we recognize the sacred in the other, we acknowledge the holy in Jesus. We take off our shoes, for it is holy ground.

I remember one of the first times I saw someone recognizing the sacred in others. In my town growing up, the local Methodist church on Main Street held a food drive and then made deliveries for Thanksgiving meals. I participated, and one year we drove to a part of town I wasn't familiar with. We entered a house with walls and floors completely made of cement or cinder blocks. Several children without shoes greeted us as we placed the boxes on their kitchen table.

I hadn't seen poverty in my own town much, and I was struck by how cold it was in the house. Then I noticed our leader smiling and talking with the family like they were royalty. She hugged them and chatted with the mother, whom she probably already knew. She interacted with the children like you would at a birthday party. The house seemed to light up with the interaction. She was recognizing the holy, the sacred, in that family. I was feeling the cold from the cement floors and watching with some trepidation. She was taking off her shoes, for it was holy ground.

I know I often miss Jesus and don't always recognize his voice in the world today, but to the best of my ability, I don't want to miss seeing him when his nearness is in others. He accompanies me. He accompanies us. And I don't want to miss that.

Recognizing the sacred in the other also shines a light on any lack there may be. I wonder if that's why the term *accompaniment* was so important to Dr. Farmer, who wrote extensively about how Father Gutiérrez's work impacted his own work. Accompaniment, by praxis and not merely by definition, exposes where there is lack or need and does something about it because of the proximity, humility, or withness with others. You don't take off your shoes with just anyone, right?

In an amazing book titled *In the Company of the Poor*, written by both Father Gutiérrez and Dr. Farmer, Dr. Farmer summarized the impact of this approach:

Liberation theology continues to be, for me, an inexhaustible font of inspiration. I see the spirituality associated with it, as, at the very least, aspirational: any of us can aspire to be better—but only if we seek to attack contemporary poverty and to remember that we live in one world, not three. Nothing that I've seen, from plague to famine to flood to quake, could persuade me otherwise.[5]

The act of accompaniment is giving a preferential option for the poor. Once we're beside or walking with the poor, recognizing the sacredness but also what makes them poor, the direct and almost unconscious next thing to do is to act. That's what's called the preferential option for the poor in liberation theology work, and it's now widely used in many other settings—theological, humanitarian, and medical, to name just a few. In doing so, we center what we have on what others don't.

This means we notice the people beside us who don't have food, shoes, or whatever else they need. We might have enough money in our bank accounts to meet that need. I can center around them and address their lack or I can use that money to buy Starbucks drinks. Don't get me wrong. I love my coffee more than most. But centering around others walking so close to me that I can see them, hear them, know them means I notice their lack and ask myself if I can help. This proximity tears down prejudices we may have and makes us people together. It's really hard not to give away our money when we notice our friend walking alongside us without shoes.

This brings me back to the Good Samaritan story. The Samaritan man noticed the hurt man on the road and stopped. That's a preferential option for the poor. I wonder what the other men in the story—the two who chose to walk by—had a preferential option for? Religious commitments? Agendas? To-do lists? Greed? Bias? Power?

The Samaritan, however, had something inside that made him notice and stop. And not only did he stop, but he attended to the man's acute need and then paid for his food and lodging during recovery. We aren't told in the story, but I wonder if he had to carry the man to the lodge. Or at the very least, support him as he walked. That's accompaniment. Being in proximity in heart and deed to notice, to act, and to give.

———

In 2008, Dr. Farmer, alongside Dr. Jim Kim, with whom Dr. Farmer worked at Partners in Health and who was the former president of the World Bank, wrote a scientific article advocating for the health community to pay attention to surgical diseases, a disease that requires surgery.[6] Over the past few decades, those of us working in global health have done a decent job of focusing on the big three diseases affecting the poorest communities:

tuberculosis, malaria, and HIV/AIDS. Although there's definitely more work to be done, what we're now seeing globally is an epidemiologic shift from communicable infectious diseases, like the big three, to noncommunicable diseases like heart disease, cancer, and conditions requiring surgery. The infectious diseases weren't going away but rather were being coupled with the noncommunicable diseases.

This translated to a double burden for the clinical deserts of the world that lacked resources, treatment, or hospitals to prevent and treat either, especially if their citizens were poor or lived in rural areas or communities with long histories of structural violence. So when Dr. Farmer and Dr. Kim, two of the greatest global health advocates of our time, published something new, the world listened.

Over the next few years, there was a swift increase in those interested in global surgery—doctors, surgeons, anesthesiologists, nurses, policy makers. And an epidemiologist fresh from earning her PhD. That was me, and this is the serendipitous part of my story.

———

After graduating from the University of North Carolina with my PhD in epidemiology, my research was focused on global surgery at the Duke Global Health Institute, where I worked. And some of my favorite collaborators were at the Program in Global Surgery and Social Change at Harvard Medical School, founded by Dr. Farmer. Over the next few years, his path and mine intersected a bit more, and eventually he had a pivotal role in my applications for national grants by writing a few letters of recommendation.

One day Dr. Farmer came to Baylor University, where he was

to speak about his new book, *Reimagining Global Health*. He was meeting with a group of faculty members before the talk, and as we were waiting, he entered the room as he probably entered every room—filling it with his joy and enthusiasm—and loudly said, "Emily!" as he started walking toward me. I tried to act cool without yelling back, "Oh my goodness, you know my name!"

We gave each other a huge hug—the kind of big bear hug that makes you feel like you're besties about to go get tacos together—and he handed me his book. Later that day, on the front inside cover I saw the exact same words he'd written to me fifteen years earlier: *In solidarity*. I took the books to his lecture later that evening, showed him the words he'd written, and told him how much they'd meant and continued to mean to me. We both teared up, me more than him.

In solidarity.

That word—*solidarity*—continues to change me, to anchor me in a world where we are all neighbors and to propel me in my work to act out that word in *expert mercy*, another one of Dr. Farmer's great phrases. He, more than anyone I've ever met, taught me what it looks like to be a neighbor by living a withness.

In solidarity, dear Dr. Farmer. Thank you.

Me with Dr. Farmer after chuckling and then tearing up about his book signatures and words—In solidarity

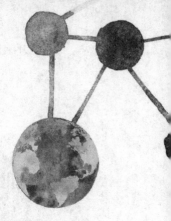

CHAPTER 8

STRUCTURAL VIOLENCE AND SINGING

Poverty is the worst form of violence.
MAHATMA GANDHI

I was a week late with my first baby, who was still plenty happy staying in the womb, and I'd been admitted to the hospital for labor to be induced in the morning. Unless, that is, something magical happened in the night.

Well, wave the wands and sprinkle some fairy dust. The magic started around 2:00 a.m. And by magic, I mean *Whoa, this is happening* labor pains. My six-foot-four hubs was sleeping on a hospital sofa made for a troll, and I promptly woke him up with something like, "I don't want to do this."

Being the incredible person he is, he grabbed my hand and started singing. And he sang for four hours, interspersed with his falling asleep because it was the wee hours of the morning and me squeezing his hand like a boss to wake him back up. Just imagine him singing "Grace, grace, God's grace" with the words trailing as he nodded off and then his loudly coming back like a Baptist choir as I gently (read: not gently) squeezed his hand.

At 6:00 a.m., the doctor told us my platelets were low, so he wasn't sure if I would be able to get an epidural. Insert my birth plan, where this development was *not* in the plan, thank you very much. *What do you mean you can't give me an epidural?* He said there were other options for pain, and in my mind that meant a cookie or half a Tylenol. Nope. Still not in the birth plan.

When he left, I looked at my pastor-husband with all the charismatic upbringing I could muster and told him—being full of the Spirit, I'm sure—"Pray." (Stat, if you're in health care.) A few hours later, the doc came back as though it was no big deal and said something like, "Well, your platelets are rock stars now. Let's get that epidural."

The anesthesiologist arrived and worked his own magic. Fast-forward a few more hours, and our gorgeous gal was born. Pink skin, ten fingers, ten toes, and one bazillion percent beautiful grace (that's what her name means) fell into our arms.

A few years later, I was pregnant with baby number four. I'd had two miscarriages, one happening at a devastating nearly fifteen weeks. But thankfully, I felt relatively fine with this pregnancy. As fine as you could be after the losses. Then at around thirty-six weeks, I lost my vision a little bit and saw stars. My doctor told me to come in for tests and an observation period, which required staying in the hospital for a full day.

Later that day, I told my husband I felt fine and bet we were about to be discharged home. Instead, the doctor walked in and said some of the tests indicated preeclampsia, which I'd never heard of at that point and didn't have any risk factors for. She also said we needed to have that baby *now* and told us to pack up our things and walk down the hallway to a birthing room.

Wait a minute. Like now? Again, not in my birth plan.

We gathered our belongings and waddled down the hall. Well, one of us waddled. A few semi-intense hours later, a sweet little boy was born. Pink skin, ten fingers, ten toes, and 1 bazillion breaths of God (that's what his name means) were placed into our arms. He was bigger than our daughter at birth even though he was four weeks early. The NICU had to bring in a full-size baby bed because after only thirty-six weeks in the womb, he was already an over-achiever. It makes me chuckle every time I think about it.

What doesn't make me chuckle is what happened next. After we went home, our son had jaundice and needed to be in the NICU for a few days. And I started feeling off while he was there. After telling my doctor about it, I was sent to the labor and delivery floor again to be checked. Turns out my blood pressure was extremely high due to the preeclampsia. Like scary high. My baby was down the hall in the NICU with my husband while I was also in the hospital with monitors and machines and medicine and dark rooms and all the post-delivery hormones surging through me. Which translated to tears. Lots of tears.

Eventually, we were discharged, a jaundiced baby and a tired mom sitting in the sunlight to recover at home. Over the coming weeks, I found myself in and out of the hospital a few more times with scary high blood pressure and just feeling awful, and I was eventually put on more medicines. It took about six months for my blood pressure to stabilize. And that's when I learned more about the true definition of structural violence.

Preeclampsia is a condition where women develop high blood pressure during pregnancy. It can lead to complications for the mom, with problems in her kidneys, liver, brain, and clotting systems, and for the baby with premature birth and poor growth. When treated by medicines and early delivery, the outcome is usually good. However, preeclampsia is a leading cause of death and morbidity among mothers and infants worldwide.[1]

But that number is not equal among all women. In low-income countries, the risk of dying from obstetric-related complications is fourteen times higher than in higher income countries.[2] In epidemiologic terms, fourteen times is a lot. Put another way, 99 percent of *all* maternal deaths worldwide occur in low-income areas, with preeclampsia a major reason. Although global health has made great strides over the past few decades in lowering the number of mothers and babies dying, preeclampsia continues to be an example of one of the starkest health disparities around.

This trend is also seen here in the United States, one of the few high-income countries in the world with worsening maternal death rates. In fact, the United States has the highest rate of mothers dying among other high-income countries, including France (the US rate is nearly three times higher), Australia or Switzerland (nearly six times higher), and Germany (eight times higher).[3]

However, the burden of maternal mortality in the US is definitely not equal. Black and Hispanic women are at a higher risk of complications such as preeclampsia. The rates of pregnancy-related mortality of Black women in 2018 was 2.6 times higher than White women (37.3 versus 14.9 deaths per 100,000 live births). Those rates have now nearly doubled in 2021 to a whopping 69.9 deaths per 100,000 live births for Black women and 26.6 for White women.[4]

Most of these deaths are preventable with medical care. But did you know that between 2004 and 2014, 9 percent of rural counties in the US lost all hospital obstetric services and also had lower numbers of family physicians?[5] Prior to 2004, 45 percent of rural counties had already lost hospital obstetric services, making this additional 9 percent feel visceral. Who lived there? Mostly women with lower household incomes and non-Hispanic Black or American Indian/Alaska Native women.[6]

Discrimination continues to play a role in provider care during pregnancy as well. Even when taking into account insurance status, income, severity of comorbidities, and age, several studies report that women of color receive a lower quality of care. One in five Black and Hispanic adults have reported unequitable treatment for any health condition in the past year because of their race and ethnicity.[7] For Black mothers, that number is even higher.[8]

Whether we're in Africa or the United States, the death rates of mothers are not equal. Why are the differences so stark? We'll get there, but first I'll introduce you to the term *structural violence*. Let me help you see why it's important, how it's often misunderstood, and how it fits in the Good Samaritan story.

———

Structural violence "refers to the avoidable limitations society places on groups of people that constrain them from meeting their basic needs and achieving the quality of life that would otherwise be possible."[9] Here's another definition of structural violence: "The arrangements are *structural* because they are embedded in the political and economic organization of our social world; they are *violent* because they cause injury to people."[10] In other words, it's when a person or group of people experience harm (there's the violence piece) *because of* power, poverty, and privilege.[11] And here's the clincher: this harm is preventable.

Let's go back to the example of preeclampsia. We've already

learned that more women and babies in low-income communities, both in the United States and globally, die from preeclampsia every year, and this difference is one of the widest in health disparities. In order to not experience complications from preeclampsia, including death, mothers need timely diagnosis and care. However, we—the collective *we*—still don't have a reliable and cost-effective screening tool for preeclampsia that can be used in clinics in areas with limited resources.

Why? That's a whole other conversation about what is deemed cost-effective in global health. But the summary of that conversation is that high-income countries still hold the majority of power on what's cost-effective or not or what goes to market or not, centering that conversation on privilege. Screening tests—like the ones I had—are needed to promptly diagnose preeclampsia so that the women affected can swiftly get care, as well as to require health facilities with laboratories. The only treatment for preeclampsia is to deliver the baby, which brings me to another dimension of structural violence—health care access.

In the event of a medical emergency like preeclampsia, delays in seeking care, reaching care, and receiving care compound on one another, resulting in increased severity of disease, complications, and death. Although the outcomes are individual for the mom, the *reasons* for these delays are strongly related to structures where the mom lives.

Let me give an example using Burundi, a wonderful country tucked in the middle of Africa, where a colleague lives. A mom in rural Burundi starts experiencing symptoms of preeclampsia. She lives four hours away from the nearest medical facility and has three other children at home. Since she doesn't have a car, she must either pay for transportation or walk. I probably don't need to remind you that she's pregnant and, though unbeknownst to her, is experiencing a potentially life-threatening condition, so walking isn't her best option. But if she decides to seek timely care by paying for transportation, that eats into the family's meager savings, or she has to sell her assets, like goats or chickens, to pay for it.

Even if she does reach the health facility in a timely manner, will they have the capability to diagnose preeclampsia? Will they have the doctors and nursing staff and anesthesiologists and a NICU team ready to perform an emergency caesarean section if needed? Will the facility's power stay on during the surgery? Will they have enough oxygen available? Will she have to pay for medical care out of pocket before any procedures are done because she lacks health insurance?

Now let's go back in time thirty years. This woman was born into poverty in the same village she currently lives in. Her family was too. The village is far away from any health facility and in a country fraught with instability, conflict, poverty, and little assistance from larger global power structures. A country without financial protections like health insurance options or universal health coverage. Burundi, located near Rwanda in East Africa, is also the third poorest nation in the world, with a gross domestic product of $246 per capita, and the mortality rate for children under five at 54 per 1,000 live births.[12] (As a comparator, the gross domestic product per capita of the US is $69,288, and the mortality rate of children under five is 6 per 1,000 live births.)[13] But why?

Burundi was colonized by Germany and then by Belgium, suffering especially hard from diseases brought by the colonizers, while also enduring a famine in 1905. Gaining independence in the 1960s, the country would live with civil war for the next several decades.

In 1993, the country was in a civil war and genocide due to the assassination of the president by Tutsi army extremists. One year later, the president's successor was killed, sparking the Rwandan genocide and a decade-long civil war with more than three hundred thousand people dying and half a million being displaced. The unstable political environment, wars hindering stable ways of livelihood (which is agriculture for Burundians), a lack of international assistance, and high numbers of droughts and floods, particularly in recent years, coalesced to send the entire country into poverty. Not only individual poverty but poverty of the country's societal and health systems.

Burundi has one doctor per every ten thousand people.[14] Most of the rest of the world, on average, has fifteen doctors per ten thousand, and the US has twenty-six doctors per ten thousand. The most startling comparison to me is when we look at the mothers. In Burundi, the rate of mothers dying during pregnancy, while giving birth, and during the postpartum period is 548 per one hundred thousand.[15] In the US, that number is twenty per one hundred thousand.[16]

This is where we go back to the mom. She was born in this country, grew up, had her own children, and here we find her with rising blood pressure coming from hours away to a health facility that only *might* be able to adequately treat her.

Through no fault of her own.

Do you see the violence of the situation playing out in this example? The societal structure of poverty into which a woman was born can result in devastation for both her and her child on an individual level. But the main players are not the individual and not necessarily the present time. They're the structures of power, poverty, policy, and history. That's structural violence.

———

In 1951, a thirty-one-year-old mom went to one of the only hospitals available to her as a Black woman. She was bleeding and felt what seemed like a "knot" in her womb. Ten years prior, she and her two young children had moved with her husband from a tobacco farm in Virginia to Dundalk, Maryland, so he could work at a steel company. Over the next few years, they had three more children, and her last delivery in November of 1950 had been fraught with complications during childbirth, including hemorrhaging.

Four and a half months later, she went to that same hospital with more bleeding. This time the doctors biopsied her cervix and soon after diagnosed her with cervical cancer. She was treated with inpatient radium tube inserts and discharged a few days later with follow-up instructions to return for X-rays.

During the inpatient treatments, two samples were taken of her cervix. One was healthy and one was cancerous. That was in January. By August of the same year, she was admitted again with severe abdominal pain and remained in the hospital until her death in early October.

Her name was Henrietta Lacks, and those biopsied cells—legally at the time, yet unethically and unjustly shared without her knowledge or consent—would become known as the immortal HeLa cell lines. They were unique, as they doubled every twenty to twenty-four hours while other cells would typically die. And because of this uniqueness, they're one of the cell lines most commonly used today in medical development for studying the human genome. The HeLa cells also played a critical role in the development of vaccines, including the ones used to combat COVID-19. Mrs. Lacks's cells continue to live on even though she died an early death.

Here's the main problem in this story though: massive profits have been made from those cells obtained unethically and without consent. Yes, they've been useful to protect tens of thousands from diseases like polio and COVID-19, and they've advanced cancer research, but most of the companies profiting from the cells have not passed earnings back to Mrs. Lacks's family. Nor has her contribution always been credited. One of her granddaughters told *Nature*, "I want scientists to acknowledge that HeLa cells came from an African American woman who was flesh and blood, who had a family and who had a story."[17]

In a notable shift, the then-director of the US National Institutes of Health, Dr. Francis Collins, who remained the director during the COVID-19 pandemic years, met with the Lacks family to discuss their matriarch's cell lines. After months of discussion, the family decided they wanted the data to be made available but under a restricted access system. A committee including Lacks's family members would review requests to use the data. In addition, all papers publishing results from the HeLa cell line would recognize Henrietta Lacks and her kin.[18]

Why do I talk about Mrs. Lacks's story in a chapter on structural violence? Many of us know her story about the injustice of obtaining her cells without her consent. I want to talk about that, for sure. But I also want to highlight where she sought care—or, more succinctly, the only place she could seek care as a Black woman. She sought care within an unequal national health system, with only a few hospitals she could go to, resulting in structural violence in the form of the system being unequal. The structural racism was the health system not being equal *for her*.

I could tell you stories of such inequity in many countries, concerning many other health conditions. Here in the United States, we see this play out within marginalized communities due to the lack of adequate health care access or poverty contributing to conditions like diabetes complications and to deaths from preventable diseases and conditions like HIV and asthma.[19] And COVID-19.

To date, race and ethnicity groups other than White and Asian have disproportionally suffered from COVID-19 the most.[20] Although Hispanic or Latino persons make up 18 percent of the US population, they make up 25 percent of all COVID-19 cases. And when we look at death rates, the differences are even more alarming.

Hispanic, Black, American Indian or Alaska Native, and Native Hawaiian or other Pacific Islander people were twice as likely to die from COVID-19 than White people, even after adjusting for age differences. During surges, these differences widened further. For example, in the summer surge of 2020, Hispanic people with COVID-19 were five times—*five times*—more likely to die than White people, while Black people were four times more likely to die than their White counterparts.

Several researchers have looked at the reasons for these disparities, and they've found that a good bit of them are not biological or individual reasons, like behavior or underlying conditions. Dr. Rashawn Ray, a senior fellow at the Brookings Institution and professor of sociology at the University of Maryland, wrote a sobering piece on disparities during the pandemic and started his article with force: "There is a saying—'When America catches a cold, Black people get the flu.' Well, in 2020, when America catches coronavirus, Black people die." He went on to argue that "structural conditions that inform pre-existing conditions and health disparities are the main culprit for the epidemic within the pandemic."[21]

Yes, underlying health conditions mattered greatly during the COVID-19 pandemic. But so do the structures supporting—or not supporting—them. I urge you to read the full article, but I want to list a few of those structures, as they're applicable to understanding structural violence in most any other health disparity.

What are some of the structures affecting COVID-19 outcomes? Living in neighborhoods with a lack of healthy food options and green spaces are "rooted in the historical legacy of redlining."[22]

Living in crowded areas, using public transportation, holding jobs noted as the essential workforce (which really means you come into contact more often with others in your job as a janitor, food store cashier, or bus driver). Criminalization and overpolicing, climate change and pollution. Racial bias in medical treatment and lack of trust with the medical system due to the "colonial legacy" of the Tuskegee experiment or the Henrietta Lacks legacy.

We all know that our surroundings affect us. Where we were born, what we have access to, what we can buy, whether we can walk safely to the store or for exercise, where we can go for medical care if we need it all matter to us as individuals. But these are structures.

In the United States, however, we don't like to talk about structural violence. That makes a lot of us feel uncomfortable. But if we pull back the curtain of people's stories and lives, we begin to see the ominous threads of these violent structures. We see the marginalized communities lacking access to timely health care or the ability to build generational wealth—not as their own fault, but rather as a result of the history in that community. Let me show you an example of redlining.

———

During the Great Depression in the 1930s, many families couldn't make their mortgage payments due to the widespread unemployment, resulting in foreclosures. In response, the federal government created the Home Owners' Loan Corporation, or HOLC, to help people stay in their homes by refinancing mortgages with lower interest rates and longer repayment times.[23]

Prior to giving out the loans, the HOLC sent representatives into neighborhoods to appraise the houses, noting the types they found and demographic information about the families living in them.[24] In the documentation, you can find a section titled "detrimental influences" indicating poor upkeep and maintenance of the homes along with "infiltration of negroes" and "mixed races." Each neighborhood was then given a designation: "best," "still desirable," "definitely declining," or "hazardous." Then banks used these classifications to determine who would qualify for a home loan. If your neighborhood received a rating other than "best" or "still desirable," you wouldn't qualify for a mortgage.

During the period of 1946 to 1959, less than 2 percent of homes insured by the Federal Housing Administration were owned by people of color. This is one of the first examples of what is called redlining ("the term has come to mean racial discrimination of any kind in housing, but it comes from government maps that outlined areas where Black residents lived and were therefore deemed risky investments").[25] In the coming decades, this policy would be somewhat reversed with equal access to mortgages in the 1977 Community Reinvestment Act. However, redlining wouldn't.

In 2018, a Brookings report found that Black neighborhoods had lower property values than White neighborhoods in similar areas, and this can only partially be explained by the neighborhood's physical characteristics or lack of amenities, such as playgrounds or green spaces.[26] On average, the loss in property values in Black neighborhoods is $48,000 per home. The result of these invisible lines drawn around certain neighborhoods prevented upward mobility for entire communities of color.

One of the best ways to build wealth is to own a home, wrapping up more and more equity the longer you own the property. Across generations, your inability to own a home hinders your ability to build generational wealth. If your family owned a home in a redlined neighborhood in 1960, over the next forty years you lost $212,000 in personal wealth generated by home ownership, which you would have accrued if you'd lived in a greenlined neighborhood. "That [redlining] has had a lingering effect on their children and grandchildren, who don't have the same economic opportunities as their white counterparts," Daryl Fairweather, a chief economist at Redfin, noted.[27]

This lingering effect is an example of structural racism from nearly one hundred years ago. Part of thinking like the Good Samaritan is to come to terms with these forms of racism and working toward a fairer future. In practical terms, let me show you how this is happening in the town I live in—Durham, North Carolina.

In the 1930s, HOLC representatives came to Durham to assess each neighborhood's risk for mortgage lending. If you look into the records of those visits, you can find neighborhoods rated as declining or risky, such as, "This was formerly a good white residential street. But negroes are gradually taking up the area." What followed over the next few decades compared with other parts of town were minimal investments in the schools, rarely if ever added amenities such as sidewalks and green spaces, and few if any health facilities close by.

Now one of those neighborhoods has one of the highest rates of food insecurity, no health clinic or pharmacy within a quarter mile, and the worst-performing school in the county. To increase the availability of affordable housing in neighborhoods like this one, Durham City Council passed a $95 million bond and is setting aside a portion of the tax rate to fund the initiative.[28]

The point of this example is to remind us that the history of a place impacts the present. Thinking like the Good Samaritan means we don't shame the neighborhood or people in it for not having enough green space or for having a poor-performing school. It's recognizing there's a history to be told. A structural violence to be accounted for.

———

Let's go back to the beginning of this chapter. I had the same condition the mom in Burundi had—preeclampsia. But I didn't experience structural violence when I gave birth to my son. I received a timely diagnosis and was fortunate to have a quick delivery with great medications. I had good health insurance, so the huge hospital bills didn't bankrupt us. I also had the ability to easily travel back and forth to the same hospital in the weeks following the birth to receive the care I needed.

And I lived.

But singing through the night with faith doesn't overcome structural violence. Lifesaving drugs, equal access to health care, person-centered policies, poverty protections, and dismantling oppressive systems does. Anyone can be sung to. Not everyone lives. Good Samaritan stopping means caring about both. Faith and also health care.

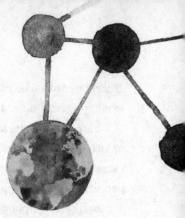

CHAPTER 9

WHEN THE MINORITY IS THE MAJORITY— AND WE MISS IT

We do not just risk repeating history if we sweep it under the carpet; we also risk being myopic about our present.
CHIMAMANDA NGOZI ADICHIE

A discourse on human rights must begin with the right to life that is the right precisely of the poor.
JON SOBRINO, *SPIRITUALITY OF LIBERATION*

If you've grown up in the Western world or as a White person or as a Christian like I did, it's easy to think most people are like you. If you're in America, where we're conditioned to be individuals or do-it-yourselfers, you can easily live in an insulated bubble where everyone looks like you do—or at least is look-ish. In other words, what you see is normal for everyone else, right?

Sure, we may have some financial problems or health problems or other real-life problems, and I don't want to negate or minimize those at all. They're very real and tangible hardships for many people. But if we're not careful to look outside our own bubbles, it seems like most people around us look as well as talk, act, think, believe, and even worship like we do. Our bubbles can produce a clouding effect on our reality, almost like those large, weird glasses they give you to block out your peripheral view during an eye exam. Or we can be like a little kid who's playing hide-and-seek and puts his hands over his eyes. *You can't see me if I can't see you*, he seems to think as he's "hiding" in the middle of the living room floor. I miss those days with my kiddos.

We do that with the world's needs, too, like inequity and racism and a lack of basic needs for millions. We can miss them entirely because they're not in our bubble. If you're reading this book, I have a hunch you care about those things, but they can still be easy to miss. If we're not careful, we won't see what we're actually walking by, passing a need like the religious leaders in the Good Samaritan story did. We think where we are is normal for everywhere, that where we are is where most everyone else is too. We think what is normal for us is, well, normal for everyone. That my center is everyone else's center too.

That's when we miss that our normal is actually not normal at all, missing reality. When we do this, we miss the opportunity to live into the reality of the world in meaningful ways. But we can take off the glasses hiding the periphery of our vision, and that, my friends, is when real change occurs. If we go to the Good Samaritan story, that's when we can see what's on the side of the road and decide to not just walk by.

We have to see it first, though. That what some of us think is normal, especially if we're in the historically powerful and privileged position of being a White Christian in the US, isn't actually the majority.

And that matters.

————

Let me start with a few examples. Do you own a car? So do 91 percent of people in America and over 80 percent of people in Germany, China, New Zealand, Britain, and a few other countries.[1] Do you own two cars? A little over 50 percent of American families do too. It's no wonder, then, that those of us living in the US think the majority of people everywhere else have a car. But the majority of people in the world *don't* have a car. In fact, globally, only 18 percent of people own a car, and I couldn't even find a statistic for two-car ownership. Whoa! This means the wealth of owning a car, even if it's a beat-up ole white Chevy with windows that don't roll down correctly, like the one I had in high school, is concentrated in only a handful of countries.

The point I'm trying to make is that something as mundane as car ownership, like a lot of things, might *look* like the majority around you, but it's actually a minority for everyone else in our world.

Let's look at another example, a little closer to home if you live in the United States. Do you have food in your pantry—even a little bit? Some of us have an extra fridge or chest freezer in the garage. Some of us shop at huge warehouse stores and stock up on four bazillion boxes of goldfish crackers. (Well, that's how many it feels like you bought when you find a third of those crackers stuffed in between your car seats.)

Fifty years ago, the White House convened a landmark conference on food, nutrition, and health and estimated that fifteen million Americans were facing food insecurity, defined as not having access to sufficient food or food of an adequate quality to meet one's basic needs.[2] (Notice I said *basic*, not *fully satisfying* or *abundant*.) Over the next nearly fifty years, this number fluctuated a bit but mainly hovered around the 11 percent mark.[3] That is, until 2020. During the same time period, nearly 15 percent of all US households reported food insecurity, almost a 40 percent increase in just a few years.[4]

But as you probably already anticipate me saying, this food insecurity, then, isn't spread evenly across all US families. And if we go to the data as an epidemiologist would, we can see who suffers the most—families with children, rural communities, single mothers, and families already below the poverty line. A whopping 32 percent of families under the poverty line could not meet their basic food needs, more than double those above the poverty line during the COVID-19 pandemic. During the pandemic, food insecurity was a staggering two and a half times higher for Black families and two times higher for Hispanic families than it was for White families.

I could give example after example of these scenarios. Do you have health insurance—even a little? Do you have stable housing? Do you have access to a library? Stable internet access? Electricity and clean water? At least five hundred dollars in savings? Do you make more than $10 per day? How about $30 per day? If you said yes to any of those questions, you are in a minority. Two-thirds of the world's people live on less than $10 per day, and 85 percent live on less than $30 per day when you adjust for the purchasing power in each country.[5] One in ten lives on less than $1.90 per day.

The *majority* of the world's people don't have health insurance—less than 40 percent.[6] For comparison, nearly 90 percent of Americans do, although I recognize that's not sufficient for many families due to exorbitant health care costs. And the majority of the world's population doesn't have clean water, a nest egg for a rainy day, enough food, or adequate housing. But the world's power and privilege are still largely centered around a minority few—namely, individuals from Western countries—and double points if you're White and male.

Now, I fit that profile except for the dude part. But I'm married to a man and I have a son, so this is no shade to the dudes. It is, however, an acknowledgment of how the world has historically worked through the lens of a minority few powerful leaders. The *real* majority are the counterparts we just described: the poor, the marginalized, those with minimal access to health care and basic human rights. In other words, who we think is the minority is actually the majority. But some of us have missed that.

———

One of the first times I saw the majority of the world correctly was on the trip with the Mercy Ships in Honduras I told you about in previous chapters. On days when I didn't have a kitchen shift, I went with the teams on their medical clinic visits to help in any way I could.

The first time we traveled a long way to a rural area, and the closer we got to the village, the more children ran beside our vehicle until it was surrounded by the time we parked. Since I wasn't qualified for any medical work, I was put in charge of the next most important task—making puppet balloons.

Now, up to this point, I had never made a puppet balloon, and as I've mentioned, I couldn't speak the language. But I mustered all the enthusiasm I had, which wasn't hard because I've always had a lot, twisted a balloon into something resembling a monkey, made a silly monkey sound in a loud voice—probably with a dance like one does in those moments—and then raised the balloon into the air. To my delight, all the kids squealed like I'd just made *Mona Lisa* from that balloon. And then the twists came apart and the balloon ended up looking like a snake. Oh well, I tried.

We had the best time giggling while the parents received the medical attention they needed. I saw lots of joy that day, but I also saw poverty like I'd never seen before. In my upbringing, most of my friends and I had never known what it was to be without shoes, enough food, or medical care when we needed it. Now I was seeing those conditions for nearly all these children and for the majority of the people in these villages. For the first time, I saw it. And the minority in my mind became the majority. I saw reality as it truly was. If we go back to the Good Samaritan story, this is the point where we have a choice to make—walk by or stop.

———

I can't leave this chapter without talking about how this viewpoint challenges some Western thinking when it comes to faith. In the United States, 70 to 75 percent of people identifying with a religious group report being Christian, depending on which research poll you view. If we zoom out to the whole world, however, people who identify as being part of the Christian faith is only 31 percent, followed closely by the percent of people who identify as being part of the Islamic faith.[7]

Let's zoom back to the United States again. Of the 70 to 75 percent of those professing to follow the Christian faith, 23 percent identify as evangelical. And over the past few years, we've seen an increase in Americans identifying as not having any religious affiliation, especially among younger ages.

Now, stay with me through this line of thinking. If you're in an evangelical church, you might hear a time gone by described as the "good old days." When you could pray openly in schools and football games began with a Christian prayer. When allegiance to

Christian family values was considered the norm. Like you see in the TV show *The Waltons*, depicting the 1930s era, and *Leave It to Beaver*, depicting the 1950s era. This was an ideal many American families strove for even in the 1990s, when I grew up with prayers at sporting events, See You at the Pole rallies around the American flag, and Fellowship of Christian Athletes meetings.

The point I'm making is that a large swath of how America functioned was according to the 23 percent of the 75 percent. In other words, a minority acted like the majority, and in many cases, they still do. And we missed the real majority. Those good old days weren't actually good at all if you were Muslim. Or Black. Or a member of any other marginalized group.

Don't get me wrong. I love being a Christian, and I'm grateful to live in America.

And also.

I can hold that identification in one hand and watch it take its rightful place when I'm at the foot of the cross of Jesus. There I see the world and who I am, individually *and* collectively, correctly. We've already talked about who Jesus centered on during his time on earth—the children, the poor, the sick, the destitute. Yes, these people were on the margins of society. But to Jesus, they were seen. *They* were the majority, and they were his center.

The Good Samaritan story gives us an opportunity to stop missing the reality of the world. To understand who the true majority is, even in our own towns and cities, we can see it through the lens of equity. And doing so realigns and recenters our eyes and giving and compassion and hearts correctly. We no longer walk by.

May his majority become my center.

PART 2

COST

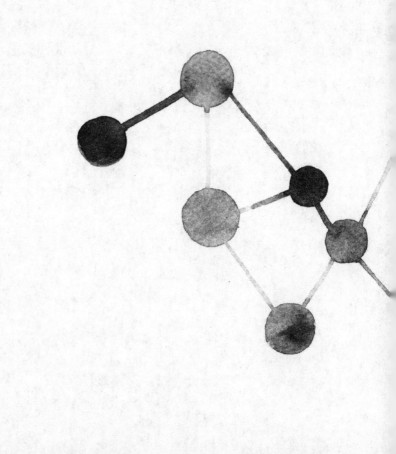

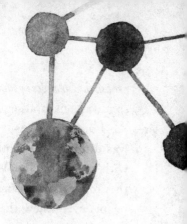

CHAPTER 10

THE NEIGHBORHOOD

These things I remember
as I pour out my soul:
how I used to go to the house of God
under the protection of the Mighty One
with shouts of joy and praise
among the festive throng. . . .
Deep calls to deep
in the roar of your waterfalls;
all your waves and breakers
have swept over me.

PSALM 42:4, 7

It was March 2020. I had just finished a busy season of traveling and speaking at my college alma mater, Wayland Baptist University, and at a global health missions conference in Houston, Texas. At both events, I was asked the same questions in hallways and at dinners and in lecture rooms: *What is happening in Wuhan, and should we worry about it?* Both lectures were about global health, so it was a natural segue to talk about the virus.

I answered, yes, we needed to pay attention to this virus. It was different from other epidemics we'd seen in the world, like with the Ebola and Marburg viruses. As awful as those are, and they're horrific, this new virus could be airborne and spread before people even knew they were infectious, as opposed to spreading after they knew they were sick, which is the case with Ebola. The other big reason we needed to pay attention to it? We would need to depend on one another to contain the spread of the virus. And the marginalized—those without access to health care, the poor, and the uninsured—would be impacted the most, like they always are during epidemics.

Both speaking engagements were for faith-based audiences, so I was also able to weave in the Good Samaritan story, encouraging those of us who followed the Christian faith to see this event as an opportunity to live that faith out loud by not just walking by. Yes, we would need to take this outbreak seriously and respond accordingly.

I drove home from the second engagement with an ominous feeling. I didn't listen to my podcasts or audiobooks like I did on most trips. During those six hours, I just sat in the driver's seat with my mind whirling. As an epidemiologist, I knew what *could* be, and I was hoping for the best.

As a global health researcher with lots of training in how pandemics work, I feared for countries that had barely weathered past epidemics and already had crumbling health systems due to historical inequities, power structures that benefited the rich and left the poor even poorer, and large swaths of their populations suffering from malnutrition, food insecurity, and poverty.

As a married mom of two, I was making a mental list of what to do just in case. Buy more disinfecting supplies, stock up on essential medicines, and call my mom and close friends to tell them to do the same. Oh, and pick up an extra bag of chicken nuggets.

By the time I got home, more information about the new virus, COVID-19, was coming in, and I heard the virus was spreading. Fast. I read the news and looked at the data points like I'd learned about in my PhD courses—the positivity rates, R0 (a calculation quantifying the intensity of the outbreak), susceptibility, incubation periods, virulence. And all data pointed toward . . . well, I'm not even sure what word to use to describe it. I still have the same awful feeling in the pit of my gut as I write this. It's like the meteorologist telling people days before a hurricane, when the sun is still shining and the weather looks great, "Board up your houses, get prepared, evacuate. This is going to be a bad storm." They're trained to look at the radars and wind speeds and a bajillion data points to predict where the storm will hit and how bad it will be.

One of the hardest parts of being an epidemiologist in early 2020—actually throughout the next two-plus years—was seeing the storm coming. And also seeing people never boarding up the house or evacuating. We also saw people who did everything right to prepare, but because of underlying health conditions or age or poverty or disparities or structural inequalities, they would be caught in the storm.

———

That brings me to my neighborhood in late March 2020, when it was still sunny outside—both metaphorically because COVID-19 hadn't yet fully hit Texas and physically because we were in the middle of the state, where the sun was usually shining. And always hot. Or at least it felt that way.

I had read and read and read the news and early scientific preprints coming out about the virus, and I needed to get outside so my kids wouldn't see me cry and to catch my breath. I could see the storm coming (*many* of us did), and it wrecked me.

I was on the front porch when my sweet neighbor drove by, rolled down her window, and said in her usual super-friendly voice, "Hey, friend! How are ya?" Poor gal was no doubt unprepared for her epidemiologist neighbor to burst into tears, but that's what I did. Then because she's that kind of friend, she cried with me when I told her about the impending storm.

I said thousands of people would die unless we as a nation acted correctly and that the toll would not be equal. We talked about our parents and older members of our church and then cried some more. Then our kiddos ran out of our houses and interrupted us with requests for food, and we tried to go back to our normal lives.

But that wouldn't happen anytime soon. The pandemic would go on to infect more than 750 million people worldwide, with nearly seven million deaths,[1] of which more than one million were from the US, an additional twenty-two million deaths due to disruptions in health systems,[2] and 10.5 million children losing a parent or caregiver to the disease.[3] A tidal wave was coming.

After that talk with my neighbor, I decided to create a social media page to help explain what was happening in real-world terms to my family and friends. *What does "flatten the curve" mean? Do we need to leave our UPS packages outside for 2.84 days in direct sunlight? And do we really need that much toilet paper?* What started for a few friends and my mom was shared to their friends. And then their friends. Pretty soon more than five hundred people were following along. Then a thousand, and then . . . well, you get the picture.

I named the page "Friendly Neighbor Epidemiologist" because I tend to be friendly, maybe too friendly at times. (My apologies if you happen to have the seat next to me on an airplane.) I also love talking about epidemiology—just ask my students. I tend to get a bit animated talking about odds ratios and spreadsheets in class, especially when you can use these tools to combat social issues.

Again, I also knew this type of virus would require us to protect one another, because certain sub-groups are at higher risk of severe disease. And again, this type of virus could spread fast before people even knew they were sick and contagious. Hence, we would have to be good neighbors to one another in both word and deed. I also strongly believed that this was a chance to live out the Good Samaritan story to our neighbors by protecting them through social distancing, using masks, and getting vaccines. To me, this would be our time to shine in what I thought was to come so naturally to us as Christians—loving our neighbors.

Over the next several months, the page's following grew to tens of thousands of people, and I frequently talked with the local news and media to help explain the virus through their outlets.

The growth of my social media page meant I could help more people. But it also meant exposure to a set of people I'd never experienced—people who would harass and threaten me and come after my family. To say I was unprepared for this would be an understatement.

A few months after I started the page, I was working at home, like we all were at the time except for health care personnel and essential workers, when my husband handed me a white piece of paper with a note handwritten in red and black marker. It was a threat, and the note was laced with biblical revelation language talking about the mark of the beast and how I was part of it because of my stance on COVID-19, along with threats I won't reveal here. The worst part was that he'd found it in our mailbox.

I nearly passed out, but then I charged out the front door and down the street like a mama bear while saying some things I don't want to repeat. I didn't know who sent the note, and what would I have done if I had known? I'd already received quite a few online threats and harassments, even a few from people I knew in town. Some included pictures of guns with statements that I or my family needed to be "taken down" or horrific comments about gas chambers with photos of Auschwitz. But these mostly came through the internet, which in and of itself was scary.

Now, though, a line had been crossed with my family. And Momma doesn't mess with that. Later that week, on TV, I would see some far-right rallies in my town with similar handwriting, biblical references, and colors, but we'll never know if there was a connection.

We called the authorities, who came over to take a statement. They said they would increase patrol around our house at different points in the day, and it felt really disconcerting in the coming weeks to see a police car parked across the street. I was thankful for it, don't get me wrong. It just felt weird. Our neighborhood had always been an area where the kids could walk around freely, and we knew most of our neighbors. If a kid fell off a bike down a certain street, they knew whose house they could go to to call their parent. We also went to church or worked with several of our neighbors. It was—well, it felt—safe.

But after that threat, we no longer let our kids walk alone in the neighborhood. My husband or I would go with them "to get more exercise," as we told them. We installed lots of cameras, and I worked with authorities on threats coming from the internet. Again, it felt weird. Now, I know that was trauma, as my body would tell me months later.

All my epidemiology friends were receiving the same types of threatening messages with varying intensities, with the worst being aimed at my female epidemiology colleagues. One of the worst messages I received was from a woman who lived within a few miles of me, went to church with us, and had her children in programs with mine. I won't share all the details, but she started sending me harassing messages, including ones about my kids. I blocked her. Then her husband came after me with even worse messages. I blocked him. Then they made a comment on one of my family member's photos on social media I'd been tagged in years ago. It was frustrating and scary.

Messages from others included pictures of guns with messages I will not publish, junk about my children or husband, threats laced with White supremacy, Holocaust-type imagery further plastered with Bible verses. It feels odd to distill down hundreds of these messages into a few sentences, and I've gone back and forth to know what level of detail to publish. I've settled on telling you it was a lot and extremely frightening, leaving me feeling woefully unprepared for how to handle this. *Where do I go and what do I do? Who can I trust? And is my family safe?* I reported them all to the correct people, including high authorities. But when it comes to social media, I don't think that goes anywhere. Free speech doesn't equal hate speech, but that's not distilled enough in social media platforms.

At least if I didn't know the person who sent the harassment or threat, it would sting, and it was scary, but a level of removal existed because they only seemed like an awful person on the internet, someone I'd never meet.

The ones that came from people I knew really hurt, though, and if they came from people of faith I knew, that was a double whammy. More than 90 percent of the threats I received were from people of the Christian faith. But when you actually *know* them and they go to church with you, it really throws you off-kilter. I'm not ready to talk about everything that happened during that time. And if I'm being really honest, it was plain scary. It was traumatizing. It was awful. It was costly.

———

What I want to say is that when you start thinking like a Good Samaritan, like we talked about in the first part of this book, your actions will follow suit, and we'll talk about that in the last part of this book. It's the in-between part that's the hardest, though, at least for me. There's a cost in shifting our worldview and actions to match. The cost could be of comfort or physical security. Or of heritage or a foundation you've been building for years that takes only seconds to unravel. Or of losing friends or community. Or of who you once were or how you were perceived. Those were my losses, but I'm sure there were more.

Yes, there is another side. Courageous living, like being the kind of neighbor Jesus talked about, redeems that cost many times over. I don't want to skip over this in-between time to get there, though. It's here we need to be first, the cost part, because it was the hardest part for me to sit with.

Jesus talked about this cost too. In Luke 14, he tells his disciples two parables to illustrate what discipleship should look like. In other words, what does it mean to follow him? One story is about a man who's building a house, then runs out of money because he didn't figure out the construction costs before he started. In the second story, Jesus talks about a king going to battle only after he makes sure he has enough troops.

I think Jesus was telling us to count the cost of following him with these illustrations. As Eugene Peterson writes in the Message translation of the Bible, "Simply put, if you're not willing to take what is dearest to you, whether plans or people, and kiss it good-bye, you can't be my disciple."[4] Now, I don't think Jesus is telling us we have to give up everything we love to follow him and live like a hermit. I fundamentally believe he wants us to enjoy life and live it abundantly. What I think he's saying is this: "Would you give it up if I asked?" Our financial security, prestige, lifelong community, time—our friends? Because sometimes, following Jesus requires that.

Dear friends of mine had all the financial security anyone would want, a dream home just built, and plans laid out for the next few decades. But then they sold everything and moved to Africa with their kids to help sick children in remote areas not many people visit. They tell stories of raising their children amid the rebel fighting at the time—some right outside their windows as they hid—sickness, and a loss of what they thought their life would look like. But just ask them if they regret any of it. Without hesitation, they and their children, who are now grown, will say no.

This couple were the main people I called during this hard part of the pandemic to ask not only for their prayers but for their advice. Several times I asked them if I should just quit, especially when the threats were increasing. (And sometimes we *should* quit for the sake of our health and family. You'll read about that in the next chapter.) That's when the story of their costs and how they're living now motivated me to keep going even amid my own costs as I experienced the loss of relationships and relative assurance of safety.

They were showing me there's another side to the costs of following Jesus, even though I couldn't see it for myself yet. Now I do see it, and I guess that's how I want to end this chapter. This is only the in-between part. For sure, it's hard, disorienting, lonely, vulnerable. It's full of loss and pain and "*what* is happening here?" It's messy and can feel long. But there's something on the other side of the cost. There's courage. And not just any type of courage. A courage that helps us be neighbors, despite the cost. We'll get there, but I don't want to move too quickly. If we do, we'll miss understanding the costs that make us truly neighbors to others.

By the way, that couple were among the first to encourage me to write a book and my husband and me to take our kids to Africa, both of which we're doing this year.

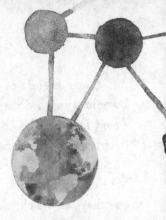

CHAPTER 11

UNTETHERING AND LOSS

*Keep watch, dear Lord, with those who work, or watch,
or weep this night, and give your angels charge over
those who sleep. Tend the sick, Lord Christ; give rest to
the weary, bless the dying, soothe the suffering, pity the
afflicted, shield the joyous; and all for your love's sake.*

COMPLINE

During the COVID-19 pandemic years, we would come to leave our church and lose a good bit of friends. It feels odd to even write that sentence because I could write chapters on those few words. This is a bigger story to tell, but it's one for another time.

We moved to another house and bought more security cameras. We did what we needed to do to keep our address from being made public or findable through a web search. I received more threats and an immense amount of harassment. And I wasn't the only one. My epidemiology and public health colleagues were also experiencing some form of harassment.

People were also experiencing unimaginable loss of life, and I want to honor that. My loss was more a loss of identity or a heritage. But it was still devastating on a personal level to lose so much so quickly. My faith tradition had always been a safe haven for me, and I'm so fortunate to have grown up in healthy faith spaces.

Then in late 2020, I was seeing some of the faith leaders I'd grown up with and mainstream Christian music artists I'd listened to attend the massive Christian prayer rally held in Washington D.C., at the height of the winter surge, two days before the world hit one million lives lost to COVID-19. I had already seen or heard many pastors I respected or musicians I supported say things I felt were dishonoring to our God, and subsequently to our neighbors, like "Faith over fear" when it came to masking or "All lives matter" when it came to Black Lives Matter rallies.

Leaving our church, no longer feeling at home in many evangelical spaces, and losing lifelong friends and traditions felt like losing the foundations I'd been building for forty years—my whole life. And I lost it. Don't hear me wrong; I didn't lose my faith or hope. But it seemed like my life as I'd known it so far was untethering. It was—and still is—gutting to me.

Friends from my childhood, lifelong friends who had hosted my wedding and baby showers, were sending some pretty horrific messages as they expressed what they were feeling about me—against me. It was devastating. I'd grown up in the same town, visited the same family for reunions and holidays, and now because I spoke up during the pandemic, that foundation was crumbling too.

Maybe the worst loss was who I had thought I was. I've always been idealistic, compassionate, and, again, probably too friendly. If you can imagine a woman walking down the streets of New York City with the song "I'm Yours" written and recorded by Jason Mraz playing in her ear, that was me. That song is full of peppy-banjo beats I still can't help smiling and bouncing to when I walk.

Prior to the pandemic, I remember my therapist telling me I didn't have to say hi to everyone I see. I also remember walking on the streets of New York so happy to be there, saying hi to people like a good Southern woman, and the first person who yelled at me with a "What do you want?" response. Ha! Maybe I'm not cut out for the big city, but again, that's me. Friendly, joyful, idealistic.

Until I wasn't during these pandemic years. Losing that part of me has been the worst to go through.

These losses were untethering. An unraveling of a gorgeous blanket woven for four decades by friends and family and faith. By safety and sameness and love. And then it was nearly gone. Or at least it felt that way.

———

During this time, I continued writing and navigating the pandemic with people on the Friendly Neighbor Epidemiologist page while also holding the tensions of the personal losses I'd suffered and was continuing to experience, plus the losses my family was experiencing. Although theirs is not my story to tell, a momma's heart wants to protect as much as she possibly can. So I tried to hold and protect and love and catch.

But at this point, it had been over a year of near-daily social media posts with too many threats and harassments to count. These big-*T* and little-*t* traumas accumulated over time, even when I tried to deal with them with therapy, exercise, the friends I still had, and hugging my dog. My body was "keeping score,"[1] and it was all about to become too much.

During Holy Week 2021, I had just finished writing a series of daily reflections; wrapped up several high-level interviews on faith and the pandemic with evangelical leaders I deeply respected (and still do), like Dr. Russell Moore and Dr. Walter Kim; worked my normal job; and baked Easter cinnamon roll bunnies. This could be called burning the candle at both ends, plus in the middle. Yet relatively speaking, I was doing okay. I felt fine physically, and I was mentally hanging in there.

I wish I'd known what was coming, but I didn't see it then. Now I do. After Holy Week, I noticed that I felt something weird in my head, which I thought was anxiety. I'd struggled with anxiety before and had definitely struggled with it more over the last several months. Yoga seemed to help on most days, so I turned on YouTube and got ready to find my zen. And oh boy, did the opposite happen.

Downward dog I went, which involves an upside-down movement where you hope to not fall over, and I suddenly felt the worst pain I'd ever felt. It was a migraine or thunderclap-type headache. I didn't pass out, but I don't remember much about that day—just getting my kids to my husband in a weird haze, and then being overcome with, again, the worst pain I had ever felt, including labor pain.

To bed I went, and I stayed there for nearly seven weeks. I visited the doctor several times, but all tests came back clear, and the preliminary diagnosis was anxiety. Later, this would be diagnosed as chronic migraine, the kind that hangs on for weeks without proper response to treatment. The kind that makes you nauseated all the time, weak because you can't get outside or have any lights on, and depressed because it's unrelenting.

I couldn't wash my hair or even put it in a ponytail, read, work, watch TV, walk around my neighborhood, cook, be in a room with the overhead lights on, laugh (oh, did I miss laughing with my kids), smile for too long, or any other normal everyday activities without my headache sending me straight back to bed with the curtains pulled and the lights off. As a person who's always loved the outdoors, not being able to go outside because it was too bright felt smothering. This health crisis was unlike anything I'd ever experienced. To a person who smiled a lot, getting a sickening headache with full-body symptoms after smiling just a little was—well, I can't even find the right word for it because it wasn't me at all. But totally out of my control.

I tried everything to fix it. I meditated every day, journaled, completely changed my diet, limited my use of screens. I went to bed early, only to be woken up by pain throughout the night. I maxed out on over-the-counter medicines my doctor had told me when and how to take.

And I cried. A lot. It felt like I couldn't crawl out of this agony even though it wasn't for lack of trying. In those months of sickness, I found myself the person on the side of the road. But slowly and surely, after spending those nearly seven weeks solid in bed, my body got better, and I could actually go into the living room to be with the kids. After that, I could walk around the block, although I needed my husband there to support my weight after about fifteen minutes.

But then I would have a setback with the headaches and have to start all over again. This ebb and flow lasted for months. I was devastated, in a tremendous amount of pain, lonely, very scared, and still trying everything possible to get better. But nothing worked. It was untethering physically on top of the other untethering. Or probably because of it. The body truly does keep score, and mine was in a deficit.

I don't remember much else during this time other than feeling really scared that this would never end. I don't remember the normal things, like celebrating Advent or taking my kids back-to-school shopping. I don't remember Christmas, even though we have pictures of me lying on the couch. I don't remember that entire summer. It's weird not to remember those things.

It was eight months before I found a neurologist who gave me the right tests and diagnoses to start a treatment plan. And seven more months before we found the correct combination of treatment. And then three more months before the treatment kicked in and began to work. For those of you with chronic illness, you know those months of testing new medicines can't be written about in one sentence like this one. The reality is that those months are fraught with side effects, weaning off medicines that don't work, waiting to see if other ones will. Lots of pain and dark rooms with any hint of light blocked out. In another summary sentence, it was hard and scary.

The worst part was still not knowing if it would ever end.

I didn't play games with my family that would be too loud or make me laugh. I didn't race my kids in the backyard or play video games with them. For a full year. Last month, though, we played the game *Guesstures*, and I laughed so hard I nearly peed my pants. I laughed hard and loud and long. I gestured in exuberant ways when it was my turn to act out the words. And it was glorious. I went to bed that night with my cheeks hurting from laughing, not my head hurting.

Here's what I know now. I will not tie up this chapter with weak, pseudo-faith platitudes like *God is so good* or *I'm so thankful I was in bed for months* or *This experience made me stronger*. I think those are silly. Nope, not gonna do it. Yes, God is good, and I am thankful (but not for being sick), but am I stronger? I don't think so.

What I am is slower at life. Not planning for the next five years. Not hustling. Not going for the gold in everything. I'm slower, and I have limits. Glorious limits of more empathy for and solidarity with others who suffer from chronic illness, including the many people with long COVID-19. I'm taking it one day at a time, and I'm thankful that it's not one hour at a time, because I remember those months too.

Here's what else I know. I made it. With a limp like Jacob's,[2] and depression and anxiety like Elijah's,[3] but with joy and belly laughs like I imagine Peter experienced after he ate the fish over that charcoal fire.[4] And again, with compassion for others who suffer. Because I *understand* it. Certainly not all of it, but more than before.

It's a combination of empathy and tears.

It's that word *withness* again.

It's accompaniment.

When I found myself as the person on the side of the road, I also found a God who stopped to help.

If there's any encouragement I can give, it's that this sounds a lot like Jesus too. He understands our suffering—not in a way that shows off power and privilege, although he certainly could have done that as God on earth. But he chose humility. He chose to come as a servant, a suffering servant, who lowered himself to us in a gesture that looks similar to the Good Samaritan lowering himself to the person in need.[5] Who understands our weaknesses, who groans with us, who prays for us. He dwelt and dwells among us.

God with us.

With us.

Withness.

Sometimes I wonder *why* the Good Samaritan in Jesus' story stopped. What gave him empathy and compassion? What propelled him toward withness and lowering himself to take care of the person on the side of the road? Was it because he'd been accompanied by someone himself and was paying it forward? We don't know, but I have a hunch.

———

I don't have a nice and neat way to tie up this chapter, but I do have the outcome of the untethering that happened to me. The outcome of the blanket unraveling, the threads becoming frayed and eventually disappearing. After months of losing what I once knew, both foundationally and physically, I found something else altogether. I found a freedom to be, well, me. You'll hear more about that in the next part of this book. Slower with more limits, a bit snarkier and more courageous than before, but wiser with my heart and filled with lots of empathy. But I also found something deeper. I found that the anchor held.[6] Was it worth those costs? Yes. And the anchor is still holding.

I'm laughing again too. Full-bellied and loud laughing.

Glory.

If the first part of this book was about changing our minds and worldviews and the second part was the cost of doing so, this next part is the "what's next," the faith meeting deeds, and the fun part. Let's finish together.

PART 3

COURAGE

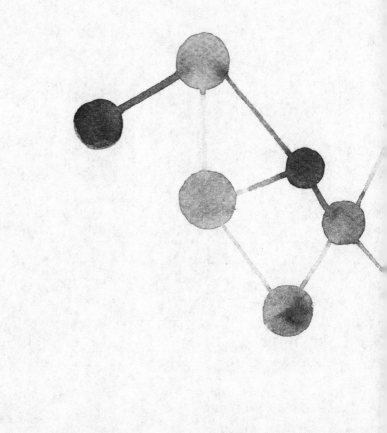

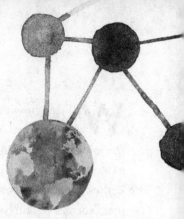

CHAPTER 12

TO BE YOU

There is in you something that waits and listens for the sound of the genuine in yourself and sometimes there is so much traffic going on in your minds, so many different kinds of signals, so many vast impulses floating through your organism that go back thousands of generations long before you were even a thought in the mind of creation and you are buffeted by these and in the midst of all of this you have got to find out what your name is.

Who are you?
REVEREND HOWARD THURMAN

I've accepted that the whole of my life will be a pilgrimage toward the sound of the genuine in me.
COLE ARTHUR RILEY

W ill you go with us?"
A global health hero of mine asked me this question in the middle of a meeting I couldn't even believe I was in, a high-level gathering on universal health coverage held in New York City at the United Nations. Just to be clear, this was not a normal Monday for me. Normal Mondays were making peanut butter and jelly sandwiches for my kids, writing research manuscripts, teaching, and figuring out what to make for supper.

Over the previous few years, I'd been working on epidemiologic projects measuring the burden of children who need surgery around the world with the long-term goal of trying to meet that need in the hardest hit areas by first determining the barriers. Over and over, our studies lined up with what others in the global health field had found or were still finding—poverty is one of the strongest predictors of poor health and death, especially for children.

I'd also been working with a wonderful organization, the Global Initiative for Children's Surgery, known as GICS. I had the honor of going to this high-level meeting with other GICS colleagues, and our mission was to advocate specifically for the inclusion of children's surgery in global health care packages. It was the highlight of my career thus far.

The first day I went to pick up my security badge from the World Health Organization's office and took approximately thirty-seven photos of the door. The next day was like a dream to walk into the historic UN building I'd previously seen only in pictures, past the row of 194 flags flying outside into the massive main room emblazoned with the UN emblem. I was meeting my favorite collabo-friend, Dr. Henry Rice, who was also part of GICS and my main research collaborator and mentor. Not only would we be meeting at the UN, but we'd be meeting in the main assembly hall.

The General Assembly Hall is a gigantic room, measuring

165 feet long, 115 feet wide, and a towering 75 feet high, just like you see in movies or in presidential press conferences or on my favorite TV show of all time, *Madam Secretary*. The hall can seat about two thousand people, with simultaneous interpretation for lots of different languages through interpreters' booths perched behind glass windows in the balconies. The shape of the hall is purposefully circular with an enormous United Nations seal over the podium in a beautiful, lighter wood panel stretching nearly the full 75 feet in height.

On the main floor are the hundreds of seats in sections of six per desk, where the delegates from different countries sit. On the desk at each seat is a digital nameplate for a country (or organization). These nameplates are what you see on TV, displaying countries' names. New Zealand, Botswana, Nepal, China, Nigeria, India, Guatemala, the United States, Finland, Ecuador—and on and on and on they go. In that one room, most countries in the world are represented with just as many languages being spoken at one time. It was magical to hear them all. And similar to the prayer and singing on the Mercy Ships I mentioned earlier in the book, the multiple languages, flags, and colors deeply reminded me of what I think heaven will be like.

The meeting would be live-streamed online, and I texted my husband and parents the link, waited for them to log on, and then nonchalantly walked across the room while trying not to wave at them or smile too much—at which I failed.

After Henry and I found seats near the middle and I officially took way too many photos and then promptly texted them to my parents, the meeting began. Each organization represented had two minutes to advocate for universal health coverage from whatever vantage point they came from. For us, it was children's surgery. During the meeting, various leaders made presentations from the main stage, and then a few people sitting in the audience were called on to make their two-minute statement.

Me with Dr. Henry Rice at the United Nations meetings on universal health coverage

Here's the deal. We didn't quite know when or if we would be called on. We were simply told we would be introduced, the microphone light would come on in front of us, the two-minute time would start, and we'd make a live statement to everyone attending and those listening to the international broadcast.

I was a ball of nerves and was thankful that we would remain seated if called on. I thought for sure I would pass out if I had to stand, and I could sit on my hands to calm my nerves if I remained seated. I was as ready as possible to make the statement. I'd rehearsed it at the dinner table. A lot. And in the pickup line to get my kids from school. A lot. So I was ready, sweaty palms, shaky voice, and all.

Me fangirling with Dr. Tedros, president of the World Health Organization

Day one went by, and it was one of the most exhilarating days I've ever experienced in my professional career. As we moved to the lunch area, the director of the World Health Organization himself, Dr. Tedros, whom I knew and admired deeply, walked by, and I didn't play it cool one bit. I said hello, and lo and behold, he stopped. We chatted for a bit—well, mostly me blubbering something about my appreciation for his work. And then I did my normal go-to when I get nervous. I got a photo. We actually had to take two since the first one is of Dr. Tedros looking at the camera while I'm looking at him with an ear-to-ear smile, full googly-eyed. I have this photo in my office, and it still makes me laugh.

After lunch, I listened to strong and powerful statements from a mom in Nigeria advocating for prenatal care, human rights advocates speaking toward the inclusion of LGBTQ and trans health care protections, and diplomatic statements from countries that weren't doing any of the above. But we weren't called on that day.

This brings me to day two. I was chatting with my friend on the right when someone sat down beside me on my left. She turned out to be one of my all-time global health "sheroes." Let's call her Dr. Shero. I totally played it cool. Okay, just kidding. I geeked out and said something like, "Oh my gosh, I love you and know all about you!" while asking for a selfie.

Dr. Shero was known in the global health world as one of the smartest, fiercest, and most tenacious advocates for health care rights for the poor. She was also from Harvard. I had some collabo-friends there, but this woman was different because she was a woman in science.

I flashed back to my senior year of high school. It was 1999, and we were all thinking about colleges, mostly those close to our small hometown. Not many of us would go off to universities like Yale, Harvard, or Stanford, but I wanted to at least try. You never know, right? So I sent an email to each university asking them to send me an application packet in the mail. (For you youngins, that's how we applied for college back in my millennial days.) I ended up letting fear get the best of me and never did apply, throwing the applications away without ever telling anyone about them.

So anyone who went to—much less *worked* at—Harvard was, to me, a huge deal. And bonus points—the Harvard professor sitting beside me was a woman like me.

Okay, back to when Dr. Shero sat down beside me. She represented one of the leading, if not *the* leading, global health organizations in the world—one that was known for pushing against barriers of colonial medicine, stigma, racism, and structural violence. In other words, she was the boss (and I mean that as in the best compliment ever) to many of us women in global health. She was loud and confident and tenacious. In other words, she was opposite to what I felt at that moment. The only thing we seemed to have in common was that we both smiled a lot.

I had two thoughts. First, I was sitting beside greatness. And second, she would see me sweating and shaking if I got called to make my statement.

I was about to ask for her autograph after she graciously took a photo with me, but then she asked the question I started this chapter with: "Will you go with us?"

She had just told all of us she was organizing a walkout in the middle of the meeting to make a statement on universal health coverage. Participants would loudly walk out of the building to a demonstration outside, advocating for health care for all. I remember her leadership and enthusiasm for making a statement by disrupting the meeting.

"Will you go with us?"

She was asking us, quite enthusiastically and convincingly, to walk out of the very important meeting with very important people with her and the others. A bit loudly and disruptively.

"Will you go with us?" she asked again.

Some people around me said yes.

Me? I don't think I even said yes or no. I just nervously chuckled and said something like, "I'm sorry, and you're still the best," and stayed in my seat.

The meeting started. Then Dr. Shero got up with others around us, said something loudly, and walked out. A ruckus they did make. Did their disruption catch the attention of the room? Yep. Did I move? Nope, other than nervously laughing and smoothing out the paper with my typed statement. I didn't want to leave in case my name was called. I wanted to make the statement on behalf of the organization I was there to represent and for the children they served. I didn't want to miss my chance. And I was a little scared too.

The rest of the meeting went like the first day. Organizations and delegates were called to make statements. I was not one of them. And that was fine. All statements would be included in the final document to be presented at the United Nations General Assembly later that year.

Here's the point of the story and what I learned that day.

You be you. Whoever that is.

If you're someone to yell, "We will prevail!" and lead a protest out of a high-level meeting, be that. (Sandra Bullock said that at the beginning of *Two Weeks Notice*, one of my favorite movies. "We will prevail" is one of my favorite lines, and you'll hear it in my house on any given Wednesday.)

If your personality is more "diplomat with a suit jacket," be that.

If you're super confident and loud, by all means be that.

If you're quieter, be that too.

If you're a strong leader by example, be that.

If you're a strong leader who listens well, be that as well.

A bit more secure in myself than I was when I attended that

meeting, I've learned my own strengths. I've learned that I like diplomacy, and I'm a bit more introverted than Dr. Shero. I really like having hard discussions with good people to get things done. And boy, do I love working in global health, evidenced by hugs and smiles.

The point of the entire event, both inside and outside the building, was to advocate for care for all. To reach that audacious goal, we need all hands on deck, everyone on board, inside and outside. So I'll end this chapter with what I tell my students: we need you to be you. Fully you, gifted and unique and . . . fine just the way you are. *You.* And then *us.* That's how the world changes.

Have the courage to be fully you. The world needs that. And that's enough, my friends. More than enough.

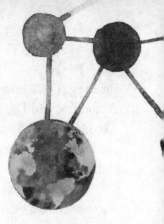

CHAPTER 13

TRICKLE-UP ECONOMICS

The poverty of the poor is not a call to generous relief action,
but a demand that we go and build a different social order.
FATHER GUSTAVO GUTIÉRREZ

Nor was there anyone among them who lacked.
ACTS 4:34 NKJV

"If you want to be perfect, go, sell your possessions
and give to the poor, and you will have treasure
in heaven. Then come, follow me."
JESUS, MATTHEW 19:21

When we start with the margins, we all thrive.

One of my first research projects out of my PhD program was in Somaliland, the beautiful country in the Horn of Africa I've told you about and also, again, one of the poorest countries in the world. (To put that in perspective, the average yearly income in the United States, measured in gross domestic product per capita, is $69,000, but it's $1,530 in Somaliland.) We'd hired a team of about ten data collectors from the country to visit a sample of households in both rural and urban areas to ask about the children's health needs: whether they needed or had had surgery, what kinds of conditions were prevalent, and whether they sought health care for their children when it was needed.

Some of my best memories are talking with the Somali data collector team via Zoom to discuss the village they would go to next for the family visits. Many of them were far away from main roads. They told me the name of the village, and then I looked it up with Google Maps and checked the route they would have to take through deserts, hills, and lots of dirt roads.

Seeing the data about health conditions these families' children were experiencing, I expected the bone fractures and congenital anomalies. But I did not expect conditions rarely seen in the US: polio, measles, and syndactyly/polydactyly, the latter congenital conditions where a child is born with extra or webbed fingers or toes.

In addition to the medical questions, they asked about the household's income level and assets they owned, such as animals—like camels and goats—which are considered currency in that part of the world.

In health research, we know some families will experience an acute health event—like an emergency room visit or emergency surgery—or a series of chronic health events—like needing expensive medication for diabetes treatment. Some families will have good insurance and be able to get that care quickly. But other families won't have good health insurance or a nest egg to help cover unexpected costs. And the closer the family is to the poverty line, the higher the risk they'll dip below the poverty line from unexpected costs like these.

Imagine this trajectory as a U-shaped timeline. Before the medical event, families are above the poverty line but quickly fall below the poverty line, like sliding down the U into poverty due to the costs. Some families are able to recover financially and climb back out of poverty. Other families get stuck below the poverty line without the ability to climb back out. Imagine this as the downward slope part of the U that's too slippery to climb back up. In the science world, we call these "poverty trajectories."

We know poverty trajectories exist and that they more accurately depict the reality of a person or family's situation rather than a one-time statistic showing how much money a family has on any given Tuesday in November does. But the questions are these: *Why do some families get stuck in poverty while others can climb out of it? And why did they slip below the poverty line due to a health event in the first place while others remain above it?* Was the family protected from poverty if they made a certain amount of money or had a specific percentage of medical costs covered by health insurance? Were they at a higher risk of getting stuck if there were more people in the home to feed or the home had only chickens rather than the higher currency of camels? What about political, social, or climate events in Somalia, like the horrific civil war in 1991, the cyclical droughts in 2016, 2017, 2018, 2019, and 2020, the lack of funding from international aid organizations?

If we could figure *that* out, then we could do something about this. That's also the point of epidemiology, in my view—measuring the problem correctly so we can do something about it. To me, this is the modern-day version of not walking by.

So we measured these aspects of how to measure poverty for families in Somaliland. Then, using fancy statistics, which are like a candy store to me as an epidemiologist, we asked ourselves, *Out of all these* [above-mentioned] *factors, which one promotes getting stuck in poverty the most?* My hypothesis was that it would be overall family income and household size since having lots of kids to feed determines what income they need to feed them all in the first place. From the families visited, we'd also heard they'd had to decide between seeking care for one child and feeding the others.

Do you want to know what *main* factor predicted descending into poverty and not being able to climb back out? Not being able to recover? Even after accounting for all the other factors?

Having a child who needed surgery, even after accounting for everything else.[1]

To me, epidemiology is the sacred work of telling people's stories through calculus and weighted metrics and integrals. A quote that Paul Farmer attributes to Saint Dominic—"Your desk is your prayer bench"—resonates deeply with me.[2] Here on the screen was the sacred work of noticing those on the side of the road because of poverty. All because a child needed surgery. The two-dimensional numbers and spreadsheets were telling a story of inequity for these families.

After running the numbers a few more times to check for accuracy and inconsistencies, the next step was to ask, *What's next? How do we not walk by?* This is where praxis meets theory or theology or data. As Dr. Paul Farmer said, "An understanding of poverty must be linked to efforts to end it."[3] From a faith perspective, Father Gustavo Gutiérrez summarized this by saying the central task of theology is not simply good theology but also a "comprehensive commitment to building a just world . . . to continue to say and show to the poor, 'God loves you.'"[4]

Since we knew these families got stuck in poverty because they'd had to pay for their child's treatment of a condition or disease with surgery, our next task was figuring out how to protect them from that poverty. Was there a way to prevent them from slipping into poverty in the first place? What would happen if they had to pay for only 30 percent of their health care costs instead of the traditional 70 percent? Or 10 percent? Would that make a difference? And would that difference be equitable to all?

We got to work. We modeled different scenarios where the health care cost for children's surgical care was reduced and then separated the data according to whether the family lived in a rural or urban area. We then stratified the data even more to determine whether the family was in the richest or poorest quintiles within each area. In other words, we were trying to get to the poorest of the poor. To the margin of the margins. This time my hypothesis was that reducing the costs would provide a buffer for all families, making the greatest impact for the poorest families. Every little bit of assistance helps, right?

But hold on to your hats, friends. That's not what we found. If you're a student in one of my classes, this is the part where I get very animated, which hopefully puts you on the edge of your seat. (This is also the part of teaching I love the most—seeing my students engage in such a way that their hearts and souls match their minds.)

After doing additional analysis of our data, we found that some families were indeed strongly protected from getting stuck in poverty if their health care costs were reduced. But to my surprise and horror, that was not equitable. The families who didn't benefit were more likely to be in rural areas. And most of the poorest families remained at a significantly high risk of poverty and medical impoverishment. Nearly *all* of them. Even when the out-of-pocket costs were reduced to the lowest amounts and most of their health care costs were paid.[5]

This was another moment in my professional career when the data rooted me in my chair. The risk was nearly solely focused within the margins. But we would have missed it if we hadn't stratified the data to get to the margins. Again, to me as an epidemiologist, this is listening to the stories in the data.

The most impoverished families in the most remote regions,

those in the margins of the margin, were most affected by poverty. Why? Because of *structural violence,* displayed as individual poverty. Do you remember that term *structural violence?* No amount of individual-level money would protect these families, because already living in poverty, they also lived within a system that kept them there. The solution, then, is more than simply throwing money at the problem, such as sponsoring a child or tithing 10 percent of our income to a food bank. All those examples are sacred and holy work, yes. But the solution to solving structural violence displayed, as I said, as individual poverty—like I was seeing in my data with the Somali families—is not an individual solution. It's a structural solution, and it will cost us much more.

We can talk about structural protections against poverty lots of ways. One is providing universal health care for all, and the question is, who will pay for it?

———

When I attended that United Nations high-level meeting about universal health coverage, the speakers included well-known leaders and philanthropists, including some of the richest people in the world. And at the end of the meeting, a panel discussed the cost and financing dimensionality of achieving universal health coverage while also recognizing the shortfalls to funding the main global health organizations of the United Nations, such as the Global Fund, set up to combat HIV, tuberculosis, and malaria, and the World Health Organization. In other words, who would pay for it? Because a lot of money was needed.

On the panel was Dr. Jeffrey Sachs, a world-renowned professor of economics at Columbia University and a global leader in sustainable development. I was thrilled he was there since years before I was inspired by his book *The End of Poverty.*[6]

Dr. Sachs was one of the final speakers, following those who had given eloquent statements about how to pay for universal health coverage but been a bit lacking in tangible plans. Dr. Sachs opened his laptop, read off the names of the ten richest people in the world—some of whom were in the room—closed his laptop, and then said something to the effect that a small percentage of those ten people's wealth would pay for the entire shortfall. All of it.

Whoa. I was a newbie professor and researcher in global health, and I'd never heard someone speak so directly about finances. Many of us sat a bit straighter to listen to the rest of the panel, and I tried not to look behind me at some of the people he called out.

Here's the deal. I agree with Dr. Sachs. He brought up a fundamental point about the world's wealth. It's distributed so very unequally.

We don't need more money; we need more equity.

If we look at all global wealth, about $418 trillion is available.[7] But nearly 50 percent of that is held by only 1 percent of the richest people in the world, defined as those with $1 million dollars or more. Nearly 40 percent is owned by the 11 percent of the second richest people in the world with $100,000 to $1 million. In 2020, the greatest increase in wealth by region was in North America and Europe (9 percent) with the greatest losses in wealth in Latin America (-11 percent) and India (-6 percent).

Let me give you one more statistic to talk about with your buddies over pizza. Have you heard of the Gini index? It's a summary measure of income inequality ranging from 0 to 100 precent, with higher numbers indicating great inequality.[8] In other words, does everyone in a particular country own the same amount of money, resulting in a score of 0, or do a few own a lot while others don't, resulting in a score closer to 100? As a rule of thumb, a score of 100 for a country indicates wide wealth inequities in the country. It isn't a perfect measure, but it's a good starting place for looking at unequal wealth distributions between and within countries.

Since 1820, except for a few years in the last half of the 1900s, the world's Gini index has risen every year.[9] To give an example, Norway, Sweden, and Belgium each have Gini indices under 30, indicating a fairly equal distribution of wealth. But to give another country example, the United States has a Gini index of 41, the highest among high-income countries.[10] (To give you a comparison, Madagascar, Togo, Uganda, and Argentina all have Gini indices of 42.) In the US, the top 1 percent of people have an income forty times higher than the entire bottom 90 percent.

Each time we've had a major health event, such as the 2009 H1N1 pandemic, the 2014 West Africa Ebola outbreak, and the 2016 Zika outbreak, the Gini index has risen in the five years following. Estimates predict that the index will increase globally 1.2 to 1.9 points each year for 2020 and 2021 due to COVID-19, meaning the rich will get richer and the poor will get poorer.

So who will pay for universal health coverage and the basic human rights of clean water, sufficient food, and access to prenatal and delivery care for babies? Again, we don't need more money; we need more equity.

To me, that sounds like a trickle-up economy. Trickle-down economy sounds upside down, doesn't it? It's like putting a hundred dollars in Warren Buffett's mailbox and then checking to see what's left once it finally makes it to the slums in Lima, Peru. It doesn't make sense. From an economic standpoint, it makes more sense to invest in the margins first and then have that investment trickle *up* to the rest of society.

Trickle-up economics is also trickle-up health. Let me give you an example.

———

In my own work, we've compared the cost-effectiveness of pediatric surgical procedures to other traditional interventions in global health that have been around for decades, such as bed nets to combat malaria, children's immunization campaigns, and HIV antiretroviral therapies.[11] In most cases, providing surgery for children is just as effective as those traditional interventions, and it costs the same amount or even less. Dollar for dollar.

But what about return on investment—ROI? This is where the trickle-up economics is trickle-up health. On a macro level, expansion of surgical care to areas that need it, such as in most low-income countries, results in substantial ROI with a 1:10 cost–benefit ratio, which remains among the most cost-effective global health interventions.[12]

In my line of work promoting surgical care in low-income countries, we know we'll need five thousand surgical procedures per one hundred thousand people by 2030 to meet the projected needs between now and then. This translates to an estimated $350 billion of investment required to increase the necessary essential surgical and anesthesia care. Although this amount is substantial, without this investment in surgical scale-up, the loss of economic productivity in low-income countries is even more—estimated at thirty-five times higher ($12.3 billion) by 2030.[13]

In other words, it makes sense to invest in health care to protect people and countries from poverty, starting with the poorest countries and communities. Trickle-up economics is trickle-up health. Who should pay for it? We think high-income countries should.[14] If this is about equitable distribution of wealth, should there be any millionaires who are also Christian? What about rich countries? Perhaps equity through Jesus means that the poorest people and countries are centered with our money too.

On a national scale, the healthier and more financially secure the families are, the more the entire country can thrive.[15] Several large studies have found that upward mobility of a country is largely dependent on the health of its citizens. So doesn't it make sense to start with those who are the sickest? When we do, we benefit more as a society than if we had started at the top. We certainly don't help people because it has any benefit to us. But I'm trying to flip our traditional capitalistic, trickle-down economy mentality on its head for a chance to reconsider. When we start with the margins, we all thrive. Trickle-up economics is trickle-up health.

———

I gave you the examples of surgery in global health because that's where I work. But you can see this return of investment story in most other development questions. In other words, it's more useful to invest in the needs of the poorest of the poor than to start with the rich and see what's left. Dollar per dollar. This is more than offering thoughts and prayers and certainly more than giving away a percent of our income. It's an upside-down way of using our money—giving and investing—and doing both to love our neighbors. This is thinking like the Good Samaritan and matching our practice to it.

Again, when we start with the margins, we all thrive. And maybe that's the way of Jesus too.

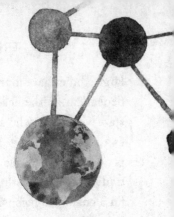

CHAPTER 14

BROADENING OUR DEFINITION OF HEALTH

Everyone has the right to a standard of living adequate
for the health and well-being of himself and of his family,
including food, clothing, housing and medical care and
necessary social services, and the right to security in the event
of unemployment, sickness, disability, widowhood, old age or
other lack of livelihood in circumstances beyond his control.

UNIVERSAL DECLARATION OF HUMAN RIGHTS, ARTICLE 25

Five billion.[1]

I start every global health course I teach with that number, followed by asking my students how many people are in the world. So I'll ask you. Pop quiz. How many people are in the world right now, in 2023? It's fine to google it. I'll wait.

As of this writing, eight billion people are in the world—and counting—and five billion is 70-ish percent of that world population number. What do you think this number corresponds to? I usually get guesses that say this number corresponds to people who have access to clean water, or live in areas most affected by climate change, or even love pepperoni pizza more than plain cheese pizza. But the real answer always surprises my students. Every single time.

Five billion corresponds to the number of people in the world without access to surgical care. Does that number seem really high to you? Same with me, friends, same. I heard that number for the first time fresh out of my PhD program at UNC Chapel Hill while easing into my first big-gal job at the Duke Global Health Institute.

My job as an epidemiologist involved working with surgeons who lived in or traveled to incredible countries like Guatemala or Uganda, Liberia or Somaliland. I hadn't heard of the term *global surgery* prior to this new job, so one of my first onboarding assignments at Duke was to educate myself on this new term and how I could contribute to the global surgery field as a population-level scientist.

This brought me to a landmark paper commissioned by the *Lancet* journal, arguably the premier scientific journal, worked on by more than two hundred scientists, doctors, surgeons, nurses, and community leaders from more than fifty countries. This commission's purpose was to estimate how many people need surgery around the world, determine where they're located, and then recommend a plan to meet the need by 2030.[2]

The first of its five key messages centered around the five billion people without access to surgical care. But that's not just *any* type of care. It's not simply getting surgery, and it's not simply having just any access. Think about what type of surgery you would want for yourself, or your kiddo, or your mom, or your best friend. You wouldn't want just any surgery, right? You would want it to be safe. You would want it to be timely. And you would want it to not bankrupt your family. In other words, you would want the surgery to be what many of us in America can get just down the road.

You would want a trained anesthesiologist and surgeon at a hospital. You would also want oxygen available, for the electricity to not cut off in the middle of the procedure, a comfortable and clean room to recover in after the surgery, and for medication to prevent infections and treat pain to be readily available. What about a place for your caregiver to comfortably sit with you as you recover? And food to eat during your hospital stay before you're discharged? You also might need physical therapy and rehabilitation post-surgery and accommodations at your work or school, including ramps and accessible bathrooms.

Do you see the picture I'm painting? You wouldn't want just any surgery for you or a member of your family. You would want it to be safe, timely, and affordable. You would want the care you needed, when you needed it, without worrying about it.

Shouldn't we expect that type of surgery for all our neighbors in the world? Sounds a whole lot like equity, doesn't it? Wanting the same care for our neighbors as we do for ourselves. But at least five billion people in the world, 1.7 billion of whom are children, don't have access to that type of surgery according to those metrics.[3] So what keeps us from achieving that? Well, a lot of things you've already read about in this book, with major finger-pointing at the historical solidifications of health inequities, poverty, and structural violence.

Those are more "big picture" reasons, though, that, if we're not careful, can be easy for us to agree are a problem but then quickly turn away from finding a solution because it's too difficult. In other words, what can one person do to actually overcome the problem structural violence or poverty poses on people thousands of miles away? What can a country do? Or a church?

Well, a lot of things. But first I want to focus on broadening our definition of health. The next chapters, including this one, talk more "big-picture" about what we can do as societies and how we can challenge our own worldviews, while the latter chapters will zero in on what we can do as individuals.

———

Over time, the definition of health has changed. Early definitions focused on merely the absence of illness or disease. But those of us who have ever been sick (read: all of us) know being "healthy" isn't simply living without a disease. It's bigger and broader than that. Then in 1948, the World Health Organization radically changed the definition of health from the ultra-biomedical definition to a more holistic, and I think more accurate, definition: "a state of complete physical, mental and social well-being and not merely the absence of disease or infirmity."[4]

Fast-forward nearly four decades to 1984, and we've hit the health promotion movement. (Jane Fonda, anyone?) The World Health Organization revised the definition of health even further, and this time they brought in more holistic aspects of a person's ability to recover from illness. In other words, there was a growing recognition that health is not static but rather dynamic through the ebbs and flows and stages of life and circumstances. This new definition of health meant a person could cope with what life brings, in and outside of their control, and adapt to still realize their dreams and satisfy the needs of themselves and their families.

Seems aspirational, doesn't it? Or isn't that what we dream for our own families and ourselves? So shouldn't it be normal? This isn't simply getting by. Nor is it merely surviving. It's living and thriving. And this type of health is what I deeply want for my kids and family and best buds. I have a hunch you do too.

So why don't we define health that way for the entire world?

Have we in the wealthier countries been conditioned to accept the rest of the world's health as *it is what it is*? That's privilege.

Now, what do we do with this? We recognize it, yes. *Then we challenge the definition.* We broaden it.

I think Jesus did this too. In the gospel of John, we read he didn't just want *life* for people, but *abundant life*—life "to the full."[5] That verse is certainly read to mean he was thinking of abundant life in a spiritual sense—an abundant life of joy and love and a double dose of peace. He did. But while I say a hearty, Southern-twang amen to all that, I started seeing a broader meaning in what he said as well. It made me think of the Good Samaritan stopping on the side of the road for a person living a nonabundant life of physical need and poverty and the consequences of actions not their fault.

This, to me, is a classic Jesus "yes and also." Yes to abundant spiritual life of joy and peace and love, *and also* yes to what physical life could be, should be, and is to be. Think of who the promise of a fuller life would have affected the most in those days. Wouldn't it have been those not yet living with physical abundance as well as a spiritual abundance? Wouldn't they have felt the ache for a fuller life even more? The ache for enough? The ache for more than enough? For their physical needs to be met as well as their spiritual need?

Jesus defines what life truly is according to his abundance, and I believe that includes a broader definition of health. Not merely an absence of illness but a shifting *toward* a wholeness of body, soul, and spirit. This isn't a health-and-wealth gospel or a "just have enough faith and you'll be healed" mentality; it's the gospel of Jesus Christ, which includes making sure people have the agency, financial means, and ability to get the care they need, when they need it, without the risk of poverty. It's an abundance of resources to live an abundant life.

That's what the Good Samaritan shows us in the story. He not only noticed; he stopped, he took care of acute medical needs, and then he proceeded to pay for food and lodging so the man could recover. I missed those details when I heard this story in Sunday school growing up. But now those details are some of the most beautiful parts to me. That's the road toward holistic, abundant health. A broadened definition of health to include the spiritual but also the physical.

By the way, did the Samaritan tell the man the gospel (or preach to him or hand out a tract)? The parable doesn't tell us anything like that. I have a hunch Jesus would have mentioned it if it were important to the point he was making at the time. But he didn't. What he modeled for us with this story is being a neighbor in word and deed. Let's challenge and definition and broaden it.

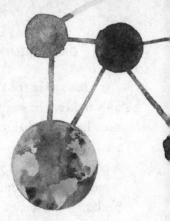

CHAPTER 15

RIVERS AND OTHERING

No, no, we are not satisfied, and we will not
be satisfied until justice rolls down like waters,
and righteousness like a mighty stream.
MARTIN LUTHER KING JR., "I HAVE A DREAM"

Equity is like a flowing river to me, and in my mind it's like the Eno River here in North Carolina. My husband and I, along with our two kids, often go there on weekends to hike and picnic. Inevitably, one kid falls in, or rather jumps in, because said kid loves getting wet, and the other kid, who likes to keep the shoes dry, just takes great photos.

To get to the part of the trail we particularly like, we have to cross the river upstream by stepping on rocks—or jumping around them like my kid who loves to get wet does—and hike to where there's an old, abandoned cabin with a picnic table in front of it. If we go in the fall, my favorite time to go, we find ourselves surrounded by a symphony of leaves. Bright yellow, burnt orange, deep red, and holding-on green leaves that haven't quite lost their chlorophyll yet.

If you sit there quietly, you can hear the sound of rushing water where the river flows the strongest. It feels rhythmically calming. I love the sound of it and would definitely notice if the water stopped flowing, which brings me back to the idea of equity.

If equity is a flowing river, strong and mighty, inequity is also a river but stagnant because it's dammed up somewhere. Here's the kicker: leave it like that, and it starts to look, well, normal. And if you visit this dammed-up river over and over, it becomes a new normal, doesn't it? Like that's how it's supposed to be and always has been.

But if we were to go back in history to see the natural flow of this water, we'd discover it's actually not supposed to be like that at all. So the biggest issue is not that we call it normal, although it's important to recognize this as an issue; it's that we miss the obstruction upstream that stopped the flow of the river in the first place. That's the real problem. And the damming has become what looks like the center of normalcy.

Normal for who though? If you're a White American, this could be like saying, "[Fill-in-the-blank] has always been like this"—the blank filled with any one of numerous examples of how we White Americans have centered the conversation around ourselves. Let me give you a few of them.

Think about what today is, or isn't, taught in schools. Who is, or isn't, in positions of power, from city boards to presidential administrations. How resources are, or are not, allocated. It may look "normal" to us because we, and generations as far back as we can track, called it normal. In reality, though, our "normal" is really a dammed-up river meant to be flowing.

Then we have a choice. Either we recenter correctly and get the river flowing again, or we reinforce an unequal normalcy with platitudes like, "This is how we've always done it." Then the obstruction becomes reinforced, especially if we say, "The good old days weren't like this," whenever the dam is challenged.

Here's an example to help explain what I mean.

During the pandemic, in March 2021, I was living in Texas when Governor Greg Abbott, on Twitter, accused the Biden administration of "recklessly releasing hundreds of illegal migrants who have COVID into Texas communities." Then he wrote, "The Biden Admin. must IMMEDIATELY end this callous act that exposes Texans & Americans to COVID."[1]

I wrote a social media post speaking out against Governor Abbott's accusations with data. He was basing his absurd tweet on a report that some migrants released by Border Patrol in Brownsville, a border city in Southern Texas, had tested positive for COVID-19 and subsequently been released into Texas communities. But the number of migrants testing positive was 108, only 6.3 percent of all migrants tested.[2] At the time, the positivity rate in the Texas county they were in was 13.8 percent, and infections and deaths due to COVID-19 in the state were growing. Fast.

New cases in the state had risen by 27 percent that week, and Texas was one of only ten states with rising new daily cases.[3] In fact, the state was still in a high-risk level of the outbreak, one of only eight in the United States. Of the top twenty counties in the US with the highest recent number of cases per capita, Texas had eleven of those counties. In the state, hospitalizations and deaths were disproportionally affecting communities of color and those living in low-income neighborhoods.

We in Texas had just come out of a massive winter storm that knocked out power and water for millions and delayed vaccinations and testing for those needing them. Texas consistently ranked in the top few states with the highest mortality rates for COVID-19, even after adjusting for population and age of the population. Texas today ranks fourth in cumulative COVID-19 deaths in the US, behind only Mississippi, Oklahoma, and Tennessee.[4]

Here's my point. The spread of COVID-19 in Texas wasn't due to 108 migrants with COVID-19 in a state with nearly 29 million people. The day Governor Abbott's remark showed up on Twitter, the seven-day average of new daily COVID-19 cases was 7,842. So the problem was not the migrants. The problem was Texans.

Out of the hundreds of social media posts I wrote as the Friendly Neighbor Epidemiologist during this time, this one most seemed to strike a chord with people the wrong way. I was bombarded with harassing comments and threats from largely my own people—White, American, Southern, and Christian. What seemed to make them so mad was my exposing the obstruction—the governor's blame-shifting the cause of the problem from Texans to migrants.

If we don't call what Governor Abbott did an obstruction, it could be easy to call what he was alluding to as "normal." Migrants were *othered*, and this belief is held, consciously or unconsciously, by thousands of others in the United States, as evidenced by the interactions following just that one post of mine.

If we go upstream in our river analogy, this obstruction of othering against migrants isn't hard to find. In the not-too-distant past of 1994, 63 percent of US citizens said migrants were a burden because they "take jobs, housing, and health care."[5] Although thankfully that number has decreased, 26 percent of Americans still hold that belief, differing strongly by political party. That's an obstruction. And if we disentangle that statistic a bit, we see that 58 percent of Republicans hold that belief compared to 16 percent of Democrats. And that was in 2017.

The reality is that migrants make up 16 percent of the US workforce, and three out of four of them held jobs deemed "essential" during the pandemic.[6] This included an estimated five million food processors, farmworkers, custodial care workers, stockers and packers, and grocery store cashiers, to name just a few occupations.

If we think words don't matter or that leadership isn't powerful or that the othering type of thinking is fringe thought, just look at the reactions to Governor Abbott's tweet about migrants and COVID-19 in Texas. More than thirty thousand people liked it, with more than 8,400 retweets. The previous year, former president Donald Trump referred to immigration as an "invasion" in more than two thousand Facebook ads viewed between 1 million and 5 million times. Obstructions are reinforced not only with anti-immigration policies, but perhaps more insidiously with words like these from leaders.[7]

———

Fast-forward a few months to August 2021. The pandemic was still going at full throttle in the US, with the Delta variant running amok, and we were also seeing an emergence of GOP leaders strongly suggesting that the pandemic was due to one subgroup in the United States—Black Americans who weren't getting vaccinated. By "strongly suggesting," I do mean blame-shifting. This is another obstruction or another example that stalls the flow of equity. But as it often does, the data told the truth of the situation.

It's important to keep in mind that the Pfizer vaccine had just been approved for distribution. By this time, the largest disparity in who was or wasn't getting vaccinated against COVID-19 was not race at all. It was political affiliation. There was a whopping 32 percent differential between Republicans and Democrats in COVID-19 vaccination rates, while only a 5 percent gap between White and Black Americans.[8] (That remains the case, although the gap between political parties has widened over time.) If you look at political affiliation, Republicans of all age groups had the highest rates of stating they would definitely never be vaccinated against the virus. For younger Republicans ages eighteen to forty-nine, one-third reported they would definitely never be vaccinated compared to 7 percent of Democrats in the same age group.

If we parse the data even further, the groups reporting they would definitely never be vaccinated were White Americans (65 percent) and Republicans (58 percent), compared to Black Americans (13 percent) and Democrats (15 percent). Now zoom in even further to Texas, where Lieutenant Governor Dan Patrick blamed the spread of COVID-19 in Texas on Black Americans and Democrats.[9]

When we compare groups of people, we have to look at the proportion rather than the total numbers. Here's an example: In Texas, Black Texans make up about 16 percent of the population, while White Texans make up nearly 50 percent. So do we see a difference in vaccination rates within each group? Not significantly. What the data in Texas at that time showed us was that the zip codes of lower-income communities, which happened to also be zip codes with Black and Hispanic families, had lower vaccine availability due to scarcer health access, and thereby lower vaccination rates.[10]

The explanation is certainly multifaceted, but the take-home point is that we can't paint a broad picture when it comes to vaccinations in any state. In other words, we can't blame-shift to groups of people; we have to look deeper at what's really going on. Where do people live? Do they have access to care? Can they take time off work to get a vaccine and a few days after if needed? What about health insurance and childcare? And for the love of all things epidemiology, please calculate a proportion with a denominator rather than the absolute numbers.

I'm not picking solely on the state of Texas. Stories of blame-shifting, of othering, can be found in many other states and communities. I chose Texas, however, because that's where I lived and also because part of going upstream to take out the obstruction means finding the truth of a situation. With data, with humility, with history—especially if that history hasn't been told correctly or been Whitewashed.

As I write this at the end of 2022, there's a clear divide for nearly every COVID-19 metric between states along political lines. COVID-19 infections, COVID-19 mortality rates, and excess death rates are higher in primarily Republican states than in primarily Democratic states. Initially in the pandemic, deaths were concentrated in urban, Democratic-leaning areas but swiftly shifted to counties more GOP-leaning. A Pew Research Center study found that "counties that voted for Donald Trump over Joe Biden were suffering substantially more deaths from the corona-virus pandemic than those that voted for Biden over Trump."[11]

And this mortality gap widened sharply by 2022, with a corresponding widening gap of unvaccinated versus vaccinated individuals. It can be hard to see the obstruction if you're in a place like Texas and think like so many of the other Texans around you. However, the data shows something different—an obstruction that's beyond political party. It's ideologies, blame-shifting beliefs, or conspiracy theories made normative by the obstruction. But certainly it's neither equity nor Jesus.

Now, some of us don't like to get political, and I get that. Equity is always political though. Part of removing true obstructions means you look at where inequities are, both upstream and downstream. Most often these involve politics, either directly or indirectly. Talking about equity usually involves talking about politics. It matters who we vote for, whether we like it or not.

Let me give you one more example that takes us global. Have you ever called a country a *Third World* country? I hear that term quite a bit in medical mission settings, churches, and even in my global health work. I see it in a hashtag on Instagram, usually from a well-meaning student who's been on their first "mission trip" overseas and taken a photo with a child in the "Third World" country, often without the child's—or the child's family's—consent. (This is one of the many reasons I tell my students who visit another country not to post photos of people there on social media. Even with consent, was the yes given in full agency of the person? This is often not the case. If you go to a country or area different from yours, be aware and empathetic, and don't Instagram what will telegraph your power and privilege. But that's a topic for another book.)

Back to the use of the term *Third World*. During the pandemic, I would hear people describe the morgue trucks, medication stock-outs, or oxygen shortages as "Third World problems." On January 6, the Capitol riots were described as what happens in Third World countries. Although we don't quite know when the term was coined, it gained speed in the 1950s as the Cold War started.

In 1952, an article titled "Three Worlds, One Planet" was published by Alfred Sauvy, a French demographer.[12] He defined First World countries as the Western NATO nations of the United States, Western Europe, and their Allies. The Second World consisted of so-called Communist countries such as China, Cuba, and the Soviet Union. The Third World was made up of the remaining nations, many of which were impoverished. These countries had widespread poverty and poor health systems, and most were former colonies of the NATO countries from the Great Scramble

I discussed in chapter 3. So the term, which became widely used, lumped poorer countries together.

The problem is that this othering of nations created a false hierarchy between countries, with Western countries at the top being centered not only in conversation but also in development aspects. The ideal for all countries became looking just like Western societies—or the First World. As a whole, the world now centered itself around the First World nations. Growing up in a country like the United States, considered among the "first," could embed supremacy overtones, even unconsciously. Consciously, this translates to othering statements like "America first" and, more insidiously, to movements like White supremacy, which nowadays isn't hard to find.

The same hierarchy comes about when we use the terms *developing* and *developed countries*. In an NPR article, Dr. Shose Kessi, a South African social psychologist at the University of Cape Town, said, "[The use of the term *developing country*] also perpetuates stereotypes about people who come from the so-called 'developing world' as backward, lazy, ignorant, irresponsible."[13] Most of my colleagues are from countries tagged as developing or Third World, and I assure you they are none of those descriptors. They are smart, deeply compassionate, capable, and tenacious.

As an alternative, I suggest saying the actual names of places and countries. Angola. South America. Rural Alabama. Durham, North Carolina. Tanzania. If we need to characterize a group of countries, consider describing that characteristic rather than characterizing the country. For example, you could say "countries with high infant mortality rates" rather than "Third World countries." You could also describe countries without centering on any particular country or trait. For example, you could say "the global South" or "the global North," which inherently centers the *globe* as the ideal.

These small changes can address any unconscious bias we likely have *and also* have a big impact on how we think or believe. And a bigger impact on our neighbors.

———

When blame-shifting happens, it places the fault on someone else. Maybe a more direct way to say it is that blame-shifting is falsely accusing someone. It's a slick way of othering, of discriminating against someone who's different, of asserting power and privilege, and in its worst form, of being racist. It might look normal to think this way because your family did or does and those around you do too. Sadly, it's not hard to find othering language even in church, where I've heard migrants called names I will not publish in a book. If you grew up in the South, you probably have too.

So what do we do? Let's go back to our example of the river. What will happen if you yell at the water to start flowing, or you push it, or you simply send it thoughts and prayers? Nothing. It will move only when you take away the obstruction. When you— when *we*—remove the obstruction, the damming, the water starts flowing again. Gushing. Like it's *meant* to. It flows like a river. Like rushing waters, loud and clear, toward the pull of gravity and design.

Equity is like that. It naturally pulls toward a design God always intended. But here, God is the center of gravity, and the systems of oppression are the obstruction. Do we see it? Or are we reinforcing it? I think it's honoring work to call out blame-shifting for an unjust, unethical, and unholy act of othering our own neighbors. Neighbors of migrants, oppressed persons, and other nations, to name a few. Neighbors all around us.

The apostle Paul describes Christians as ambassadors of a new reality.[14] I think of it as being conduits to bring heaven to earth, like the way Jesus taught people to pray.[15] That includes doing the hard work of clearing the obstructions.

Gravity and rivers will do the rest.

This work of equity is not a onetime task. Just like freedom from Egypt for the Israelites wasn't just leaving Egypt but freedom gained by going *to* something. Like where a river takes us when it's actually flowing. Maybe that's why the prophet Amos said, against the obstructions at the time, "Take away from me the noise of your songs; I will not listen to the melody of your harps. But let justice roll down like waters, and righteousness like an *ever-flowing* stream."[16]

Probably the most famous use of this quote was on August 28, 1963, when the Reverend Martin Luther King Jr. proclaimed, "We will not be satisfied until justice rolls down like waters, and righteousness like a mighty stream" in his "I Have a Dream" speech and echoed in his letter from the Birmingham jail: "Was not Amos an extremist for justice: 'Let justice roll down like waters and righteousness like an ever flowing stream.'"[17]

Justice flowing like a river.

Just like it was designed to do.

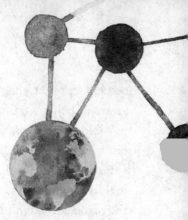

CHAPTER 16

TOPICS TOO MANY EVANGELICALS DON'T WANT TO TALK ABOUT

Dear old world, you are very lovely,
and I am glad to be alive in you.
ANNE SHIRLEY, *ANNE OF GREEN GABLES*

And God saw that it was good.
GENESIS 1:10

Are you a socialist?"

I wasn't asked that question in a school classroom or over coffee or in a grocery store. I was asked in church, and I was so caught off guard that I think I stammered some sort of churchy answer like, "Jesus is my friend," while nervously giggling.

My husband served on staff at our large church and had been

serving in other churches for nearly twenty years, so I was well aware of being a pastor's wife and all that entailed, including the possible expectation that I would follow certain socially accepted norms in that role. I'd never really fit those norms, though, because I didn't want to work in the children's ministry (I love kids, but mainly my own, and I didn't want to teach a group of them) or play the piano (although I love to do that) or sit in the front row (which I have adamantly requested to not do). To be clear, my hubs and none of the churches he worked in and their staffs had ever put those pressures on me. I've been really fortunate to have the space to just be me—all science, PhD, full-time working, talking-a-lot me.

But in that moment, when I was asked if I was a socialist in Sunday school, the social conditioning of what a pastor's wife is supposed to traditionally do or not do or how she's supposed to act or not act was strong—even with none of the pressure and all of the space. Would my answer affect my husband's job? And then there were the deeper internal questions: *Why is anyone even asking that question in the first place, and why does it matter? Especially in church?*

Let me give you the context of that day. I had just returned from the New York trip to the United Nations. As I already explained, we were there to advocate for universal health coverage for all, which in turn meant someone would have to pay for it. The point of this chapter is not to go into all those nuances, but the sticky point for many evangelicals comes when we talk about money.

Capitalism weaves a strong web for us in the United States and similar countries. So it feels weird when someone from an organization like the UN says, "Did you know your country has 70 percent of the world's wealth? But we could wipe out the lack of health care or food insecurity or extreme poverty if you gave an extra 10 percent."

Yes, that means some taxes, but it also means other cost-saving mechanisms, such as energy consumption savings and buying eco-friendly products and a myriad of other opportunities to give. The problem is that it's not what we're used to in higher-income countries, especially if we're rich-ish. That goes against the hard-work, individual ethic we tend to praise. More importantly, that's certainly not capitalism.

In a weird, ironic twist, the day I went to that high-level summit was also the day a summit was held for religious freedom at the UN right down the hall. On a break, I snuck down there, popped my head in for a bit, and heard about religious freedom seen mainly through a Western viewpoint. I also noticed that the US delegates attended the religious freedom summit more often than the universal health coverage summit I was attending.

This was in 2017, and it was a reminder that some people don't like to talk about faith and science. Or poverty and faith. Or the interconnectedness of all three.

White evangelicals aren't necessarily anti-science, although a few blatantly are. Some of the worst emails I got from Christians during the pandemic—all male and some of them pastors—were when I used the word *equity*. I know this is an issue, and I don't think it's just a fringe issue, but why are we so scared to talk about things that challenge our beliefs, especially real-life issues like global warming and poverty and equity?

We can have both, friends. Faith *and* science. In fact, when we live out our faith in ways that love our neighbors, as Jesus' second greatest commandment says we should, I think we'll automatically be pro-science. And pro-faith. To really love our neighbors, to live like the Good Samaritan did, we (and by *we*, I mean mainly White evangelicals) need to be okay with being challenged.

What if we're wrong about some things? If you've grown up

in the church like I did, especially in America, you weren't really taught anything other than capitalism. As evangelicals, we were taught to have faith, which subtly compounded over time to be pro-faith at all costs. I wonder if that also translated to be against anything other than faith, including science, even unconsciously. Just say *climate change* or *global warming* when you're at lunch with your church buddies and see what happens.

The point I'm trying to make is that God cares deeply about our faith and trust in him. *And also.* He cares about how we spend our money and how we care for the earth. I think he cares about how we vote and whether we strive for equity. So I wonder if those words we don't like to say at church like *global warming*, *wealth*, and *politics* are actually holy words indicating faith made alive by deeds.

———

Let me illustrate through the example of climate change. Look at it through the lens of the Good Samaritan and how our taking care of the earth can be a collective choice to not walk by.

Climate change is a live conversation in the church and has been for some time. Some really smart scientists, like Dr. Katharine Hayhoe, are engaged in the issue. She's a brilliant climate scientist with more than 125 peer-reviewed publications, who consults with leading agencies such as the US National Academy of Sciences and is the chief scientist for the Nature Conservancy. She also happens to be another Christian pastor's wife. Dr. Hayhoe, along with other scientists, has written entire books on the realities of global warming and climate change in our world over time.

The point of this chapter is not to convince you that climate change is real, although in my mind that's an undisputed truth. This is to tell the story of *why* the reality of climate change and its close friends power and money matter to us and to God—and, because of that, to our neighbors.

I don't remember hearing about climate change as a looming crisis during my formative teen years back in the 1990s. My apologies to my teachers if you covered that topic and I missed it. I was probably folding a note, fortune-teller style. Or maybe it just wasn't talked about a lot where I grew up, which is more likely. It should have been, though, because it was a threat even back then. What was once only a threat, though, is now on us. In spades.

Did you know 2020 was one of the *three* hottest years since 1850, when they started keeping records?[1] (If you lived in Texas, as I did in 2020, and still live there, you're likely sitting by a fan with an iced tea, saying, "Yes, yes, it was *hot*.") And do you know the other two years were almost as recent—2016 and 2019?[2] Hold the door, 1850 to 2020 is . . . let me do the math . . . 170 years. So *three* of the hottest years in all that time have come in only a recent four-year span. In fact, the past decade has been the hottest on record.[3] And this isn't due to better measurement of temperatures or new technology. The truth is, it's hot, and the earth is getting hotter.[4]

We need to focus in on why this matters. It's not only that the earth is getting hotter; it's that the increase in temperatures in even small increments increases the risk of events like hurricanes, droughts, floods, and wildfires by increasing sea levels. Did you know that over the past two decades, when the majority of earth's temperatures have increased, we've seen a 26 percent increase in storms and a 23 percent increase in floods—and an increase in intensity in both?

Also, the rise in temperature shifts the risk of diseases, or more accurately, expands the risk of vector-borne and water-borne diseases, like the Zika virus, dengue fever, or cholera, which all need warmer climates to survive, multiply, and thrive.[5] It's affecting the margins more. It's affecting the already vulnerable in the world due to poverty, food insecurity, war, and conflict. It's affecting those already living in areas of fragmented health systems or systemic injustice or structural racism from before their own lifetimes.

Do you once again hear the common theme throughout this book? Systems affect people, and this relationship is illustrated by climate change.

Pretend you're at my kitchen table with Google Earth pulled up on my laptop. Do you love Google Earth? We in the Smith household can spend way too much time zooming in and out of places all over the world. Pretend I've made coffee (because it's 10:00 a.m. or 2:00 p.m.) and apricot scones (because God is good) and I've already showed you all 538 photos of my kids (because Momma's cool like that). Let's use Google Earth to zoom in on three locations to illustrate the story we're telling of climate change—Nicaragua, the Horn of Africa, and North Carolina.

———

Let's go first to Nicaragua. Warmer sea temperatures and rising sea levels intensify hurricane and tropical storm wind speeds, resulting in more Category 4 or 5 hurricanes, dropping 10 to 15 percent more precipitation than expected, which results in flooding.[6] So we're experiencing more hurricanes at higher intensities with increased risk of flooding.

Let's go to the people now. In 2020, a record number of hurricanes ripped through Central America. For the previous five years, the region experienced above-average hurricane and tropical storm activity. On November 3, 2020, Hurricane Eta made landfall as a Category 4 storm in Nicaragua, causing devastating damage and displacing thousands of people with 240 kilometers per hour winds. Only two weeks later, Hurricane Iota barreled through as a Category 5 hurricane with unimaginable windspeeds of 260 kilometers per hour in the already fragile country before hitting Honduras, Guatemala, and other parts of Central America.

A staggering 7.5 million people were affected. It was reported that most people in these indigenous communities lost everything in the double whammy of hurricanes Eta and Iota. Even before the pandemic, the areas affected by the hurricanes in Nicaragua were some of the most affected by high levels of violence and poverty. Then came the COVID-19 pandemic on top of everything else. And then the hurricanes.

More than two months later, 1.5 million children still had access only to contaminated water due to damaged wells or water systems.[7] What happens when there's contaminated or standing water? Disease—but this time it wasn't COVID-19. Well, COVID-19 was still there in full force, since Latin and Central America were some of the hardest hit areas in the world. But I should say on top of COVID-19 came the risks of dengue fever, malaria, Zika, and other tropical diseases due to the flooding.

———

Now let me take you to the Horn of Africa, where I work. If you watch the news, you've probably at least heard of the drought happening in East Africa. In 2016, prophetic voices at humanitarian organizations such as UNICEF, Save the Children, and the United Nations started sounding the alarm on the growing and increasing crisis. Now in 2022, it's the region's worst and longest-lasting drought in forty years, with the sixth—and counting—failed rainy season in a row.

In this part of the world, currency is measured largely by the assets a family owns. I'm not talking only homes or TVs or motorcycles; I'm talking about the region's main source of currency:

camels and livestock. In addition, families in the Horn of Africa rely largely on food they grow themselves to feed their family or to sell. In other words, the physical nature of where they live impacts how they live—and *if* they live. Enough rain but not too much; fertile soil, not arid clods; thriving food sources, not leaves wilted from the sun; healthy and multiplying camels and goats, not depleted animals that cannot reproduce.

Rain, soil, food—the natural circle of life that many of us take for granted if we get our food from grocery stores is a live conversation during periods of drought. A family can get through one failed rainy season if they're frugal, or have other means to get food, or have a drought-day fund. Two missed rainy seasons, and things become tighter. Three missed rainy seasons starts affecting the margins of poverty or nomadic communities with disease, malnutrition, and death. Four rainy seasons extends that to more and more of the country. And five in 2021? The result is a devastating humanitarian crisis.

Where was the tipping point at which we could have intervened? Better said, when we *should* have intervened?

As I write this, we're entering what should be the rainy season in the Horn of Africa, the time between October and December, when 70 percent of the region's annual rainfall is received. However, the forecast from the UN's World Meteorological Organization, commissioned to sound alarms on how climate affects people, shows that this next rainy season will have a high probability of drier conditions.[8] The region has already lost more than 7 million livestock, and herders are having to migrate with their families in search of pasture and water sources to areas that look similar to where they've just come from—dry and arid.

Remember, the drought is expanding and worsening, with the effects spreading outward to the more nomadic regions. In Somalia alone, livestock production contributes to nearly 50 percent of the country's gross domestic product and more than 60 percent of its revenue from exports.[9] If those statistics were in the United States, that 50 percent would be equivalent to all real estate and the business world (think huge corporations and conglomerates like Walmart and Amazon) combined.[10] So the loss of livestock in the region is like 50 percent of the US real estate and businesses crashing at the same time. With the expanding drought in Ethiopia, Somalia, Somaliland, and Eastern Kenya, the fertile landscapes are disappearing.

Now let's use Google Earth to take us farther into East Africa to Somaliland. On my desk at work and at home, I have a photo of two children in Somaliland from when I first started working there in 2016. I think they're about three and five or six, and they're running and smiling, just like my own kids did at that age. In the background is their home, shaped like an oval and covered in sticks that in turn are covered with blankets, sheets, tarps, and various other cloths sewn together. It looks like a bright, multicolored patchwork quilt. A few dry trees stand around, but mostly the land is dirt and rock.

Although the patchwork catches your eye, there's a stark reality in this image. It's near a refugee camp. This is also one of the families we talked to who were living in extreme poverty, hours and hours from the nearest medical facility. And that was in 2016 as the country was entering the historic multiyear drought.

Somaliland is a country of four million people, half of them children. As we said earlier in the book, Somaliland is the fourth poorest country in the world and relies heavily on livestock for income. Although an independent country, Somaliland does not have international recognition with the United Nations, the World Health Organization, the African Union, or the Arab League. These organizations do a massive amount of good in the world but typically only to recognized countries. That means the money

Somalia receives must funnel to the northern part of the country to reach Somaliland. So a country without international recognition rebuilding from war is the setting I'm talking about.

Now pretend you have a transparency of how climate change impacts the country and overlay that on the setting. What happens? Drought upon poverty. As of this writing, in Somaliland alone, 810,000 people have been displaced due to the severe drought, usually on foot. That's almost the equivalent of South Dakota's entire population having to move somewhere else for survival. According to the Horn of Africa Voluntary Youth Committee, 59 percent of families reported losing all their livestock.[11] And that was only after three rainy seasons, ending in 2020.

Of course, by now you can see this also leads to massive food shortages. In the Horn of Africa, at least twenty million people are at risk of extreme food insecurity, more than six million of those in Somalia.

———

Let's zoom to the last place on Google Earth: Durham, North Carolina, where I live. In Durham, one in six individuals is food insecure—without enough food to meet basic needs—and 20 percent of those are children.[12] We know the pandemic increased food insecurity across the country for those who had not previously been affected by it and then deepened the levels for those already in it. Same with poverty. In the US, 11 percent of homes were food insecure prior to the pandemic. That number rose to nearly 15 percent in 2020, with the highest risk among families with children under twelve and even more among families below the poverty line.

I could go on and on with statistics, but I think you probably get what I'm trying to say. Climate change, health, and poverty are all related and unequally distributed.

Let's zoom back out, close the laptop, and get some more coffee. I want to close this chapter talking about what we can do, individually and collectively.

If we look at the example of food insecurity, Russia's unconscionable current war in Ukraine is a major disruptor in food distribution, since the two countries account for 30 percent of all global wheat exports (20 percent for Russia and 10 percent for Ukraine).[13] But it's most acutely felt in areas that need food the most. Both Russia and Ukraine play a main role in supplying wheat to regions where it's the main staple food, such as the Middle East and North African regions. The disruption in wheat supplies is also pushing food prices to record levels.

As another example, the COVID-19 pandemic disrupted global supply chains and shipments in unprecedented ways. If your holiday presents were late or unavailable for a few months, or if eggs weren't available in the grocery store, that's the result of poor pandemic control, mainly by high-income countries, directly affecting global supply chains. But it didn't have to be that way. If we in countries of power had contained the pandemic at its onset, by following the public health tried-and-true precaution playbook, we wouldn't be where we are today. One of the repercussions and consequences was global food insecurity due to an already stressed pipeline.

Going back to the issue of global warming, we're at an inflection point. We're told by climate scientists, however, that that window is narrowing. In 2015, 192 countries plus the European Union signed an international treaty with a goal of limiting global warming to below two degrees Celsius, preferably to 1.5 degrees Celsius, which would peak global greenhouse gas emissions, thus slowing down climate change. The trickle-down effects of reducing increasing temperatures include protecting the poor, making sure families can make a living in pastoral societies like Somaliland.

I remember when that treaty was signed and being so grateful for the call to action for my children and their children and their children to come. But in 2017 the United States formally pulled out of the Paris Climate Agreement. The official reason was that it wouldn't benefit the US economy.[14] In part, that might be valid, and I'm all about local jobs. But the way of capitalism is not friendly to the poor in the world. When we pull out of agreements like the Paris Agreement, the downstream consequences affect those on the margins more.

In other words, our energy consumption and fossil fuel usage undeniably matter. And who we vote for matters. Our responsibility if we live in a high-income country is to take account of how we're contributing to the diseases, poverty, and global climate disasters I just discussed. If you live in a high-income or upper-middle income country like I do, 86 percent of all carbon emissions comes from us.[15]

That's a huge responsibility and fault, so of course we would need to be accountable to offset what those emissions are doing in the rest of the world. It matters what car we drive, whether or not we have a gas stove, and, arguably most importantly, who we vote for. We can't, as just one person, change the world. But we can do our part and join the collective others who are bending the world's arc toward justice.

What do we do? We give. We vote. We don't walk by. And we don't get scared by words and phrases like *science, climate change,* and even *socialism.* Instead, we let them challenge worldviews that reflect more of a Western mindset than a Jesus mindset. We hold the words up to the cross and see if they reflect heaven.

Let it be here as it is in heaven.

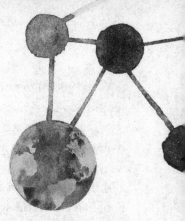

CHAPTER 17

TRUE INNOVATION IS EQUITY

And also.

ME

*How many things, too, are looked upon as quite
impossible, until they have been actually effected.*

PLINY THE ELDER, *NATURALIS HISTORIA*

There was no more oxygen in the hospital.

This was in India during the second surge of COVID-19. You likely remember this surge from the photos like I do. In particular, I remember the rows and rows of burning makeshift funeral pyres as seen through a drone camera—a scene permanently stamped on my mind. In April, May, June, July, and August of 2021, COVID-19 hit India hard. And as the world's leading populous nation with densely populated cities, low hospital bed capacity, and high rates of poverty, the country was entering into a second wave.

Really, the wave was more like a tsunami from the roller-coaster-like increase in cases they were about to experience. In four weeks, cases exploded from 419 per day to over thirteen thousand—and that was only in Delhi, India's largest city and the fifth most populous city in the world with 18.6 million people.[1] The country's case count as a whole mirrored this surge, peaking at over four hundred cases in a single day in early May, and those were only reported cases with likely thousands more going unreported in rural and remote areas that didn't have access to testing. Within an eleven-day period ending at that peak, India saw over 3.5 million cases.

The next two weeks would show an additional 180,000 to 200,000 cases per day. The unimaginable magnitude of the pandemic on the country took its toll on the health care system, leaving families unable to even properly bury those who died.

One of the most-read articles during this time was a *New York Times* piece titled "The Night the Oxygen Ran Out."[2] The opening paragraphs describe alarms going off in the intensive care unit at Jaipur Golden Hospital in New Delhi during the surge of what I just described. The unit was already full, with more than twenty-four COVID-19 patients needing oxygen and ventilator support, overflow areas being added, and new patients being turned away, just like it was with nearly every other hospital during that surge.

"Nobody can forget that night," said Shaista Nigar, the hospital's superintendent. The hospital had run out of oxygen, indicated by multiple alarms, leaving patients gasping for air. By the next morning, twenty-one patients had died. Another report said twenty-six died.[3] We likely all remember the threat of running out of medical oxygen here in the States, too, but never, ever at this magnitude.

If you had a family member struggling to breathe from

COVID-19 and you weren't able to be there with them, I am so sorry. I know this is the case for many people, since some of you sent me emails, messages, or comments.

A year after the second India surge, I was speaking to a group of students and went through the above statistics with them. One student later told me a family member had passed away in India during the surge because of a lack of oxygen. This was a sober reminder that our neighbors are all around us. If you were like that student and lost someone to COVID-19, we—the collective *we*—want to make space upon space for you and your family.

Again, I'm so sorry.

———

It's estimated that at least six hundred people in India died from oxygen shortages in the two months prior to the surge, not even counting most of the deaths attributed to oxygen shortages from the second surge.[4] The crisis left people scrambling to try to find oxygen cylinders they could buy and bring to their hospitalized family members. For moderately ill patients, some hospitals used portable oxygen concentrators.

And that's where we need to focus. These oxygen concentrators are small, portable bedside machines that take in the surrounding air, remove the nitrogen, and deliver oxygen to the patient continuously. I had seen these in Africa, providing lifesaving oxygen to tiny babies. Each concentrator can be used for five children or two adults with mild to moderate infections. For severe infections, the patients need higher levels of respiratory support.

With oxygen shortages around the world during the worst of the pandemic, including many of the shortages concentrated in Asia, Africa, and India, an all-hands-on-deck approach delivered thousands of concentrators to the poorest countries. UNICEF alone, one of the leading global organizations for children's health, shipped more than 62,000 oxygen concentrators to more than one hundred countries.[5]

Here's the point I want to make about this. We applaud UNICEF and many other individuals and organizations for stepping in during an acute crisis to provide lifesaving oxygen to the hardest hit areas, the overwhelming majority being low-income countries. And rightly so, as these health champions are some of the heroes of the day. For those of us not directly involved, however, it's easy to see this heroic act of compassion and solidarity as a one-and-done event. Meaning, we call it innovative and problem-solving and troubleshooting.

If we stop there, though, we've stopped too soon. If we stop at calling this innovative, we take a default posture of solidarity that may make us feel good but doesn't go the full mile. It's like putting a small Band-Aid on a palm-sized gaping wound. But why wasn't there enough oxygen there in the first place? Instead, real innovation is when the storm has passed and the acute crisis is over, we're still there to pick up the pieces and see the root of the real problem behind the acute problem. The person behind the curtain. The *why* and *how* behind the *what happened*.

If we stay long enough, we'll see that providing oxygen concentrators is not innovative. It was necessary because adequate amounts of oxygen weren't there in the first place, but true innovation would be what we saw in the US when there were much smaller oxygen shortages. We had a safety net. We didn't need oxygen concentrators to be shipped in the thousands because we already had stockpiles of the rest of the world's supply.

Do you see the inequity and how easy it is to miss? This is an example of being careful to not pat ourselves on the back too quickly. Sit, wait, accompany those most in need so that you're there when the storm passes. Then you can see the root causes more clearly and solve the real problem—in solidarity, by not walking by, just like we see in the Good Samaritan story.

That is real innovation. What does that look like? Think through what you would want for your own family in a health crisis and start there. True innovation is asking why there wasn't enough oxygen in the country in the first place. If we use the easier, cloaked definition of innovation, we miss the equity portion because we haven't solved the root of the problem. We've just cut the tops off the weeds. The real problem was that oxygen wasn't there sufficiently to begin with.

———

Let me give you another example. Have you heard of gastroschisis? I hadn't until my research taught me the word. Gastroschisis is a congenital condition—one of the most common congenital conditions—where "the baby's intestines, and sometimes other organs, are found outside of the baby's body, exiting through the hole [the belly button]."[6] Those of you in the medical field will understand how serious this condition can be.

As a mother, I can't imagine how heartbreaking and scary this would be. Since my prenatal care was in the US, however, I would likely have known this was going to happen through antenatal ultrasound scans, probably several of them. At the time of birth, the obstetric team and surgical crew would have been there to deliver the baby and perform the surgery needed to tuck the intestines inside, sew up the wound, and then let my child heal a bit before sending us both home. And my baby's chance of survival would have been greater than 96 percent.[7] Done, done, and done.

That's in the US, though. Most sub-Saharan African countries report survival rates of 4 to 25 percent.[8] That means the same number of babies surviving from gastroschisis in the US (96 percent) were dying in some African countries. This disparity in children's deaths from high-income countries to low-income countries is one of the widest in global health problems. Why is this the case? Since the 1960s, mortality from gastroschisis has drastically fallen from 60 percent to around 4 percent in the US and UK.[9] A good bit of that reduction is due to improved detection of the condition through ultrasound, timely and safe surgical and anesthesia care, and improved nutrition for the mother and child.

But timing matters the most here. In low-income countries, if a mother gives birth far away from a hospital equipped to care for the baby, she then travels by foot, boat, wheelbarrow, or some other mode of transportation to get to care. If she can. Once the baby arrives at a facility, the condition, which worsens quickly—hence the need for swift and timely care—now includes hypothermia, dehydration, sepsis, and/or swollen bowels, all which strongly impact the baby's overall chance of survival. It's a horrific disease. But only if untreated. Clearly, we need to talk about treatment.

I've already told you how surgical teams treat this condition in the US. Sub-Saharan African countries have an absence of what Dr. Paul Farmer dubbed the five *S*'s needed for a strong and healthy health care system: *staff* (well-trained and adequate surgical staff, such as neonatologists and nurses); *stuff* (such as breathing support and equipment); *space*; *social support*; and *systems* (such as a NICU or referral systems from more rural hospitals).[10]

One of the main ways to care for these babies is to use what's called a preformed silo to hold and protect the bowels from infection for a few days as the organs are slowly tucked safely back into the abdominal cavity. Then the wall is surgically closed, and the enclosure heals over a few more days. This use of a silo is highly successful with an over 96 percent survival rate.

In sub-Saharan Africa, though, these silos are hard to come by due to a lack of the five *S*'s, but also because of poverty. The preformed silos cost approximately $240, which is already higher than the monthly income of people in most sub-Saharan African countries like Tanzania ($146) and Kenya ($188).[11] Even if the silos are provided by charity organizations, the staff, spaces, and systems still need to be there.

In the absence of a preformed silo, surgeons have to improvise with something to hold the bowels in place, like a disposable exam glove, IV bag, or female condoms, and then sew the makeshift bag in place. Although these improvisations have some success, there's still a higher risk of infection, inflammation of the abdominal wall, and damage to where the sutures are. Definitely higher than with the preferred gold standard version of the preformed silo.

Here's the point. It's easy for people in high-income countries to stop here and call these improvisations innovation. Slap a "wow" sticker on it as problem-solving, Instagram a picture of it with a #nailedit and then stop there. The problem, though, is that while it's certainly quasi-innovative, is it equal? Maybe another way to say that is, would you want that improvision if your child was born with their bowels outside their body?

So why do we stop at the version that might be cheaper but doesn't work as well rather than push toward the best one? True innovation is a silo that works just as well as the gold standard one to keep those babies alive and healthy *and* doesn't bankrupt families or the health care system. Why not reduce the cost of the silo from $240? I have some friends working to develop a low-cost way to treat gastroschisis.[12] In fact, the silos are estimated to cost less than one US dollar, and they work just as well as the gold standard silos. Also, these low-cost silos can be placed cot-side for the children under local anesthesia rather than under general anesthesia, which is often not found in low-income settings.

I understand the need for interim treatments in places without a single surgeon available. I work with smart, capable, incredibly talented and passionate colleagues in many of these places. But these should be short-term treatment solutions toward long-term sustainable and equitable building of care. The real solution— the real *equitable* solution—is high-level care, regardless of what country or region you're in, supported by strong surrounding health systems. True innovation is building strong health systems that provide care toward strong, healthy babies. In this case, that means the gold standard silo or one that works just as well for a fraction of the cost.

———

A friend of mine transported COVID-19 vaccines by boat via the Amazon River and through the jungle to some of the hardest-to-reach places. The photos are incredibly cool, reminiscent of what you would see in *National Geographic*. This is an example of a modern-day hero, for sure. *And also.* One of the problems of this scenario, though, and many others playing out daily in hard-to-reach places, is that the vaccines (or food or lifesaving medicines, in other situations) have to be kept cold. Transportation can take a long time for someone who's sick. True innovation heralds the heroes meeting the need while also asking why roads, ambulances, and medicines weren't there in the first place.

True innovation also makes sure vaccines are available equally. As I write this, nearly three years after the start of the pandemic, three billion people in the world have yet to receive a COVID-19 vaccine dose, including many health care workers still fighting the pandemic, with early inequities set in place when high-income countries gobbled up massive stockpiles of available vaccines, later thrown away. True innovation for vaccines looks like Dr. Peter Hotez and Dr. Maria Elena Bottazzi at Baylor College of Medicine, both of whom I have the honor to know, developing a low-cost, patent-free COVID-19 vaccine made in India and Africa. They were later nominated for the Nobel Peace Prize for that work, which I wholeheartedly applaud.[13]

If we're privileged with access to health care and the ability to pay for it, we have to be really careful not to call something innovative in low-income settings because it looks cool or makes us feel better when the reality is pushing the needle only a few points when we need it to push a hundred. When treatments or the availability of medicines looks different around the world, when we would ask lots of questions before our own child gets a treatment, that's not true innovation. That's *inequity*. Courage is knowing there's a difference and reaching higher.

———

I want to introduce you to a small, sweet bundle of joy born in Northern Ghana, held by a beaming mother with a surgeon, a health care team, and friends, all smiling. One of my favorite colleagues, a pediatric surgeon from the UK, developed a low-cost intervention study for gastroschisis, the condition I told you about earlier, with a team of more than seventy country partners, mainly in low-income countries. I saw she posted a photo of the child on social media with the caption *Here is our star boy*. He was the first survivor born with gastroschisis in Northern Ghana at this hospital that provides most of the care in the region.

Since that post, my friend has reported that sixty babies with gastroschisis have survived at the study sites in Malawi, Zambia, Tanzania, and Ghana, whereas only three had survived in the two years prior to the study. She and her team lived out the true definition of innovation and didn't stop at simply providing *something*. They offered a high level of care for that child while also lowering costs. Now, *that's* innovation for the star boy.

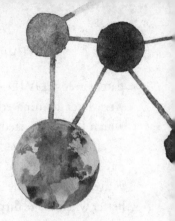

CHAPTER 18

HOW DO WE MEASURE THE WORTH OF A LIFE?

If access to health care is considered a human right, who
is considered human enough to have that right?

DR. PAUL FARMER, *PATHOLOGIES OF POWER*

As I write this, Ebola is quietly spreading in Uganda. Well, quietly for some in the world and loudly for people in global health work trying to sound the alarm and for those living there. On September 26, 2022, a thirty-seven-year-old doctor from Tanzania tested positive for Ebola.[1] Within a week, he died while receiving treatment at a regional hospital's isolation facility. He had been working toward a Master of Surgery degree in Kampala, the capital of Uganda, when he became the second health care worker to die of Ebola in the country during the outbreak. But history tells us more deaths will likely be coming without aid.

Ebola, although a highly contagious disease, is often misunderstood as a highly fatal disease. Let me clarify. When left untreated, Ebola is highly fatal, at least 50 percent, and has even hovered at around 80 to 90 percent in past outbreaks.[2] But Ebola is *not* highly fatal with proper treatment. The mortality rate under those circumstances? Ten percent.

So what's the holdup? The problem? More pragmatically, what's the treatment?

Proper medical care for Ebola includes aggressive hydration, electrolytes, and fever-reducing and anti-vomiting/diarrheal medications. But the real heroes are the big dogs in Ebola treatment: monoclonal antibodies. The development of monoclonal antibodies was a game changer in the Ebola outbreak in 2014 to 2016 in Sierra Leone, Guinea, and Liberia. But only some patients received this treatment. Who was worthy of getting the best chance at survival during the outbreak? How are lives valued?

———

In 2013, a child between one and two years old started running a fever and had diarrhea in his home in Guinea.[3] This was in early December, and by the end of the month, he'd died. His sister, who was three or four years old, died a few days later. Then their pregnant mother and her unborn child, the maternal grandmother, and other extended family members succumbed to the illness within weeks. In the next year, 30 percent of the population of their village died from the disease or became sick. However, the decimation of a family and other community members in a small, rural village in Guinea did not result in alarm bells reaching international aid organizations or authorities.

Then the disease started hitting health workers. The grandmother had sought care, taking a local taxi to a health facility, but she was misdiagnosed with malaria and sent home. Others who sought care were misdiagnosed as having cholera or other febrile illnesses typically seen during rainy seasons in the country. Not until late spring of 2014 was a field team from the Centers for Disease Control and Prevention (CDC) deployed to Guinea to respond to early reports of the viral hemorrhagic fever.

By July of the same year, the disease had spread to the densely populated capital cities of Guinea, Sierra Leone, and Liberia, and by August 2014, Ebola was formally declared an outbreak of PHEIC (Public Health Emergency of International Concern) by the World Health Organization. By the time the outbreak was finally declared over almost two years later, in June 2016, 11,325 people had died and 28,600 people had been infected. Those were the documented cases and fatalities, with more likely dying in the villages or remote areas in the countries without access to health facilities with reporting systems.

The 2014 to 2016 outbreak in those three countries was the largest Ebola outbreak ever, eclipsing the other thirty-four documented outbreaks by magnitudes.[4] More than a thousand health care workers were infected, and 50 percent died. In Sierra Leone alone, 221 health workers died, accounting for 21 percent of the entire country's health workforce.[5] The risk of health workers dying from the disease was at least ten times higher than for the general population, whose risk was already high.

Let me tell you about two people in West Africa from 2016. See each of them through the lens of the Good Samaritan story. And then let's ask ourselves how we measure the worth of a life.

———

Dr. Sheik Humarr Khan, who was Sierra Leone's top Ebola physician and lauded as "a national hero," was deeply respected in his own community and by others he worked with at leading organizations in the United States and Geneva.[6] Powerful people, such as health ministers and global health legends like Dr. Paul Farmer at Partners in Health, knew of Dr. Khan, worked with him, and loved him.

To me, Dr. Khan is equivalent to the household names we all now know because of the COVID-19 pandemic, like Dr. Anthony Fauci and Dr. Sanjay Gupta. He might not have been Insta-influencer famous like a movie star, but he was famous, esteemed, and a legendary physician.

If you rewind time a few years prior to the outbreak, Dr. Khan and his team, including his high-level and well-known colleagues, had already been advocating for a new isolation unit to treat hemorrhagic-type fevers, including Ebola. As one of the most in-depth and poignant narratives of this story puts it, "Even the U.S. Navy had pledged to help. There were a few false starts, and a foundation was half-laid and a wall or two were thrown up."[7] At the beginning of the 2014 to 2016 outbreak, Dr. Khan had already treated more than one hundred patients with Ebola at his facility where many of the nurses, physicians, and other frontline workers had fallen ill.

A few months earlier, a sick pregnant woman had come to his hospital and was eventually diagnosed with Ebola. Dr. Khan informed the World Health Organization, setting off a chain of events in what can be called just a "wall or two" facility. Soon the isolation unit was filled, then the hospital, then another tent serving as a makeshift treatment unit. Those who died were placed in a shed, "stacked like corkwood."[8]

I want to mention that the team did have personal protective equipment (PPE) brought by Dr. Khan's friends, who arrived to help when the first Ebola patient showed up. But this gear takes time to put on and take off, also known as donning and doffing, with precision and accuracy as well as with assistance. In the poorly resourced ward, however, the spread of Ebola was hard to contain as buckets of excrement and crowded beds permeated the crowded nursing areas. Those who were there described it this way: "Ward A had never smelled good, but now it was swimming with shit and vomit and urine and chlorine."[9] The same colleagues who were sending him PPE were also sounding the alarm to health authorities here in the US, including testifying before Congress.[10]

Even with protective gear, health care workers started getting sick, including Dr. Khan. On July 19, he was transported to a Doctors Without Borders unit for the treatment of Ebola hours away and given the standard therapy—fever-reducing medications, oral rehydration and electrolytes, and diarrheal antibiotics. No intravenous drugs were given, though, due to existing protocols, as they were thought to pose a hemorrhage risk—a risk that has now largely been debunked. For patients with profuse vomiting and diarrhea like Dr. Khan experienced, the use of IV hydration could have been lifesaving.

Three days after Dr. Khan was diagnosed, the health minister intervened and asked for two drastic interventions—a medivac to a better-equipped hospital and the use of an experimental drug called ZMapp that had not yet been tested on humans but had shown promising results to prevent death with Ebola.[11] ZMapp, though, wasn't readily available, like Tylenol, NSAIDs (nonsteroidal anti-inflammatory drugs) or even the MMR vaccines most children in the United States receive in their early years. Only a few vials of the drug were in the world, making it extremely limited to administer.

How do you decide who gets it? How do you value a life?

A very limited supply of ZMapp (one course for one person) was stored in the Ebola treatment unit where Dr. Khan was. I wrote that last sentence with very politically correct nouns and verbs. Let me say it in a more human way, using Dr. Paul Farmer's words: "A few of [ZMapp doses], providentially, were in a refrigerator not more than a few hundred paces from Humarr Khan's cot."[12]

After three intense days of debating, assessing risk and benefit, and engaging in discussion with Ebola experts from the World Health Organization, Doctors Without Borders, and health authorities in Canada, Sierra Leone, and the United States, much of which was reported as traumatizing, emotional, and heated, it was decided to not give Dr. Khan one of the doses.[13]

I won't get into the intricacies of this decision, but you can read about it in the incredible investigative reporting from Joshua Hammer, the reporter I cited above who wrote about the stacked bodies at Dr. Khan's hospital,[14] or in Dr. Paul Farmer's extraordinary book, *Fevers, Feuds, and Diamonds: Ebola and the Ravages of History.*

Dr. Khan continued to deteriorate, unable to keep down food or oral rehydration, still not receiving intravenous rehydration to compensate for the loss of fluids. A medevac plane was arranged to take him to Germany or Switzerland, but the pilots and crew refused when they learned Dr. Khan was sick with vomiting and diarrhea even though this was arranged through emergency efforts by the government of Sierra Leone.

On July 29, ten days after being diagnosed and about a week after being transferred to the Ebola treatment unit, Dr. Khan died without anyone by his side other than the medical team and a friend who was allowed to see him near the end.

———

Two days later, a physician in Liberia did receive ZMapp—the only course in Sierra Leone.[15] The vial or vials were flown about five hundred miles south to Liberia on a private plane and then transferred to a helicopter before reaching the patient's home. The first dose was administered by a nurse in full PPE as the medical team watched through a bedroom window.

Do you remember watching all this unfold? It was reported via TV as well as in print. As an epidemiologist, I followed stories of Ebola closely, including this outbreak. I also followed them as a friend since several of my colleagues were in the heart of the outbreak providing care in Ebola units in Sierra Leone and Liberia at the time, many taking significant risks of their own.

I vividly remember watching this event. The house wasn't a hut or a makeshift home like the ones you see throughout Africa. It had walls, rooms, and windows. Everyone except the patient wore PPE, and communication was achieved through that bedroom window covered by a simple curtain. I held my breath, knowing ZMapp was still a highly experimental drug. It was historic and scary. This was July 31—likely around the time discussions about who should get the ZMapp treatment were happening at the treatment center where Dr. Khan was and two days after he died.

Let's back up. Nine days earlier, on July 22—the day after Dr. Khan got sick—the physician in Liberia woke up feeling ill, followed by developing a fever, vomiting, and diarrhea—classic Ebola symptoms—in the days ahead. Another health care worker at the same hospital developed the same symptoms. They'd been working long hours at an Ebola treatment center in Monrovia, the capital of Liberia, which was one of the hardest hit areas in the country.

They were an American physician and nurse working with Samaritan's Purse, a large humanitarian organization headquartered in the US, in a country where one of the Ebola treatment centers runs like a well-oiled machine. The donning and doffing areas, isolation units, and protocols in that health care center are to be commended. I've been in one of the units, and they're incredibly efficient. Even with the right protocols and procedures in place, though, Ebola is relentless.

One of this doctor's colleagues reported there was a course of ZMapp in Sierra Leone, enough for one person. In one of the most haunting lines of Dr. Farmer's book on the ordeal, he writes, "The Kailahun doses of ZMapp [the doses at the Doctors Without Borders facility where Dr. Khan was] went by private plane to two American missionaries in Liberia, crossing flight paths with a UN helicopter sent from Liberia to collect the precious vials for the Americans."[16]

After the experimental drug arrived in Liberia, the American doctor took a turn for the worse and, as I mentioned above, was started on ZMapp, along with the IV hydration and antibiotics he was already receiving. The next few days were a whirlwind of activity, including medevacking him to Atlanta. The plane was equipped with an Aeromedical Biological Containment System, with HEPA filtered air, a containment tent with negative pressure, and air ambulance capabilities such as oxygen and IVs. It had been built to transport patients during the 2003 SARS outbreak.

By August 2, that doctor walked from the back of an ambulance in full PPE gear into the state-of-the-art isolation unit at Atlanta's Emory University Hospital. Again, did you see that? I remember it vividly.

At the time, only one other facility in the US was capable of handling highly contagious pathogens like Ebola. The American doctor, along with the other US health worker at the same hospital, would receive ZMapp and spend the next few weeks receiving aggressive treatment administered by a team of five infectious disease doctors, twenty-one nurses, two pathologists, and five medical technologists. On August 19 and 21, both the American doctor and the nurse walked out of the hospital, about three weeks after Dr. Khan died in Sierra Leone.

———

Two doctors contracted Ebola on nearly the same day, five hundred kilometers apart. Both worked the front lines, providing care in a burgeoning crisis to the sickest of the sick. One was African and one was American. One lived and one died. One was medevacked, given the type of medical care all of us would want for our families, and one wasn't. The differentiation wasn't just about who got ZMapp, though. It was also about who received adequate treatment, such as replacing lost fluids through intravenous measures and quickly treating any infections that might result from an Ebola infection.

How do you determine the value of a life?

I know, I know. It's complicated, fraught with unanswerable questions and unimaginable decisions. But come up from the ground to a ten-thousand-foot view with me. This is a story of equity. And worth. Value and dignity. And who gets to assign that.

We, those of us in the American church or who live in a high-income country, have to be careful here. At this point in the conversation, it's easy to stop with this comment: "Well, if it were you, you would want medical care for your family, too, wouldn't you?" The answer is always a resounding yes to that. Of course I would. But that comment misses the point.

If a colleague or a family member were sick with Ebola during this outbreak, I would move heaven and earth to do what I could to get them the best care possible. You better believe I would be calling contacts with contacts and then calling those contacts. I would try to raise enough money to pay for what was needed, and I bet you would too.

But that's not the point of these stories, is it? One person was American with a host of contacts in high and highly resourced places—some of the same contacts you might have if you live in the US. Or at least you could call someone who might know somebody who could help.

And also.

Why weren't one-of-a-kind planes and helicopters deployed five hundred kilometers away to Sierra Leone?

———

I distinctly remember when my husband-to-be and I prayed at a picnic table by our college before we were married and told the Lord we would go wherever he wanted us to go and do whatever work he had for us. He had been to Africa and I'd been to Honduras, and we knew part of our calling or one of our life goals was to do mission work of some kind. (In my efficient-planner mode, I likely also snuck in *help me get into medical school and let us go to Africa* somewhere during that earnest prayer.)

Then early in our marriage, I talked to a recruiter at Samaritan's Purse, the organization I mentioned earlier with the American doctor. We discussed possibilities for us to serve with them, including an option for married couples. My husband was a pastor and I was in public health, so it seemed like a good fit. I can't remember if we applied and weren't accepted or we never applied for one reason or another, but we never served with them. Several of my friends did, though, and they continue to serve there.

My purpose for telling the stories of Dr. Kahn and the American doctor, who worked for Samaritan's Purse, is not to call out that organization, although I no longer agree with some of its key tenants and I strongly called out its president and CEO, Franklin Graham, for how he responded to the pandemic—especially in the context of the November 2020 prayer rally at the Capitol he both organized and participated in. The point is to learn if and how our hearts react to the two stories.

Part of being courageous is coming to terms with the fact that these inequities happen all the time. Some get treatment and others don't. Some live and others don't. Some countries get more while others don't. Again, it's a common misconception that most people die from Ebola if they become infected. Well, that might be true if you live in Africa, but not if you live in the United States or the

United Kingdom or Denmark or Belgium. The case fatality rate for Ebola during the 2014 to 2016 outbreak in Africa ranged from 45 percent in Liberia to 67 percent in Guinea to a whopping 74 percent in the Democratic Republic of the Congo.[17] During the same period, eleven people were treated for Ebola in the United States. One died.[18]

Were those in the US healthier, younger, or stronger? No, they weren't very different in general. The ones who lived just received supportive care in non-fragmented medical facilities. In hospitals not overflowing with other sick patients. In hospitals not reaping years of war and systemic injustice resulting in understaffing or underequipping to begin with. In countries with expensively equipped hospital-type planes and powerful contacts.

They weren't different; *the systems surrounding them were.*

Courage like that of the Good Samaritan works to see and share this reality, naming the injustices and then changing the narrative, the arc toward justice. This brings me back to our initial question in this chapter: How do you measure a life? The value and worth of one. The dignity and honor. If you're a Christian, like me, our humanity is rooted in the image of God. All of us. To God, then, measurement is equal. Grace and mercy aren't apportioned according to the world's metrics. Compassion and care aren't either, but they're given overflowingly—out of an abundance of his presence.

Like when God passed by Moses on the mountain. Do you know the story of when Moses asked to see God?[19] God told him no because no one can see God and live. But he said he would pass by him if he turned with his face into the cleft of the rock. While God passed Moses, he didn't proclaim his power or might; he proclaimed his character. Gracious. Compassionate. Slow to anger. Rich, oh so rich, in love. Abounding in love and faithfulness. And care.

It takes courage to do our valuing of others according to God. This doesn't come naturally for some of us, and we'll need to dismantle our own unconscious biases. Others of us have done the hard work of courageous relearning, and now we must do the equally hard work of living that out by advocating with love.

How do we measure a life? Graciously. Compassionately. Abounding in love and faithfulness.

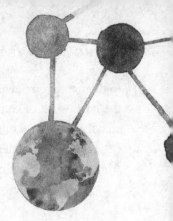

CHAPTER 19

WISDOM, WORSHIP, AND OLAF

I am doing a great work, and I cannot come down.
NEHEMIAH

You sure you want to do that?
DR. HENRY RICE, MY REAL-LIFE MENTOR
AND COLLABO-FRIEND

We don't have to enter every fight we're invited to or stumble upon. Just like there's wisdom in where we put our energy, there's wisdom—perhaps an even harder-won wisdom—in what we resist pouring our energy out for. It reminds me of when the apostle Paul counseled not to get into silly fights or to avoid godless chatter.[1] Or when Jesus said to be wise like a serpent or walked straight through crowds that were trying to get him to stay.[2] How did he know what to do or, better yet, what not to do?

Nestled at the end of the historical narrative portion of the Hebrew scriptures, the book of Nehemiah takes place in the fifth century BC. It reads more like a memoir than a history book, written by a dude named Nehemiah who found himself in the right place at the right time for some right-ish people. We'll talk more about why I call them right-ish later, but for now, let me set the stage.

At this time in history, the walls of Jerusalem have been destroyed, and captivity is rampant. Then comes one of my favorite parts of the Bible—one of those passages that stops me every time I read it. In chapter 1, when Nehemiah hears about the walls being destroyed, he does something private and tender, almost raw. He sits down. And weeps. And then he prays,

> Lord, the God of heaven, the great and awesome God, who keeps his covenant of love with those who love him and keep his commandments, let your ear be attentive and your eyes open to hear the prayer your servant is praying before you day and night for your servants, the people of Israel. I confess the sins we Israelites, including myself and my father's family, have committed against you. (verses 5–6)

Before I go on, I want us to hear the remnants of justice in that prayer. Yes, Nehemiah declared the great and awesome characteristics of God, but he also confessed his own sins *and those of his father's family.* Even Nehemiah recognized that the present is impacted by history. That the sins of his father's family, over which he had no control, could continue infusing the present. That past individualistic actions could become structural.

Does this remind you of our discussions on structural violence? That's what Nehemiah's opening prayer reminds me of. There's a deep humility in Nehemiah's prayer of his own sins, yes. But perhaps also a more powerful wisdom and humility in acknowledging his family's sins of the past. We, especially those of us in privileged societies or positions, would do well to acknowledge the same.

Let's keep going in the chapter, though, because the best part is coming.

Nehemiah prays a few more stanzas where he reminds God of what he said about his promises and the consequences of a rebellious people, and then again asks God for an attentive ear.

At the end of chapter 1 is the clincher: "I was cupbearer to the king" (verse 11).

After an incredible prayer of remembrance, confession, and worship, Nehemiah remembered his place. A simple cupbearer to a powerful king. This passage anchors me in whatever season I find myself in. At the end of my own prayers, I'm still, well . . . me. Emily. Known by not many people and fully loved by a few. In the margins of my Bible beside this verse, I write a descriptor of myself each time I reread it, with a date. I now have several years of new descriptors, since 2014. Instead of *cupbearer to the king*, I've written *a new mom of children, a PhD student in North Carolina, a new professor*.

Nehemiah was a simple cupbearer to a king. And not just any king but one powerful enough to control an entire people group's success or demise. I wonder if, at the time, Nehemiah felt like "just" a cupbearer. Did he realize he was in a strategic position right next to power that he probably couldn't have planned if he'd wanted to? I wonder if we recognize our simple positions of whatever we're doing as strategic and impactful as well.

Nehemiah was where he needed to be.

You are too.

In the next few chapters of this book in the Bible, Nehemiah goes on to rebuild the wall with a team of likeminded people. Well, most of them were. A few, led by Sanballat and Tobiah, didn't like what Nehemiah was doing and stirred up trouble. At first they were blunt in their verbal attacks, calling the work weak enough that children or foxes could break it, or saying the stones they were building with were merely piles of trash and dirt. (Okay, I see you with your sass, San and Tob!) Over time, the words became more like sneak attacks of passive aggressiveness and weird reasoning. Let me show you how.

The biggest attack took place in chapter 6 when Sanballat sends a message to Nehemiah: "Come, Nehemiah, let's chat. Come meet with us. Everyone is talking about a rumor going around, it involves you, and Geshem says it's true. Something about the Jews planning to turn against the king. Come on, let's have lunch and chat." Well, that's not a direct quote, but it's how I imagine the message sounded.

Do you see the sneakiness here? This isn't a blatant threat to hurt Nehemiah or an attack on his character like the initial ones that would have made anyone angry and defensive. This attack is more like a distraction to get Nehemiah to worry about rumors or what so-and-so said. Instead of trying to get him upset in a 90-degree turn, they tried a more subtle 10-degree turn of a lunch meeting. We all know a 90-degree turn will put you in a very different end-place miles down the road than where you originally planned to be.

Here's the deal, though. So will a 10-degree turn. It will just be more discreet. More subtle.

And here's my second favorite part of this story. Nehemiah saw the road that turn would take, and he didn't take the bait. He sent a message back to the naysayers: "I am doing a great work, and I cannot come down."[3]

Oh, snap. (Okay, Nehemiah. I see you!)

It's drama time now, friends. Better go grab some popcorn. Nehemiah had the wisdom to not let the blatant attacks get to him.

But he also had the deeper wisdom to recognize the sneakier attack. He kept first things first, which was building the wall. He could have tried to set the record straight on what Tobiah was believing or Sanballat was spreading. He would have been justified in doing so, wouldn't he? Nehemiah's reputation was on the line, and I don't know about you, but I don't like it when false words are said about me. I want to roll up my sleeves and set the record straight.

But Nehemiah knew something. He saw *through* the distraction and remembered his job. It wasn't to defend himself or his fellow coworkers at that time; it was to keep working toward rebuilding: "I am doing a great work, and I cannot come down."

Again, this passage is such an anchor for me. So much so that my husband will text this verse to me when he knows I'm nervous while writing a paper (or this book) or before I teach a class or when I do something that takes courage. Or when people say dumb things about me on social media. Most often, though, we need the wisdom to remember that the Sanballats and the Tobiahs of the world are trying to distract us from the good—even great—work we're doing. I need periodic reminders that I am doing a good work and don't have to answer everything and everyone.

———

There's no lack of things that need to be fixed, is there? Just go on social media for ten minutes, and you can be angry or frustrated for days on end about issues like climate change. (Or even about far less important things, like a rumor that your McDonald's might not bring back Shamrock Shakes this year.) If we're not careful, we can easily spend hours on social media responding to what's made us angry—or at least stewing over it while washing the dishes. It's not worth it, though, is it? The anger and frustration get inside us and affect our centering. It distracts us and takes away our energy.

I've become much better at choosing what I read and who I listen to. Sometimes I audibly say, "Nope!" as I scroll past ugly words or crazy talk on social media or news sites. I've learned those steal my peace and my mind. And I'm in control of both. I don't have to go to every fight I see or hear. I'm doing a good work and cannot come down. For those of us with empathetic tendencies, there's more than enough hurt in the world to throw us on our backs over and over again. If we can't fix it all, what issue do we choose? What issue do we let others choose? And how do we know the difference?

Therein lies the wisdom, friends.

In the middle of the COVID-19 pandemic, I had to choose what I would let be distractions and what were my places to keep building. I'd been speaking out about the church's response to the pandemic and how it—mainly the White evangelical church, my own people—wasn't acting like Jesus would. So much of American White evangelicalism had become more discipled by Donald Trump than by the Beatitudes. I've heard people say that Christian nationalism is just fringe and will slowly die out. I don't think that's true though. I've seen it creep into our mainstream churches in sneaky and not so sneaky ways. I've also watched it grow insidiously rather than slowly die out. It's not fringe anymore. I was also speaking out against poverty, structural violence, and global vaccine inequities. That's three more battles.

Here's the point. All the injustices are important to combat, but of course, the battles are too much for just one person. We each have to choose wisely because we cannot carry the weight of all of them. Not even a few of them. And not all battles or issues or arguments are ours to jump into and fight anyway. The real question for us, then, is this: what is my good work that I cannot and will not come down for?

Thank goodness for the wisdom of my husband and others to constantly remind me that I am doing a good work and don't have to accept that lunch invitation with the Sans or the Tobs. Or even a coffee date, for that matter.

If I can impart any wisdom about this hard world we live in, it's this: remember that you, in your unique place with your unique personality and quirks and limitations and giftings, are doing a good, even great, work. Don't come down from that. Don't let the fight of the day distract you. Fight your fight. Keep building. Do your good work, and don't come down for the rest.

To get super practical on what this looked like for me, I got off social media entirely for a year, and now I use it only with strong boundaries and limits. I didn't really notice this until I got off, but social media got me all frustrated and mad. Why? I think in part because it's full of Sans and Tobs, and it's hard to discern that through a screen. We end up going to lunch with them by scrolling. And, friends, that does something to our hearts and distracts us from our good deeds.

I'm so much calmer, wiser, and, well, more peaceful since I've taken steps to protect myself. And I'm also a better mom, wife, and researcher because now I have more room in my mind and heart to think and love. If you're considering getting off social media or setting strict boundaries for yourself, I highly recommend it. It's a lot easier to keep building whatever you're meant to build when you don't have that distraction.

———

Let me show you the end results of this wisdom—what happens when we do our great work and don't come down together. One is personal, marginal, secular, neighborly; the other is corporate, holy, worshipful, like collective solidarity. Put this together, and it sounds a lot like the Good Samaritan story.

In the building process, some marginalized and impoverished

people came up to Nehemiah and complained that they didn't have enough food for their families and were being unfairly taxed.[4] They couldn't afford the taxes, had to borrow money just to pay them, and had already lost their fields and vineyards.

Now, think through this problem with me. We've already established that we don't have to enter every fight that comes our way.

Nehemiah could have chosen to delegate here, asking the marginalized group to figure it out for themselves. Or he could have sent thoughts and prayers along with a fruit basket. Instead, in chapter 5, he confronted the "nobles and officials" about their unjust actions with a speech fit for more popcorn: "Give back to them immediately their fields, vineyards, olive groves and houses, and also the interest you are charging them" (verse 11).

If you look closely at verses 14 through 16, you'll see the *why* behind Nehemiah's strong reaction. He'd seen this type of oppression before and chosen not to follow suit even though he was in a position of relative power and wealth for the king. Now look closely at verse 16: "I devoted myself to the work on this wall." Sounds a lot like what he said in chapter 6, doesn't it? "I am doing a great work, and I cannot come down."

This brings me to the other end result. While the first is personal, tangible, on-the-ground taking care of the poor, the second is corporate worship. In the final few chapters of the book of Nehemiah, when the building was completed, Nehemiah ensured that every family's name was recorded in one of those really long genealogy sections of the Bible we usually skip over in our yearly reading plan, am I right? (Well, I used to skip those. Now I read them, especially the ones where the women are mentioned.)

In Nehemiah, the list represents families who were once in captivity and now were free. Families, named along with the number of household members, that had lost everything and were now being restored. The descendants of Parosh, 2172; Arah, 652; Adin, 655; Hashum, 328; and on and on and on. The unnamed and the uncounted and the poor were now named and gathered.

In chapter 8, we're given this beautiful picture of all the people gathering in the square. Ezra, a leader of the rabbinical law, read the law again. Then they shared a meal and confessed both past and present wrongdoings before Nehemiah rose and reminded them that the day was holy. He also told them, "The joy of the LORD is your strength" (verse 10). That's a phrase some of us learned as a kid in Sunday school or have adapted for display on our walls: "The joy of the Lord is my strength."

In other words, they worshiped. Corporately. And I wonder if that was an extension of the individual work of taking care of the poor, which was itself an extension of choosing wisely what we are building. Wisdom and the work of a cupbearer turned into the worship of a God who takes care of the poor—and us.

We are doing a great work. Let's not come down. And that's what I want to talk about next. What happens when a group of people are doing their own "works," and together it changes the world? I've already mentioned that I had lost most of my community and tradition. So I needed a new community that I didn't even know was out there. A new group of people who are working and worshiping too. I just wasn't sure I would find it. And goodness, was I about to be surprised!

———

When my daughter was five-ish, the worldwide phenomenon *Frozen* came out. If you had a kid between the ages of three and thirteen then, there's a high likelihood you watched that film over and over and over, especially as soon as it was available on DVD. Did you have the dress-up clothes? The sing-along videos? The books? The [*insert lots of Disney stuff here*]? We did too. We weren't a huge Disney family. In fact, my hubs changed the Disney stories a bit to make the guy in need of rescuing and the gal the awesome hero.

One night I walked into my daughter's room and saw her six-foot-four father lying with half his body inside a tiny pink play castle, waiting to be rescued by the fierce and strong Bella, our daughter. To this day, it's one of my favorite memories of them. I think he actually fell asleep in there that night, because, well, parenting is hard.

Okay, back to the story. One day our local movie theater was offering a 10:00 a.m. (read: before naptime) showing of *Frozen*, and you bet your bottom dollar I bought tickets. When I told my daughter, she promptly ran into her room to change into her best theater attire. You guessed it: full *Frozen* outfit. And off we went.

I thought the theater would be less than half full since that's what we'd found when we'd been to these early movie showings before, but when we got there, it was packed. Like no-seats-between-anyone packed. Loads of little people and their bigger caregivers, all with the same love for this story. And to my pleasure, lots of other little people dressed like Elsa or carrying stuffed Olafs. It was the epitome of adorable.

The lights lowered, and the movie started. Then *the song* began. You know, the one that gets stuck in your head. Do you know that one? Oh well, I'll let it go. (See what I did there?)

Now, I need to tell you something about my daughter. She's always loved to sing. Loudly. We didn't even need a monitor in her room during her crib days because we could hear her announcing she was awake by singing. This happened most often between 2:00 and 3:00 a.m. She would wake up, sing "Jesus Loves Me" or "ABCDEDaddyyyyyy" (because she thought those were the words) at the top of her lungs for a few—ahem, twenty—minutes and then go back to sleep. It was so sweet. And tiring. Again, parenting is hard.

Back to the movie theater. *The song that gets stuck in your head* began, and my gal jumped out of her seat in her Elsa outfit and started belting every single word. Every. Single. Word. But just as I was about to try to get her to sing with her inside voice, the other little people in the room started singing too. Then more. And more. Before you knew it, this giant movie theater was full of kids out of their seats having the time of their lives.

What did I do? I sang too. Well, I also started crying. This was pure joy. I looked at the other adults in the room, and most of them were singing too. A few were teary-eyed like me. And several were just smiling with a "this is the life" look.

The rest of the movie brought one big party Olaf-in-the-summertime would be proud of. There was dancing and lots more singing. Some giggles and cheering. It was a surprising, collective exhale of joy.

———

If you're like me, you may have lost friends and traditions and faith over the past few years. You may have needed courage to speak up for what you know is true, even at a cost. And now it can feel unstable or vulnerable and just be lonely. Let me give you some hope, since I've been there and inching toward the newness on the other side of the loss. Once you get to what's on the other side of whatever you needed courage for, once you find what your good work is—the one, like Nehemiah, you're not coming down for—you'll find it's bigger than you expected. You'll find an entire theater of people singing the same song you are. And you'll look around, take more courage from them, and be swept up in the joy. You'll sing and cry. And no one will care. Because everyone else is doing it too.

You'll find yourself in a new theater. For me, that was a new church with new friends. I found a whole slew of people working to bend the arc toward justice when to me it had looked like only a few before. Now it's stadiums full.

Of justice and tears and collectivity.

In the most unseen places where you didn't think it would ever come again.

There's joy. And solidarity.

Having the courage to work for justice can be scary when you've risked or lost so much. It can be lonely too. In reality, though, an entire new world of people is out there. They're singing and smiling and working on their good deeds, just like you are and Nehemiah did. A world of people who, like you, are not walking by.

And there's probably singing.

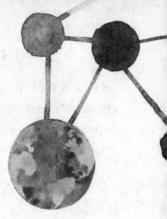

CHAPTER 20

A GARDEN

And the LORD will continually guide you,
And satisfy your soul in scorched and dry places,
And give strength to your bones;
And you will be like a watered garden,
And like a spring of water whose waters do not fail.

ISAIAH 58:11 AMP

It's still hard to see photos of us at our old house. The one with the mailbox mentioned earlier in this book. We thought it would be our forever home. It had room to grow and my dream fireplace of old stone and a massive wood mantel. It's the house where I lived in the "before times." Before the pandemic. Do you call the years before 2020 that too? When I look at photos from that time, a bit of my heart still hurts. Now I see TV shows or documentaries or read books that talk about the pandemic in a thousand different ways, and my heart twinges with those too. In many ways, it's still hard and triggering.

I have a feeling it is for many of you as well. None of us will be the same after the collective trauma.

In other ways, though, I'm seeing how I've changed after the personal disappointments and losses. I notice it the most when I'm gardening. Gardening allows me to dig out my frustrations in the dirt and cry into the soil. Then a few months later, stalks shoot up from the ground, cracking with intensity as the flower or tomato or spinach seedling finally pushes through. It's magical and poetic.

I come by my love of the outdoors and gardening honestly from the cardinal-loving grandma I told you about. But mostly, I get it from my dad. As I was growing up, our backyard in the dry heat of New Mexico was like an oasis, much like my grandparents' backyard had been in Oklahoma. Our yard had a tiny pond, flowers upon flowers, walkways, and even trees that made you feel like you were in the mountains of Colorado. I can still smell the ivy right after my dad watered it, and some of my favorite memories are from when he and I spent time together on our porch swing late into the evening, talking about the weather or life.

I still like to go to one of the big-box hardware stores with him to buy the reject plants at the back of the store, and my dad and I can usually bring those back to life just by giving them some tender lovin' care and talking to them.

During my growing-up years, I had a special place in the main tree, which stood in the middle of the backyard. I sat up there for hours to read or write like Jo from *Little Women*. It had one branch to hold my pencil and another to hold my journal and bag. Maybe that's when my dream of one day writing a book was birthed. Years later, that tree had to be taken down due to disease, and my dad cut off part of the bark for me. I still have it in my living room.

———

When I got sick with chronic migraines, one of the hardest parts was being unable to go outside. The sunshine was too bright or I would get dizzy if I bent over or walked for too long. Nonetheless, in an act of defiance, when we moved to North Carolina, the first thing we decided to do—even though the house needed lots of updates—was put in a garden.

Not any garden, mind you. I wanted one just like Psalm 16—spacious, safe, a refuge with boundary lines in pleasant places, a reminder of a glad heart and restful body. I needed that garden. It has a few beds with a fence to keep the deer out, gates on either side that I think look just like the ones at Green Gables, and solar lanterns that glow at night. I needed this garden.

One of my favorite things to do is walk the garden at dusk or at night to the glow of those little lanterns. Do you remember me telling you about those birdhouses my grandma made? They're in each bed in the garden, one painted red like the cardinals she loved.

I felt well enough in the spring to plant vegetables and flowers with the help of my family. We planted an exorbitant amount of kale, broccoli, spinach, and more spinach. We planted grapevines and lots of blackberry bushes. In the summer we planted tomatoes and watermelon, zucchini and yellow squash. I also knew I needed flowers like my grandmother had in her garden, so I planted dahlias, zinnias, and gladiolus from bulbs.

On days when I felt okay, I would walk the garden, kneeling to see if any of the flowers had burst through. Finally, one day I saw the first shoot. Then the second, third, and fourth. Obviously, I did what any good gardener does and made my family come look. Every time. On days when I didn't feel well, I could still see the garden from my bedroom. Then I hit a rough health patch for a few months that laid me up enough that I couldn't water or weed or tend the garden at all. Here's what happened, though, without me knowing: the garden burst open and overproduced. Again and again.

My garden of abundance during my sabbath year, 2022

One day after I was feeling a little better, my daughter and I went out to pick tomatoes, and we picked at least fifty of them, with many still left on the vine to ripen. The dahlias and glads were as tall as my eleven-year-old, and I had never seen such a beautiful bouquet as the one we made for our kitchen table—just like the bouquet I mentioned in the introduction of this book. What in the world was happening even when I couldn't get out there?

This year, 2022, was a sabbath year for me, also known as the *shmita* in Judaism. When I finished my PhD in 2015, I remember saying that I would take a sabbath year, a year of rest from productivity and hustle, in seven years. This was based on the biblical principle of the Sabbath to rest in God's provision weekly but also for an entire year every seven years. Even the land was to lie still, knowing that what was needed would be provided.

It's not lost on me that the seventh year hit in 2022, when I needed it the most. And my garden was a gentle reminder of the principle of the year. During the sabbath year, the land is to lie fallow with no plowing, planting, pruning, or harvesting, but the people would be taken care of from the bounty of the previous six years. It's a powerful lesson in hustle culture to just . . . be. So the fact that my garden was overproducing in abundance—*even in the midst of* me being sick and coming out of the height of the pandemic years—was such a gift. This was a tangible picture of the *and also* I've talked about again and again in this book.

———

Perhaps the main gift is what was happening in my heart though. If you look at the first time a sabbath year is talked about in Scripture, you have to go to Exodus 23. The sabbath year certainly was designed for us and the land. But there's a deeper principle that applies to what my heart was doing at that time. Verse 11 of Exodus 23 tells us that during the sabbath year the poor among the people will be able to eat. Perhaps the deeper lesson is that all of us are taken care of, but only when some of us stop striving. Stop producing. Stop consuming. Stop wanting or taking too much of what is not ours. There it is again—the principle of *collective solidarity*. My garden helped remind me of that and of the importance of loving my neighbors through recentering my heart around the sabbath.

That garden taught me one more thing I want to share with you, which is even more tender to me. Many times when I was homebound, I would walk in the garden simply to get out of the house and try to get outside of my head and away from the pain, but it never worked. It was really hard to pray or read during those times, which was new for me since prayer and reading have always been central in my life. Digging in the dirt and pulling weeds, I found myself lamenting with the earth in a Romans 8–type of groaning way without words, just tugs and pulls of weeds and dirt.

A GARDEN

One day at dusk, when the lanterns were barely twinkling, I was resting my chin on my arms, which were perched up on the fence, wondering if I would ever get back to the person I once was. I remembered one of my favorite stories in the Bible. The Bible opens with a garden and closes with a garden. And tucked away in the middle is a story about a gardener and a woman named Mary. In this story, Mary is approached by a man she thinks is a gardener and expresses her sorrow when she tells him about her grief at losing Jesus, who had been put to death on a cross. You can hear the deep lament and disappointment of a woman who had just lost what she thought would be her future. It wasn't until the man, who was Jesus, spoke her name—"Mary"—that she realized her hopes were still right there inside her. They just looked different from the way she thought they would look.

My garden did the same thing with me. It taught me about the needy, and the Gardener met me when I was needy when he called my name—Emily—and helped me see my true identity in this world as Emily, a courageous neighbor, fully known and fully loved, just as I am. In my garden, I was reminded of who I had always been but needed some courage and centering to see it fully. The Good Samaritan story had come full circle for me.

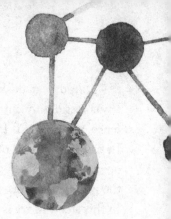

CHAPTER 21

A NEW TABLE

Nor was there anyone among them who lacked.

ACTS 4:34 NKJV

This book started with a table and will end the same way. But this time I'm outside, writing on a massive picnic table my husband built for me using wood deep with pine knots that remind me of my grandparents' old house. I wanted one as big as I could fit into the yard so lots of neighbors could sit around it, and he delivered! He also knows how much I love nature and art and poetry and anywhere that looks like a secret garden meadow. So he lugged this table along with its benches to the very back of our yard, where it's nestled in the trees in a tiny meadow of our own.

Okay, technically it's not a meadow, but I'm imagining that's what this patch of grass surrounded by trees is. It's October here in North Carolina, with changing leaves everywhere. Some of those leaves fall on my computer or notebook from above me—even in my coffee that's close by—and it makes me smile every time. If you need a visual of where I wrote the majority of this book, it's out here on this table.

I've been thinking a lot about tables lately. Tables are where we gather our families to share a meal and life together. For me while I was sick those dark months, I wasn't able to even cook supper, much less sit at our dining table, because even a little laughter would have been too loud and the sunset too bright. Maybe that's one reason tables mean so much to me now. I caught myself this week getting teary during supper. Nothing spectacular was going on. It was simple talk of "please pass the bread" or "don't feed the dog." But to me, it was like one of those scenes in a movie where things blur in and out as the background music swells. A scene where you know the person the camera zooms in on is overwhelmed and grateful for the mundane nature of a simple meal. That person was me this week. We have a tradition where we say something we are thankful for before we eat dinner. That night, I said through tears that I was thankful to just be there with them. As neighbors and family.

This week was Easter week. I was apprehensive and anxious, since Holy Week two years ago was the last "normal" week I would have. That year, a few days after Easter my body told me that enough was enough, and it fell apart for eighteen months. This falling apart would feel like one very long, dark, and silent Saturday between Good Friday and Easter Sunday but Sunday never comes. When we walked into our new church this year, I asked my husband if I had attended Easter the year before. He said I had, but I don't remember anything about it from being so sick. I was there but had to leave because of the noise and light and movement. This year, however, I stayed while we rang little bells every time we heard the word *hallelujah*. I stayed while we placed our flowers on the cross. I stayed and thought of the table from a few weeks ago and the cross alongside it. That table, full of bread and wine, broken for me and my own brokenness. I have taken Communion five times since the pandemic and cried every single time. I think it's out of grateful-ness, yes. But I wonder if something about the table reminds me of being welcomed, of being brought near to love. Perhaps it reminds me of being neighbored.

It is not lost on me that Jesus spent much of his life around tables or teaching about them. He dined with all sorts of people around tables. It was at a table where he was prepared for his death by a grateful woman with an alabaster vial. It was at a table that the holy work of breaking bread and sharing a cup was carried out for the disciples as a reminder of a newness about to spring forth. That newness meant those disciples years later would share all they had so there would be no lack of food among the rest of them. Food eaten together around shared tables.

Jesus does that, doesn't he? Transforms us into people who share, who add more chairs, who squeeze in too many people on the bench, who set a few more plates out, who break bread believing that our few loaves will be enough and that this shared table is one of abundance rather than scarcity.

Let me tell you about one more table though.

When my first child was born, I bought a book with the Lord's Prayer written in more than twenty different languages. On the front cover was Norman Rockwell's famous painting *The Golden Rule*, created as a cover illustration for the *Saturday Evening Post* in 1961 during the peak of the Cold War.[1] The painting portrays sixty-five people of different ages, races, ethnicities, and religions representing the nations of the world. Ascribed at the bottom is the Golden Rule of the Good Samaritan: "Do unto others as you would have them do unto you." I've loved that painting from the first time I saw it on the cover of that book.

Eight years later at the United Nation meetings, which were life-centering for me, I was headed back to my seat when I rounded a corner and abruptly stopped. On the third floor of the building was Rockwell's *Golden Rule* painting, re-created in Murano mosaic glass tiles, stretching 10 feet by 9 feet. It halted me straight in my boots. (Just kidding, I was wearing heels, but I was halted either way.)

For some reason, I, a simple woman who came from a small town in New Mexico, was living a life with a job and a family I wouldn't have even known how to dream about. And there in the middle of it, I was reminded again of what I believe the heavenly table will look like. A new table of neighboring and neighbors, colors and countries, sizes and shapes. Neighboring had made my ordinary life extraordinary.

I used to tell my students that to get a seat at "the table," someone had to give up their chair. While I understand the underlying message of that statement, I no longer believe it. That table now seems like one of scarcity, with just enough seats or food for some but not for all, and elbows of power needed to get a seat there. That table is where not everyone is welcome or heard, and you have to be loud and assertive to get there. It's exhausting. It's not friendly to everyone. And if you're marginalized for any reason, it likely hasn't been safe. Sure, it may be the reality of the world we live in, but should it be?

Now I tell my students—and myself—to find a new table. To create our own table and leave behind the one that doesn't have enough room for everyone. To create a table that has enough seats for all and then some. Where everyone has their turn to speak and listen with dignity and agency. A table where deeds meet faith, just as silence fills empty spaces between words to form our stories or water fills cracks on boulders to form waterfalls. A liminal space between the "already and the not yet" where there is room at this table. A table that looks like what I think heaven will look like.

Neighboring does that to us. It interrupts us and invites us to the new table, with Jesus showing us the way. A table in the middle of a wilderness or in the presence of our enemies. Where bread and wine, body and blood are broken. Where tears and laughter are shared equally. Where the lowest person sits at the head and the marginalized are brought to the center. Where all have enough to eat, to share, and to be satisfied, with basketfuls left over. A table of color and equality.

A table of neighbors and neighboring.

Who *was* the neighbor?

Let it be us.

ACKNOWLEDGMENTS

How do you sum up an abundance of gratitude in a few paragraphs when even a thousand thank-yous won't suffice? I don't know the answer, but I'm going to try to say thank you to those who have been a neighbor to me.

First and foremost, without hesitation, I name my husband. Mike, you have loved and cherished me beyond words for more than twenty years, making me feel seen and heard and safe. More importantly, you've been right there as I've stood up into myself, at my full height. And applauded the whole time. In very real ways, I am me because of who we are. You are more than I could have asked for and my greatest gratitude beyond grace. I love this life we've made together.

To my children, you have had to rise to your own heights in ways you did not choose as your mom was rising to hers, and you've done that beautifully. If all the children in the entire world were lined up, I would still pick you two in a millisecond. Thank you for nothing more than being you, which in reality is everything, and for applauding right alongside your dad. I love this life you, Bella and Jonathan, are making with us, and I'm beyond honored to be your mom. In everything most important, you are our life.

To our dog, Charlie, thank you for the constant bumps of my

hands off the keyboard and onto you. If this book has any typos no one caught, I joyously blame you.

Thank you to the many teachers who encouraged a gal from a small town in New Mexico to dream and love the world at the same time. Mr. Acosta, thank you for introducing me to science in the form of that nerdy genetics college textbook (did I ever return it to you?). And to the first woman scientist I ever met, Dr. Strahlendorf, thank you for watching over my shoulder and encouraging a sixteen-year-old girl to become a scientist too. Mrs. Dodd, now that I'm older, I understand the sacrifice it takes to drive a group of students to countless science fairs and an even greater one to drive just one—me. Mr. Acosta is the reason I got into science, and you are the reason I stayed there. Thank you for your encouragement, including reminding me of Isaiah 43 at one of those science fairs. I still have that note from all those years ago.

I've been fortunate to have a long line of strong female teachers, scientists, and professors after Mrs. Dodd, including Ms. Streber, Mrs. Ballinger, Mrs. Rutledge, Dr. Swann Adams, Dr. Annelies Van Rie, Dr. Frieda Behets, Dr. Shukri Dahir, and Dr. Edna Adan Ismail. On their shoulders, thousands of us women scientists now stand too, including my own students. And to my students, your joy and tenacity to make this world a better place are on every page of this book.

Speaking of those scientists, I have to give a huge shout-out to a group of women who surrounded one another during the pandemic years when we all found ourselves in a fight we didn't see coming but needed each other to get through.

The Nerdy Girls, especially Malia and Lindsey, I'm so grateful I found you all, and I'm thankful for your continued friendship. And giggles.

Your Local Epidemiologist, Katelyn, I've found one of my favorite friends in you. Several people were convinced we were the same person, like a good ole conspiracy theory, which still makes me chuckle. If I was going to be mistaken for anyone, though, I'm glad it was you. Thank you for the solidarity, for being a sounding board during the pandemic years, for reading an early version of this book, including the parts where I was just mad, and laughing at my silly memes to this day. You are strong and brave and made me the same.

I also need to give a huge shout-out to my favorite collabo-friends, who continue to do the hard work of neighboring in their own work or have opened up opportunities for me to join: The departments of public health at Baylor University and emergency medicine at Duke University, specifically Chuck, Catherine, Joao, and Henry. Catherine and Joao, it is such a joy to come to work with you two, because it doesn't feel like work at all. It feels like equity building and friendship.

To my favorite collabo-friend, Dr. Henry Rice, I will always be grateful that you are both mentor and sponsor, friend and family. Your integrity, kindness, and friendship have provided a safe place for me to become who I am. I'm just glad I get to become the person I am alongside someone like you. You started as a colleague but have become a best friend, someone who is like family to me. Dedicating this book to you was one of the easiest decisions I made as I began my writing. You deserve all of that and more. There's no one else I'd rather have an hours-long meeting with because we laugh too much or you listen to all my fears, tears, and dreams. And thanks for putting up with my endless selfies. You're stuck with me, and I will always be grateful to be stuck with you.

If the previous paragraphs were about saying thank you to those formative to my science, this one is saying thank you to those formative in my faith journey, starting with Dr. Vaughn Ross. Dr. Ross, I first heard the word *epidemiology* in your class at Wayland Baptist University. Mike and I are forever grateful to you for taking the time to invest in us, as well as in the entire science department at WBU.

Thank you to the two faith communities that surrounded and held my family after we lost so much. To Dayspring and Watts Street, your welcoming a battered and weary epidemiologist into your fold was a gift I wasn't sure was possible. To the numerous other faith communities I had the immense pleasure to work with during the pandemic years, I know the deep costs those years had for you as you shepherded your congregations. Your resilience and strength, humor and tears are sprinkled throughout this book.

Finally, I want to thank several people who have been immensely formative for me. Granny Ruth and Pop, Mrs. Juanita, Mrs. Lillian, Mrs. Eileen, Mr. and Mrs. Byrd, thank you for loving and encouraging my family and me. When I think of the hall of faithers, I think of you all. Dr. Paul and Jennifer Osteen, thank you for being one of the first to encourage me to write a book and to take our kids to Africa, both of which my husband and I are doing this year. Drs. Mark Shrime and Malcolm Foley, thank you for reading early versions of this book and for your incredibly empowering works of solidarity in the world. You make the world a better place.

Thank you to the incredible Zondervan and Bindery Agency team. When I first got that email from Andrea Heinecke, my agent, I thought it was spam (because why would someone want a book on faith and science, and why me?), and I'm so glad I was wrong. Andrea, thank you for neighboring in a way that only you can to those of us who have words burning in our souls. It's a deeply vulnerable process to write something and let a team read it first, knowing the first draft was more of a journal entry than a polished book.

To my editor Carolyn McCready, thank you for holding those words with grace, honoring the story, and making sure I'm not yelling too much in the final product—yes some of that first draft needed to stay in a journal. I will always be grateful that you gave me a chance and saw what this book could be before I could. I'm still convinced that editors should be paid double for editing and counseling. You made my dream as a nine-year-old come true. Thank you to the entire Zondervan marketing, editing, and design team for taking a complicated topic and making it shine. More importantly, I've gained a host of friends along the way as well!

To my real-life neighbors, thank you for being our neighbors in tangible ways. When we experienced the scary threats at our house, I felt bad that cop cars were patrolling the streets you lived on too. Yet instead of judgment, you protectively surrounded us. I created a list of homes my kids could run into if they ever needed anything or felt unsafe, and your houses were places of refuge. To the Gustafons, the Everetts, the Burnses, and the Quorzals, thank you. When I think of best friends who lived far away but made themselves a refuge as well, I think of Alison Alford, Gayla Partin, Katie Lesko, and Ashley Mangrum. If I'm Anne Shirley, you're my Dianas.

I can't leave without acknowledging the Friendly Neighbor Epidemiology (FNE) community. Never in my wildest dreams did I think the site's readers would grow to include more than my mom, who is still my biggest fan, and my Sunday school friends. We—you in the FNE community and I—rode that tsunami wave of the worst pandemic years together and in real time watched one another grow in courage and solidarity. You are also the reason I got a book deal and decided to say yes to that deal. Mr. Knick, you were the first FNE community member to encourage me to write a book. Curtis Freeman, you have been a constant encouragement to me, even before we knew one another in real life.

Although I've never met most of you in the FNE community, if you know me in real life, you know I'd love to address that by having a huge party in my backyard with endless nachos. I found a whole new community to lean on and walk with in the FNE group, and I will forever be thankful for that. You're deeply compassionate and a bit snarky at times; you love (or pretend to love) my jokes and memes; and you're scrappy. This book is indeed because of and for you. Thank you for coauthoring it with me. I carry your stories and our collective neighboring in these pages. I hope the words honor them.

I can't help but think of the long lineage of love I've been given, starting with my grandparents. To my grandmothers, thank you for being the first author I met and the first one to encourage me to be one. With everything in me, I want to send you the first copies of this book, but that will have to wait a while. I'll save a copy for you—signed, *Love, Emi*.

Angela and Joe Bailey, you are as close to family to us as anyone has been. Thank you for always loving us—definitely through the hard pandemic years. You two are a treasure beyond words to the Smith family.

To my parents and parents-in-love, thank you for watching our kids on countless writing weekends or sick weeks, for answering the phone calls to simply say hi, and for raising us. Parents are the ones who hold our first dreams, protecting them with fierce love, nurturing them with joy and safety. (That's what you did for me, Mom and Dad, and those dreams tucked away years ago are now coming to fruition in my work. And more.) If Mike and I have flown high, it's because you made a safe nest to begin with.

Daddy-o, being your "Emi" is one of my greatest joys. Thanks for being the type of dad who will go into bookstores and make sure your daughter's book is front and center. Mom, you are dearer to me than I can adequately put into words. You are my Marmee, and thanks for letting me be Jo.

Last but not least, this is a book about solidarity with our neighbors. Dr. Farmer, I have an entire chapter dedicated to your resounding influence in my life. But I have to say it again—thank you for your solidarity with the world, including students like me who needed to see that the impossible was indeed possible. We are forever changed.

Me writing as a little girl

APPENDIX

A SIMPLE PLAN TO GET YOU STARTED ON THE NEIGHBORING JOURNEY

So *how* do you *be* a neighbor? Some of you reading this will have a job in a humanitarian organization or the like and will live this book every day. For most of us, though, we will live Monday through Sunday as normal as can be. So *how* do *we* be neighbors?

PRACTICAL TIPS

We've already established that it takes a lot of heart and soul work to center correctly for our neighbors so that our actions match what's true and important. Although that work can't be boiled down to an eight-step plan, I want to share a few practical tips I'm using to help live a life of neighboring.

APPENDIX

Practical Tip #1: Post-its

You know the people who love buying new Post-its and love the new version that are sticky on all sides? Those are my people. Throw in new highlighters in your basket? Chef's kiss. One way to become more of a neighbor is by constant learning. Let me give you an example. A colleague who works with me in Tanzania ended her email this week with the Swahili phrase "Asante Sana." I looked it up and found that it means "thanks a lot." So I pulled out my trusty, olive green Post-it pad, my preferred color, and wrote those words and meaning on it. My family and I are headed to live in Tanzania for a few months the next several summers, so we are learning a bit of Swahili on these Post-it notes over the dinner table. It's not fancy and doesn't take an hour to do. It's just a simple, easy way to love our neighbor's culture and language over our own dinner table. When you hear a new term in another language you don't understand, write it down and look it up. When you hear a quote you love that helps you center your heart correctly, write it down on a Post-it and stick it on your fridge. When you hear something you want to tell your family over dinner about your neighbors, like a story on the news about Malaysia or sharks in Australia, write it on a Post-it note so you'll remember later. Here's my favorite. When you hear someone mention a country, city, or town and you have no idea where it is on a map, write down its name on a Post-it. This brings me to . . .

Practical Tip #2: A Map

Buy a cheap map you can find at most big-box stores, but make sure you get the version that has the accurate country sizes. When maps were first printed, some used the biased, Mercator versions which inaccurately portray land masses. For example, Africa in those maps is depicted as the size of the United States when it is actually much, much bigger and accurately drawn in the newer

234

versions. Once you get an accurate map, take the Post-it notes of the places you don't know the location of, google the location or better yet have your kids find it on the map as a race, and then put the Post-it note on the location. If you put the map on your fridge, that's even better. Then every time your family wants a drink of water or fifteenth snack of the day, they will see that map and spend a few seconds reading the locations on the Post-its, hopefully leaving them wanting to know more. Here's my favorite activity to do with my own kids. We google earth the location to learn a little about it and use the fun tools, like being able to "walk" through some of the streets or see the overall topography. It becomes a teaching moment for them and for me. Just this week, I was walking down the hall at work to get some coffee when I met someone from Ethiopia. Right down the hall are colleagues from Peru, Britain, Guinea, and South Sudan. Over dinner, I've told my family about these places, and we looked up pictures of most of them. If you can couple this with a story, the Post-it and pictures become even more alive which brings me to practical tip number three: Reading.

Practical Tip #3: Reading

Reading opens us up to worlds we might never get to go to ourselves and to people we might never meet. This year, I've made a goal to read a certain number of books, at least 75 percent of which are written by diverse authors. I learned many things I didn't learn in school. One example is a memoir written by a Muslim American woman named Linda Sarsour titled *We Are Not Here to Be Bystanders*. Until I read her book, I had never heard about the profiling which occurred against thousands of Muslim men after the attacks, and the fear the families experienced simply for wearing a hijab. Reading these stories made me see reality through their eyes, and in doing so, helped me center on their stories with compassion. As a neighbor. I could mention so many other books that have changed me, and I've noted several at the end of this book. I think this changes us deeply if we choose carefully what we listen to. Although this is slowly changing, there are many of us millennials (and older people) who never heard of Tuskegee or Henrietta Lacks or Fannie Lou Hamer or Howard Thurman until we were well in our twenties—if at all. The point I want to make is that reading helps us listen well and learn the truth about history, and sometimes we need a concerted plan to do that.[1] Reading slows us down enough to be not the one talking, but rather the one listening, which brings me to the final tip.

Practical Tip #4: Listening

Listening is a powerful tool in our compassion reservoir to learn empathy, to deepen humility, and to anchor one's self to other people's experience. I think this is the most powerful tool we have toward neighboring well. Let me give you an example of how listening transforms us toward being better neighbors. Have you heard of Be the Bridge? It's a program designed for churches to go through together and explore the complexities of racial reconciliation and systemic justice. One of my favorite parts of the program is that you, if you are a White person, are to listen for at least the first half of the program which is around six weeks. Why? Because we've had the microphone for centuries anyway, and we need to hear voices that have been wrongly silenced.

The power of listening to stories unlike our own experiences changes us from the inside, and that effects our outside actions as well. It's very hard to hear someone's story and experience and not have your own preconceived notions or assumptions challenged. The more we do that, the more our biases, unconscious or not, start crumbling, making room for equity and compassion. This has happened to me when I listen to the stories of my own friends and colleagues. I hear the story of one friend who was not able to go to medical school because he doesn't have a birth certificate or know his birthday. You see, he was a child during a ruthless civil war in Africa and lost everything he owned. That changes me toward neighboring better. I hear stories of friends who can't travel to conferences with me due to visa issues. To get a visa, they have to travel to their home countries, often costing hundreds of dollars, travel back and wait for approval. I, on the other hand, can travel much more freely simply because of what country is on my passport. That causes me to shift any privilege I might have toward changing the system. I hear friends who are not Arab but have been profiled as looking Middle Eastern. So they get stopped in the airport every time they fly. That changes me—but only if I listen with humility and solidarity.

In summary, listen, read, and get yourself a map for the fridge. And Post-its notes to go with it. Preferably in olive green.

TOP 10(ISH) BOOKS

Go to my website (https://emilysmith.substack.com) to see the full list of books I update periodically. Here are my top 10(ish) books, in alphabetical order.

Andrews, Kehinde. *The New Age of Empire: How Racism and Colonialism Still Rule the World*. New York: Bold Type, 2021.

Benjamin, Ruha. *Viral Justice: How We Grow the World We Want*. Princeton, NJ: Princeton University Press, 2022.

Faloyin, Dipo. *Africa Is Not a Country: Notes on a Bright Continent*. New York: Norton, 2022.

Griffin, Michael, and Jennie Weiss Block, eds. *In the Company of the Poor: Conversations with Dr. Paul Farmer and Fr. Gustavo Gutiérrez*. Maryknoll, NY: Orbis, 2013.

Hochschild, Adam. *King Leopold's Ghost: A Story of Greed, Terror, and Heroism in Colonial Africa*. New York: Mariner, 1998.

Ismail, Edna Adan. *A Woman of Firsts: The Midwife Who Changed the World*. London: HQ, 2019.

RESOURCE LIST

Kendi, Ibram X. *How to Be an Antiracist*. New York: One World, 2019.

Kidder, Tracy. *Mountains beyond Mountains: The Quest of Dr. Paul Farmer, a Man Who Would Cure the World*. New York: Delacorte, 2013.

McCaulley, Esau. *Reading While Black: African American Biblical Interpretation as an Exercise in Hope*. Downers Grove, IL: IVP Academic, 2020.

Mirza, Fatima Farheen. *A Place for Us*. New York: SPJ Hogarth, 2018.

Nayeri, Daniel. *Everything Sad Is Untrue (A True Story)*. New York: Levine Querido, 2020.

Shilts, Randy. *And the Band Played On: Politics, People, and the AIDS Epidemic*. New York: St. Martin's, 1987.

Tisby, Jemar. *The Color of Compromise: The Truth about the American Church's Complicity in Racism*. Grand Rapids: Zondervan, 2019.

Washington, Harriet A. *Medical Apartheid: The Dark History of Medical Experimentation on Black Americans from Colonial Times to the Present*. New York: Doubleday, 2006.

For a full list of my scientific articles, please visit my website or the National Library of Medicine website at www.ncbi.nlm.nih .gov/myncbi/emily.smith.9/bibliography/public.

NOTES

Author's Note

1. "Land Acknowledgement," Eno River Association, www.eno river.org/land-acknowledgement, accessed April 10, 2023.

Chapter 1: Two Questions Asked

1. See Matthew 18:1–3.
2. See Matthew 9:20–22.
3. See Luke 4:14–21.
4. See Luke 2:1–20.
5. See Matthew 8:3; Mark 8:22–25; Matthew 21:14 (among many others); Luke 8:26–29; Matthew 9:20–22.
6. See Matthew 5.
7. See Matthew 25:40–45.
8. See Hebrews 13:2.
9. See John 19:25–27.
10. See Luke 19:28–40.
11. See Philippians 2:5–8.
12. James 2:17.
13. Edna Adan Ismail, *A Woman of Firsts: The Midwife Who Changed the World* (London: HQ, 2019).

NOTES

Chapter 3: What History Reveals to Us

1. "General Act of the Berlin Conference on West Africa, 26 February 1885," https://loveman.sdsu.edu/docs/1885 GeneralActBerlinConference.pdf, accessed April 10, 2023.

2. See Iraklis Karabatos, Christos Tsagkaris, and Konstantinos Kalachanis, "All Roads Lead to Rome: Aspects of Public Health in Ancient Rome," *InfezMed* 29, no. 3 (September 2021): 488–91, www.ncbi.nlm.nih.gov/pmc/articles/PMC 8805493; see also Carolyn Wazer, "The Cutthroat Politics of Public Health in Ancient Rome," *The Atlantic*, April 2016, www.theatlantic.com/health/archive/2016/04/the -tricky-politics-of-ancient-romes-aqueducts/479298.

3. Stephen Neill, *A History of Christian Missions*, 2nd ed. (New York: Penguin, 1990), 121.

4. See Alfred W. Crosby, *Ecological Imperialism: The Biological Expansion of Europe, 900–1900*, 2nd ed. (Cambridge, UK: Cambridge University Press, 2004).

5. "Case Studies: Hispaniola," Yale University Genocide Studies Program, https://gsp.yale.edu/case-studies/colonial-genocides -project/hispaniola, accessed April 10, 2023.

6. Noble David Cook, "Disease and the Depopulation of Hispaniola, 1492–1518," chapter 2 in *Biological Consequences of the European Expansion, 1450–1800*, ed. Kenneth F. Kiple and Stephen V. Beck (London: Routledge, 1997), www.taylor francis.com/chapters/edit/10.4324/9781315261522-2/disease -depopulation-hispaniola-1492%E2%80%931518-noble-david -cook, accessed April 10, 2023.

7. Tzvetan Todorov, *The Conquest of America: The Question of the Other* (1984; repr., Norman: University of Oklahoma Press, 1999), 45.

8. See David S. Jones, *Rationalizing Epidemics: Meanings and*

Uses of American Indian Mortality Since 1600 (Cambridge, MA: Harvard University Press, 2004), 36, 53.

9. Quoted in Adam Hochschild, *King Leopold's Ghost: A Story of Greed, Terror, and Heroism in Colonial Africa* (New York: Mariner, 1998), 6.

10. See Joyce E. Chaplin, *Subject Matter: Technology, the Body, and Science on the Anglo-American Frontier, 1500–1676* (Cambridge, MA: Harvard University Press, 2003).

11. See Philip D. Curtin, "Epidemiology and the Slave Trade," *Political Science Quarterly* 83, no. 2 (June 1968): 194, www.jstor .org/stable/2147089.

12. See Norimitsu Onishi and Melissa Eddy, "A Forgotten Genocide: What Germany Did in Namibia, and What It's Saying Now," *New York Times*, May 28, 2021.

13. See Tim Whewell, "Germany and Namibia: What's the Right Price to Pay for Genocide?," BBC News, April 1, 2021, www.bbc.co.uk/news/stories-56583994.

14. See Martin S. Staum, *Labeling People: French Scholars on Society, Race, and Empire, 1815–1848* (Montreal: McGill-Queen's University Press, 2003).

15. See Dipo Faloyin, *Africa Is Not a Country: Notes on a Bright Continent* (New York: Norton, 2022), 280.

16. For a rich and thorough discussion on the history of stolen artifacts from Africa, I encourage you to read Dipo Faloyin's incredible book *Africa Is Not a Country*.

17. See Crosby, *Ecological Imperialism*.

18. See "Introduction: Disease, Medicine, and Empire," in *Imperial Medicine and Indigenous Societies*, ed. David Arnold (Manchester, UK: Manchester University Press, 2013), 1–26; Nancy Rose Hunt, "Review of *The Colonial Disease: A Social History of Sleeping Sickness in Northern Zaire, 1900–1940* by

Maryinez Lyons," *Journal of Southern African Studies* 19, no. 4 (1993): 736–38, www.jstor.org/stable/2636997.

19. See "Introduction: Disease, Medicine, and Empire."

20. See Hochschild, *King Leopold's Ghost*.

21. Hochschild, *King Leopold's Ghost*, 11.

22. Faloyin, *Africa Is Not a Country*, 28.

23. See Tullio Scovazzi, "The Italian Approach to Colonialism," in *A History of International Law in Italy*, ed. Giulio Bartolini (New York: Oxford University Press, 2020), https://academic .oup.com/book/36893/chapter-abstract/322133346.

24. Aryeh Y. Yodfat, "The Soviet Union and the Horn of Africa," *Northeast African Studies* 1, no. 3 (1979): 1–17, www.jstor.org /stable/43660018.

25. See George James, "Somalia's Overthrown Dictator, Mohammed Siad Barre, Is Dead," *New York Times*, January 3, 1995, www.nytimes.com/1995/01/03/obituaries/somalia -s-overthrown-dictator-mohammed-siad-barre-is-dead.html; Chris Mburu, "Past Human Rights Abuses in Somalia: Report of a Preliminary Study Conducted for the United Nations (OHCHR/UNDP-Somalia)," 2002, https://search works.stanford.edu/view/6330721.

26. Quoted in Hilke Fischer, "130 Years Ago: Carving Up Africa in Berlin," *DW*, February 25, 2015, www.dw.com/en /130-years-ago-carving-up-africa-in-berlin/a-18278894.

27. See Pierre Englebert, Stacy Tarango, and Matthew Carter, "Dismemberment and Suffocation: A Contribution to the Debate on African Boundaries," *Comparative Political Studies* 35, no. 10 (2002): 1093–1118; Nicola Gennaioli and Ilia Rainer, "The Modern Impact of Precolonial Centralization in Africa," *Journal of Economic Growth* 12, no. 3 (2007): 185–234.

28. See Elias Papaioannou and Stelios Michalopoulos, "The Long-Run Effects of the Scramble for Africa," Voxeu, January

6, 2012, https://cepr.org/voxeu/columns/long-run-effects
-scramble-africa-0.

29. For more detail, I suggest Nic Cheeseman, *Democracy in
Africa: Successes, Failures, and the Struggle for Political Reform*
(New York: Cambridge University Press, 2015). Note: I chose
to use a lowercase *g* in god in this sentence. At the time, the
colonizers were motivated by their faith and would have used
a capital *G*. However, that's not the God I know and believe
in—the God of the Good Samaritan story. So I'm using a
lowercase *g* instead.

Chapter 4: Systemic Racism and Lucy

1. Does anyone else love the library as much as I do? Some kids
dream of going to Disney World. Me? My dream place was
the Scholastic Book Fair in the school library. Aw, can't you
see it and smell the new books with me? A bit musty, with
old books pushed back and the rows of new books laid out by
genre. If you were lucky enough, you might have money left
over for a cat poster and a pencil that smelled like an overripe
watermelon. Solidarity to all of you who loved the Scholastic
Book Fair and the elementary school library. And to all of you
librarians, including my dad.

2. See Frederick Douglass, "The Race Problem: The Great
Speech of Frederick Douglass," October 21, 1890, National
Humanities Center, http://nationalhumanitiescenter.org/pds
/maai2/politics/text2/douglass.pdf, accessed April 10, 2023.

3. Frederick Douglass, "What to the Slave Is the Fourth of
July? 1852," *American Yawp Reader*, www.americanyawp.com
/reader/democracy-in-america/frederick-douglass-what-to-the
-slave-is-the-fourth-of-july-1852, accessed April 10, 2023.

4. See "This Month in Physics History: November 8, 1895:
Roentgen's Discovery of X-Rays," *APS News* 10, no. 10

(November 2001), www.aps.org/publications/apsnews/200111 /history.cfm.

5. Theodor Waitz, *Introduction to Anthropology* (London: Longman, Green, Longman, and Roberts, 1863), 93.

6. See Itai Bavli and David S. Jones, "Race Correction and the X-Ray Machine—The Controversy over Increased Radiation Doses for Black Americans in 1968," *New England Journal of Medicine* 387 (September 2022): 947–52, www.nejm.org/doi /full/10.1056/NEJMms2206281.

7. See Isadore Meschan, *An Atlas of Normal Radiographic Anatomy*, 2nd ed. (Philadelphia: Saunders, 1959).

8. See Bavli and Jones, "Race Correction."

9. For other examples, see Kelly M. Hoffman et al., "Racial Bias in Pain Assessment and Treatment Recommendations, and False Beliefs about Biological Differences between Blacks and Whites," *Proceedings of the National Academy of Sciences* 113, no. 16 (April 2016): 4296–4301, www.ncbi.nlm.nih.gov /pmc/articles/PMC4843483. For the best book I've read on this topic, see Harriet A. Washington, *Medical Apartheid: The Dark History of Medical Experimentation on Black Americans from Colonial Times to the Present* (New York: Harlem Moon, 2006).

10. See Michael W. Sjoding et al., "Racial Bias in Pulse Oximetry Measurement," *New England Journal of Medicine* 383 (December 2020): 2477–78, www.nejm.org/doi/pdf/10 .1056/NEJMc2029240.

11. See Valeria S. M. Valbuena et al., "Racial Bias and Repro- ducibility in Pulse Oximetry among Medical and Surgical Inpatients in General Care in the Veterans Health Adminis- tration 2013–19: Multicenter, Retrospective Cohort Study," *BMJ* 378 (July 2022), www.bmj.com/content/378/bmj-2021 -069775.

12. John W. Severinghaus and Poul Astrup, "History of Blood Gas Analysis. VI. Oximetry," *Journal of Clinical Monitoring* 2, no. 4 (October 1986): 270–88, https://pubmed.ncbi.nlm.nih.gov/3537215.

13. See Amal Jubran and Martin J. Tobin, "Reliability of Pulse Oximetry in Titrating Supplemental Oxygen Therapy in Ventilator-Dependent Patients," *ScienceDirect, CHEST* 97, no. 6 (June 1990): 1420–25, www.sciencedirect.com/science/article/abs/pii/S0012369216320293.

14. See Martin J. Tobin and Amal Jubran, "Pulse Oximetry, Racial Bias and Statistical Bias," *Annals of Intensive Care* 12, no. 2 (January 2022), https://annalsofintensivecare.springeropen.com/articles/10.1186/s13613-021-00974-7.

15. See Ashraf Fawzy et al., "Racial and Ethnic Discrepancy in Pulse Oximetry and Delayed Identification of Treatment Eligibility among Patients with COVID-19," *JAMA Internal Medicine* 182, no. 7 (May 2022), https://jamanetwork.com/journals/jamainternalmedicine/fullarticle/2792653.

16. See Fawzy, "Racial and Ethnic Discrepancy."

17. See "COVID-19 Science Update Released: September 21, 2020, Edition 44," Centers for Disease Control and Prevention, www.cdc.gov/library/covid19/090120_covidupdate.html, accessed January 27, 2022.

18. Cited in Fawzy, "Racial and Ethnic Discrepancy."

19. See L. L. Wall, "The Medical Ethics of Dr J Marion Sims: A Fresh Look at the Historical Record," *Journal of Medical Ethics* 32, no. 6 (June 2006), www.ncbi.nlm.nih.gov/pmc/articles/PMC2563360.

20. Quoted in Maura Hohman, "How This Black Doctor Is Exposing the Racist History of Gynecology," *Today Show*, June 29, 2020, www.today.com/health/racism-gynecology-dr-james-marion-sims-t185269.

NOTES

21. See J. Marion Sims, *The Story of My Life* (New York: Appleton, 1884), 239, https://ia800303.us.archive.org/1/items/storyofmy lif00sims/storyofmylif00sims.pdf.

22. See Camila Domonoske, "'Father of Gynecology,' Who Experimented on Slaves, No Longer on Pedestal in NYC," NPR, April 17, 2018, www.npr.org/sections/thetwo-way/2018 /04/17/603163394/-father-of-gynecology-who-experimented -on-slaves-no-longer-on-pedestal-in-nyc.

23. See Sarah Kuta, "Subjected to Painful Experiments and Forgotten, Enslaved 'Mothers of Gynecology' Are Honored with New Monument," *Smithsonian Magazine*, May 11, 2022, www.smithsonianmag.com/smart-news/mothers-of -gynecology-monument-honors-enslaved-women-180980064.

24. To see photos of the statue, visit Michelle L. Browder and Dr. Beth Harris, "Michelle Browder, *Mothers of Gynecology*," *Smarthistory*, March 21, 2022, https://smarthistory.org/seeing -america-2/mothers-of-gynecology.

25. Quoted in Dennis Pillion, "Monument to 'Mothers of Gynecology' Unveiled in Montgomery," AL.com, September 27, 2021, www.al.com/news/2021/09/monument-to-mothers -of-gynecology-unveiled-in-montgomery.html.

26. See J. A. Kenney, "Second Annual Oration on Surgery: The Negro's Contribution to Surgery," *Journal of the National Medical Association* 33, no. 5 (September 1941), https:// pubmed.ncbi.nlm.nih.gov/20893044.

27. See "The Syphilis Study at Tuskegee Timeline," Centers for Disease Control and Prevention, www.cdc.gov/tuskegee/time line.htm, accessed April 10, 2023.

28. See Robert Gaynes, "The Discovery of Penicillin—New Insights after More Than 75 Years of Clinical Use," *Emerging Infectious Diseases* 23, no. 5 (May 2017), www.cdc.gov/eid /article/23/5/16-1556_article.

29. See "Memorandum Terminating the Tuskegee Syphilis Study," National Archives Catalog, November 16, 1972, https://catalog.archives.gov/id/650716; Jean Heller, "AP Was There: Black Men Untreated in Tuskegee Syphilis Study," AP News, May 10, 2017, https://apnews.com/article/business-science-health-race-and-ethnicity-syphilis-e9dd07eaa4e74052878a68132cd3803a; "Final Report of the Tuskegee Syphilis Study Ad Hoc Advisory Panel," U.S. Department of Health, Education, and Welfare Public Health Service, April 28, 1973, https://biotech.law.lsu.edu/cphl/history/reports/tuskegee/complete%20report.pdf.

30. See "Remarks by the President in Apology for Study Done in Tuskegee," White House Office of the Press Secretary, May 16, 1997, https://clintonwhitehouse4.archives.gov/New/Remarks/Fri/19970516-898.html.

31. See "A Nation's Story: 'What to the Slave Is the Fourth of July?'" National Museum of African American History and Culture, https://nmaahc.si.edu/explore/stories/nations-story-what-slave-fourth-july, accessed April 10, 2023.

Chapter 5: Getting Along Isn't the Goal

1. John 17:22.
2. Psalm 133:1.
3. Johannes Hoekendijk, "The Call to Evangelism," *International Review of Mission* 39 (April 1950): 163.
4. Suzanna Krivulskaya, "The Diminishing Importance of Personal Morality in Politics, 2011–2020," PRRI, November 21, 2022, www.prri.org/spotlight/the-diminishing-importance-of-personal-morality-in-politics-2011-2020.
5. Be the Bridge exists "to empower people and culture toward racial healing, equity and reconciliation," BetheBridge.com, https://bethebridge.com, accessed April 10, 2023.

Chapter 6: Unknown Is the New Fame

1. Psalm 27:4.
2. Philippians 3:7–10.

Chapter 7: Solidarity and Sneaking In

1. See "Book Page: Gustavo Gutiérrez: A Theology of Liberation," Liberation Theologies Online Library and Reference Center, https://liberationtheology.org/gustavo -gutierrez-a-theology-of-liberation, accessed April 10, 2023.
2. Quoted in "Apostolic Exhortation: *Evangelii Gaudium* of the Holy Father Francis," 133–34, www.vatican.va/content /dam/francesco/pdf/apost_exhortations/documents/papa -francesco_esortazione-ap_20131124_evangelii-gaudium _en.pdf.
3. See Matthew 25:37–40.
4. See Hebrews 13:2.
5. Michael Griffin and Jennie Weiss Block, eds., *In the Company of the Poor: Conversations with Dr. Paul Farmer and Fr. Gustavo Gutiérrez* (Maryknoll, NY: Orbis, 2013), 19.
6. See Paul E. Farmer and Jim Y. Kim, "Surgery and Global Health: A View from Beyond the OR," *World Journal of Surgery* 32, no. 4 (April 2008): 533–36, www.ncbi.nlm.nih .gov/pmc/articles/PMC2267857.

Chapter 8: Structural Violence and Singing

1. See Carl H. Backes et al., "Maternal Preeclampsia and Neonatal Outcomes," *Journal of Pregnancy* (2011), https:// www.ncbi.nlm.nih.gov/pmc/articles/PMC3087144.
2. See "Maternal Mortality," World Health Organization, February 22, 2023, www.who.int/news-room/fact-sheets /detail/maternal-mortality.
3. See Donna L. Hoyert, "Maternal Mortality Rates in the

United States, 2020," NCHS E-Stats, 2020, https://dx.doi.org/10.15620/cdc:113967; Munira Z. Gunja, Evan D. Gumas, and Reginald D. Williams II, "The U.S. Maternal Mortality Crisis Continues to Worsen: An International Comparison," Commonwealth Fund, December 1, 2022, https://doi.org/10.26099/8vem-fc65.

4. See Donna L. Hoyert, "Maternal Mortality Rates in the United States, 2021," NCHS E-Stats, 2021, www.cdc.gov/nchs/data/hestat/maternal-mortality/2021/maternal-mortality-rates-2021.htm; E. E. Petersen et al., "Racial/Ethnic Disparities in Pregnancy-Related Deaths—United States, 2007–2016," *Morbidity and Mortality Weekly Report* 68, no. 35 (2019): 762–65, http://dx.doi.org/10.15585/mmwr.mm6835a3.

5. See Peiyin Hung et al., "Closure of Hospital Obstetric Services Disproportionately Affects Less-Populated Rural Counties," Policy Brief April 2017, University of Minnesota Rural Health Research Center, https://rhrc.umn.edu/wp-content/files_mf/1491501904UMRHRCOBclosuresPolicyBrief.pdf, accessed April 10, 2023; Lan Zhao, "Why Are Fewer Hospitals in the Delivery Business?," NORC – Health Policy and Evaluation Division, April 2007, www.norc.org/PDFs/Walsh%20Center/Links%20Out/DecliningAccesstoHospitalbasedObstetricServicesinRuralCounties.pdf.

6. Cited in Peiyin Hung et al., "Access to Obstetric Services in Rural Counties Still Declining, with 9 Percent Losing Services, 2004–14," *Health Affairs* 36, no. 9 (September 2017), www.healthaffairs.org/doi/10.1377/hlthaff.2017.0338.

7. See Latoya Hill, Samantha Artiga, and Usha Ranji, "Racial Disparities in Maternal and Infant Health: Current Status and Efforts to Address Them," *KFF*, November 1, 2022, www.kff.org/racial-equity-and-health-policy/issue-brief/racial

-disparities-in-maternal-and-infant-health-current-status-and
-efforts-to-address-them.

8. See Liz Hamel et al., "KFF/The Undefeated Survey on Race and Health: Main Findings," *KFF*, October 13, 2020, www .kff.org/report-section/kff-the-undefeated-survey-on-race -and-health-main-findings.

9. Bandy X. Lee, *Violence: An Interdisciplinary Approach to Causes, Consequences, and Cures* (New York: Wiley-Blackwell, 2019), 123.

10. Paul E. Farmer et al., "Structural Violence and Clinical Medicine," *PLoS Medicine* 3, no. 10 (October 2006), https:// journals.plos.org/plosmedicine/article?id=10.1371/journal .pmed.0030449.

11. To read more about cost-effectiveness research, see Paul Farmer, *To Repair the World: Paul Farmer Speaks to the Next Generation* (Berkeley: University of California Press, 2013).

12. Cited in "Mortality Rate, under-5 (per 1,000 Live Births)," World Bank, https://data.worldbank.org/indicator/SH.DYN .MORT, accessed April 10, 2023.

13. Cited in "Mortality Rate, under-5."

14. See "Physicians (per 1,000 People)," World Bank, accessed April 10, 2023, https://data.worldbank.org/indicator/SH .MED.PHYS.ZS.

15. See "Maternal Mortality Ratio (Modeled Estimate, per 100,000 Live Births) – Burundi," World Bank, https://data .worldbank.org/indicator/SH.STA.MMRT?locations=BI, accessed April 10, 2023.

16. Cited in Donna L. Hoyert, "Maternal Mortality Rates in the United States, 2019," National Center for Health Statistics, April 2021, www.cdc.gov/nchs/data/hestat/maternal -mortality-2021/E-Stat-Maternal-Mortality-Rates-H.pdf.

17. See "Henrietta Lacks: Science Must Right a Historical

Wrong," *Nature* 585, no. 7 (September 2020), www.nature
.com/articles/d41586-020-02494-z.

18. See "Henrietta Lacks: Science Must Right a Historical
Wrong."

19. See Mario F. Perez and Maria Teresa Coutinho, "An
Overview of Health Disparities in Asthma," *Yale Journal of
Biology and Medicine* 94, no. 3 (September 2021): 497–507,
www.ncbi.nlm.nih.gov/pmc/articles/PMC8461584; "2022
National Healthcare Quality and Disparities Report,"
Agency for Healthcare Research and Quality, www.ahrq
.gov/research/findings/nhqrdr/nhqdr22/index.html, accessed
April 10, 2023; Brian D. Smedley, Adrienne Y. Stith, and
Alan R. Nelson, eds., *Unequal Treatment: Confronting Racial
and Ethnic Disparities in Health Care* (Washington, D.C.:
National Academies Press, 2003), https://nap.national
academies.org/read/12875/chapter/1.

20. See Latoya Hill and Samantha Artiga, "COVID-19 Cases
and Deaths by Race/Ethnicity: Current Data and Changes
Over Time," *KFF*, August 22, 2022, www.kff.org/coronavirus
-covid-19/issue-brief/covid-19-cases-and-deaths-by-race
-ethnicity-current-data-and-changes-over-time.

21. Rashawn Ray, "Why Are Blacks Dying at Higher Rates from
COVID-19?," Brookings, April 9, 2020, www.brookings.edu
/blog/fixgov/2020/04/09/why-are-blacks-dying-at-higher
-rates-from-covid-19.

22. Ray, "Why Are Blacks Dying?"

23. See "First Annual Report of the Federal Home Loan Bank
Board, from the Date of Their Creation through December 31,
1933," Fraser, https://fraser.stlouisfed.org/title/annual-report
-federal-home-loan-bank-board-70/first-annual-report-federal
-home-loan-bank-board-23532, accessed April 10, 2023.

24. See Amy E. Hillier, "Redlining and the Homeowners' Loan

Corporation," University of Pennsylvania, Penn Libraries, May 1, 2003, https://repository.upenn.edu/cgi/viewcontent .cgi?article=1002&context=cplan_papers.

25. Candace Johnson, "What Is Redlining?" *New York Times*, August 17, 2021, www.nytimes.com/2021/08/17/realestate /what-is-redlining.html.

26. See Brad Plumer and Nadja Popovich, "How Decades of Racist Housing Policy Left Neighborhoods Sweltering," *New York Times*, August 24, 2020, www.nytimes.com/interactive /2020/08/24/climate/racism-redlining-cities-global-warming .html.

27. Quoted in Brenda Richardson, "Redlining's Legacy of Inequality: Low Homeownership Rates, Less Equity for Black Households," *Forbes*, June 11, 2020, www.forbes.com /sites/brendarichardson/2020/06/11/redlinings-legacy-of -inequality-low-homeownership-rates-less-equity-for-black -households/?sh=4d39dc1e2a7c.

28. See Jasmine Gallup, "Historic Redlining and Discriminatory Policies Have Had Lasting Effects on Black Homeowners in the Triangle," *Indy Week*, February 23, 2022, https:// indyweek.com/news/durham/mapping-inequality-redlining -discriminatory-housing-practices.

Chapter 9: When the Minority Is the Majority— and We Miss It

1. Cited in "22nd Annual Global Automotive Executive Survey 2021," KPMG Global, https://kpmg.com/xx/en/home /insights/2021/11/global-automotive-executive-survey-2021 .html, accessed March 1, 2023.

2. See "White House Conference on Food, Nutrition and Health (White House Central Files: Staff Member and Office

Files)," Richard Nixon Presidential Library and Museum, www.nixonlibrary.gov/finding-aids/white-house-conference -food-nutrition-and-health-white-house-central-files-staff, accessed April 10, 2023; Eileen Kennedy and Johanna Dwyer, "The 1969 White House Conference on Food, Nutrition and Health: 50 Years Later," *Current Developments in Nutrition* 4, no. 6 (June 2020), www.ncbi.nlm.nih.gov/pmc/articles/PMC 7279882.

3. Cited in "Food Security and Nutrition Assistance," Economic Research Service, US Department of Agriculture, www.ers .usda.gov/data-products/ag-and-food-statistics-charting-the -essentials/food-security-and-nutrition-assistance, accessed March 1, 2023.

4. Cited in Niyati Parekh et al., "Food Insecurity among Households with Children during the COVID-19 Pandemic: Results from a Study among Social Media Users across the United States," *Nutrition Journal* 20, no. 73 (August 2021), https://nutritionj.biomedcentral.com/articles/10.1186/s12937 -021-00732-2.

5. Cited in Max Roser, "Extreme Poverty: How Far Have We Come, How Far Do We Still Have to Go?" Our World in Data, November 22, 2021, https://ourworldindata.org /extreme-poverty-in-brief.

6. Cited in Brady Hooley et al., "Health Insurance Coverage in Low-Income and Middle-Income Countries: Progress Made to Date and Related Changes in Private and Public Health Expenditure," *British Medical Journal Global Health* 7, no. 5 (May 2022), https://gh.bmj.com/content/7/5/e008722.

7. Cited in Anshool Deshmukh, "Mapped: The World's Major Religions," *Visual Capitalist*, February 11, 2022, www.visual capitalist.com/mapped-major-religions-of-the-world.

Chapter 10: The Neighborhood

1. Cited in "WHO Coronavirus (COVID-19) Dashboard," World Health Organization, https://covid19.who.int, accessed March 1, 2023.
2. Cited in Charlie Giattino et al., "Excess Mortality during the Coronavirus Pandemic (COVID-19)," Our World in Data, https://ourworldindata.org/excess-mortality-covid, accessed April 10, 2023.
3. Cited in "Global Orphanhood Associated with COVID-19," Centers for Disease Control and Prevention, www.cdc.gov /globalhealth/covid-19/orphanhood/index.html, accessed April 10, 2023.
4. Luke 14:33 MSG.

Chapter 11: Untethering and Loss

1. See Bessel van der Kolk, *The Body Keeps the Score: Brain, Mind, and Body in the Healing of Trauma* (New York: Penguin, 2014).
2. See Genesis 32:31.
3. See 1 Kings 19.
4. See John 18.
5. See Isaiah 53; Hebrews 2:9.
6. See Hebrews 6:19.

Chapter 13: Trickle-Up Economics

1. See Emily R. Smith et al., "The Contribution of Pediatric Surgery to Poverty Trajectories in Somaliland," *PLoS One* 14, no. 7 (July 2019), https://pubmed.ncbi.nlm.nih.gov/31348780.
2. Quoted in Michael Griffin and Jennie Weiss Block, eds., *In the Company of the Poor: Conversations with Dr. Paul Farmer and Fr. Gustavo Gutiérrez* (Maryknoll, NY: Orbis, 2013), 22.
3. Griffin and Block, *In the Company of the Poor*, 21.

4. Griffin and Block, *In the Company of the Poor*, 34.

5. To read more about the findings, see Emily R. Smith et al., "Does Reducing Out-of-Pocket Costs for Children's Surgical Care Protect Families from Poverty in Somaliland? A Cross-Sectional, National, Economic Evaluation Modelling Study," *BMJ Open* 13, no. 5 (May 2023), https://pubmed.ncbi.nlm.nih.gov/37130683.

6. See Jeffrey Sachs, *The End of Poverty: Economic Possibilities for Our Time* (New York: Penguin, 2006).

7. Cited in Anshool Deshmukh, "This Simple Chart Reveals the Distribution of Global Wealth," *Visual Capitalist*, September 20, 2021, www.visualcapitalist.com/distribution-of-global-wealth-chart.

8. See "Metadata Glossary," World Bank, https://databank.worldbank.org/metadataglossary/gender-statistics/series/SI.POV.GINI, accessed April 10, 2023.

9. See "Poverty and Shared Prosperity 2020: Reversals of Fortune," World Bank, www.worldbank.org/en/publication/poverty-and-shared-prosperity-2020, accessed April 10, 2023.

10. Cited in "Gini Coefficient by Country 2023," World Population Review, https://worldpopulationreview.com/country-rankings/gini-coefficient-by-country, accessed April 10, 2023.

11. See Vivian Vigliotti et al., "Modeling the Scale-up of Surgical Services for Children with Surgically Treatable Congenital Conditions in Somaliland," *World Journal of Surgery* 46, no. 10 (October 2022): 2489–97, https://pubmed.ncbi.nlm.nih.gov/35838776; Anthony T. Saxton et al., "Economic Analysis of Children's Surgical Care in Low- and Middle-Income Countries: A Systematic Review and Analysis," *PLoS One* 11, no. 10 (October 2016), https://pubmed.ncbi.nlm.nih.gov/27792792; Emily R. Smith et al., "Is Global Pediatric

Surgery a Good Investment?," *World Journal of Surgery* 43, no. 6 (June 2019): 1450–55, https://pubmed.ncbi.nlm.nih.gov/30506288; Smith, "Does Reducing Out-of-Pocket Costs."

12. See John G. Meara et al., "Global Surgery 2030: Evidence and Solutions for Achieving Health, Welfare, and Economic Development," *Lancet* 386, no. 9993 (April 2015), www.thelancet.com/journals/lancet/article/PIIS0140-6736(15)60160-X/fulltext; Charles N. Mock et al., "Essential Surgery: Key Messages from *Disease Control Priorities*, 3rd edition," *Lancet* 385, no. 9983 (May 2015): 2209–19, www.ncbi.nlm.nih.gov/pmc/articles/PMC7004823.

13. See Meara, "Global Surgery 2030."

14. See Joshua S. Ng-Kamstra et al., "Global Surgery 2030: A Roadmap for High Income Country Actors," *BMJ Global Health* 1, no. 1 (April 2016), https://pubmed.ncbi.nlm.nih.gov/28588908.

15. See Francis S. Collins, "Growing Importance of Health in the Economy," World Economic Forum, https://widgets.weforum.org/outlook15/10.html, accessed January 23, 2023; "Sustainable Health Systems: Visions, Strategies, Critical Uncertainties and Scenarios," World Economic Forum (January 2013), www3.weforum.org/docs/WEF_Sustainable HealthSystems_Report_2013.pdf; "How Prioritizing Health Could Help Rebuild Economies," McKinsey Global Institute, July 8, 2020, www.mckinsey.com/industries/healthcare/our-insights/how-prioritizing-health-could-help-rebuild-economies; Suchit Arora, "Health, Human Productivity, and Long-Term Economic Growth," *Journal of Economic History* 61, no. 3 (September 2001): 699–741, www.jstor.org/stable/2698133; Masagus M. Ridhwan et al., "The Effect of Health on Economic Growth: A Meta-Regression Analysis,"

Empirical Economics 63 (April 2022): 3211–51, https://link
.springer.com/article/10.1007/s00181-022-02226-4.

Chapter 14: Broadening Our Definition of Health

1. This number was calculated in 2015 using the world's
population at the time of 7 billion. Thus it is likely an
underestimate of the true value now that the world's
population has exceeded 8 billion.
2. See "The Lancet Commission on Global Surgery," *Lancet*
386, no. 9993 (April 2015): 569–624, www.thelancet.com
/pdfs/journals/lancet/PIIS0140-6736(15)60160-X.pdf; www
.thelancet.com/commissions/global-surgery.
3. Bhargava Mullapudi et al., "Estimates of Number of Children
and Adolescents without Access to Surgical Care," *Bulletin of
the World Health Organization* 97, no. 4 (April 2019): 254–58,
www.ncbi.nlm.nih.gov/pmc/articles/PMC6438256.
4. "Constitution," World Health Organization, www.who.int
/about/governance/constitution#, accessed April 10, 2023.
5. John 10:10.

Chapter 15: Rivers and Othering

1. Greg Abbott, Twitter post, March 3, 2021, 5:40 p.m., https://
twitter.com/GregAbbott_TX/status/1367243450140086274.
2. Cited in Damià Bonmatí and Martha Alicia López, "After
Border Patrol Release, Asylum-Seekers Test Positive for
Covid in Brownsville, Texas," NBC News, March 2, 2021,
www.nbcnews.com/news/latino/after-border-patrol-release
-asylum-seekers-test-positive-covid-brownsville-n1259282.
The 6.3 percent is known as the positivity rate, the number of
migrants testing positive for COVID-19 out of all migrants
tested.

NOTES

3. See "Tracking Coronavirus in Texas: Latest Map and Case Count," *New York Times*, updated March 23, 2023, www.nytimes.com/interactive/2021/us/texas-covid-cases.html; "Coronavirus in the U.S.: Latest Map and Case Count," *New York Times*, updated March 23, 2023, www.nytimes.com/interactive/2021/us/covid-cases.html.

4. Cited in Grace Ratley, "States Ranked by Age-Adjusted COVID Deaths," Bioinformatics CRO, updated December 7, 2022, www.bioinformaticscro.com/blog/states-ranked-by-age-adjusted-covid-deaths.

5. "Views on Race and Immigration," Pew Research Center, December 17, 2019, www.pewresearch.org/politics/2019/12/17/views-on-race-and-immigration/.

6. Cited in Tom Jawetz, "Immigrants as Essential Workers during COVID-19," Center for American Progress, September 28, 2020, www.americanprogress.org/article/immigrants-essential-workers-covid-19.

7. See Julia Carrie Wong, "Trump Referred to Immigrant 'Invasion' in 2,000 Facebook Ads, Analysis Reveals," *The Guardian*, August 5, 2019, www.theguardian.com/us-news/2019/aug/05/trump-internet-facebook-ads-racism-immigrant-invasion.

8. See Liz Hamel et al., "KFF COVID-19 Vaccine Monitor: September 2021," *KFF*, September 28, 2021, www.kff.org/coronavirus-covid-19/poll-finding/kff-covid-19-vaccine-monitor-september-2021; William A. Galston, "For COVID-19 Vaccinations, Party Affiliation Matters More Than Race and Ethnicity," Brookings, October 1, 2021, www.brookings.edu/blog/fixgov/2021/10/01/for-covid-19-vaccinations-party-affiliation-matters-more-than-race-and-ethnicity.

9. See Patrick Svitek, "Lt. Gov. Dan Patrick Blames Democrats

NOTES

for Low Vaccination among Black Residents, but More White Texans Are Unvaccinated," *Texas Tribune*, August 20, 2021, www.texastribune.org/2021/08/20/dan-patrick-black-democrats-vaccine-white-republicans.

10. See Colleen DeGuzman and Mandi Cai, "COVID-19 Is Spreading Fast among Texas' Unvaccinated: Here's Who They Are and Where They Live," *Texas Tribune*, August 3, 2021, www.texastribune.org/2021/08/03/unvaccinated-texas-demographics.

11. See "The Changing Political Geography of COVID-19 over the Last Two Years," Pew Research Center, March 3, 2022, www.pewresearch.org/politics/2022/03/03/the-changing-political-geography-of-covid-19-over-the-last-two-years.

12. See Alfred Sauvy, "Three Worlds, One Planet," in *Encyclopedia of the Developing World*, vol. 3, ed. Thomas M. Leonard (New York: Routledge, 2006).

13. Quoted in Marc Silver, "If You Shouldn't Call It the Third World, What Should You Call It?" NPR, January 4, 2015, www.npr.org/sections/goatsandsoda/2015/01/04/372684438/if-you-shouldnt-call-it-the-third-world-what-should-you-call-it.

14. See 2 Corinthians 5:20.

15. See Matthew 6:5–14.

16. Amos 5:23–24 NRSVue, italics added.

17. "Read Martin Luther King Jr.'s 'I Have a Dream' Speech in Its Entirety," NPR, January 18, 2010, www.npr.org/2010/01/18/122701268/i-have-a-dream-speech-in-its-entirety; "Letter from a Birmingham Jail [King, Jr.]," African Studies Center: University of Pennsylvania, www.africa.upenn.edu/Articles_Gen/Letter_Birmingham.html, accessed April 10, 2023.

261

Chapter 16: Topics Too Many Evangelicals Don't Want to Talk About

1. See Rebecca Lindsey and Luann Dahlman, "Climate Change: Global Temperature," NOAA Climate.gov, January 18, 2023, www.climate.gov/news-features/understanding -climate/climate-change-global-temperature.
2. See "Global Average Surface Temperature," NOAA Climate .gov, June 28, 2022, www.climate.gov/media/12885.
3. See Lindsey and Dahlman, "Climate Change: Global Temperature."
4. I've simplified the reality of climate change to a paragraph here. For a longer and more thorough discussion, consider reading Dr. Hayhoe's book *Saving Us: A Climate Scientist's Case for Hope and Healing in a Divided World* (New York: One Signal Publishers / Atria, 2021).
5. Camilo Mora et al., "Over Half of Known Human Pathogenic Diseases Can Be Aggravated by Climate Change," *Nature Climate Change* 12 (August 2022): 869–75, https://doi.org/10 .1038/s41558-022-01426-1.
6. See "Hurricanes and Climate Change," Center for Climate and Energy Solutions, www.c2es.org/content/hurricanes-and -climate-change, accessed April 10, 2023.
7. See "Back-to-Back Hurricanes in Central America Left at Least 1.5 Million Children at Risk of Severe Diseases Due to Water Contamination," UNICEF, January 22, 2021, www .unicef.org/lac/en/press-releases/back-to-back-hurricanes-in -central-america-left-1.5-million-children-at-risk-of-severe -diseases.
8. See "Greater Horn of Africa Faces 5th Failed Rainy Season," World Meteorological Organization, August 25, 2022, https://public.wmo.int/en/media/news/greater-horn-of-africa -faces-5th-failed-rainy-season.

9. Cited in Hannah Button, "Drought-Induced Loss of Livestock in Horn of Africa Will Impact Communities 'For Years to Come,'" *Agrilinks*, July 8, 2022, https://agrilinks.org/post/drought-induced-loss-livestock-horn-africa-will-impact-communities-years-come.

10. See "Ranking the Biggest Industries in the US Economy—with a Surprise #1!" Blue Water Credit, March 18, 2017, https://bluewatercredit.com/ranking-biggest-industries-us-economy-surprise-1.

11. Cited in "IFAW Responds to Disaster in Somaliland as Water Scarcity Destroys Livelihoods," IFAW, June 3, 2022, www.ifaw.org/international/news/disaster-drought-somaliland.

12. "2019–2020 Durham County Profile," Food Bank of Central and Eastern North Carolina, http://foodbankcenc.org/wp-content/uploads/2020/09/2020-2021-County-Profiles_Durham.pdf, accessed April 10, 2023.

13. Cited in "The Impacts and Policy Implications of Russia's Aggression against Ukraine on Agricultural Markets," Organisation for Economic Co-operation and Development, updated August 5, 2022, www.oecd.org/ukraine-hub/policy-responses/the-impacts-and-policy-implications-of-russia-s-aggression-against-ukraine-on-agricultural-markets-0030a4cd.

14. The United States, under the Biden administration, rejoined the Paris Agreement in early 2021.

15. Cited in Hannah Ritchie, "Global Inequalities in CO_2 Emissions," Our World in Data, October 16, 2018, https://ourworldindata.org/co2-by-income-region.

Chapter 17: True Innovation Is Equity

1. See "Tracking Coronavirus in India: Latest Map and Case Count," *New York Times*, updated March 10, 2023, www.nytimes.com/interactive/2021/world/india-covid-cases.html.

NOTES

2. See Jeffrey Gettleman et al., "The Night the Oxygen Ran Out," *New York Times*, June 28, 2021, www.nytimes.com /2021/06/28/world/asia/india-coronavirus-oxygen.html.

3. See Joanna Slater and Shams Irfan, "India's Hospitals Run Out of Oxygen as Surging Coronavirus Count Passes 346,000 a Day," *Washington Post*, April 24, 2021, www .washingtonpost.com/world/asia_pacific/india-pandemic -record-coronavirus-oxygen/2021/04/24/3afea474-a4f3-11eb -b314-2e993bd83e31_story.html.

4. See Udani Samarasekera, "India Grapples with Second Wave of COVID-19," *Lancet Microbe* 2, no. 6 (June 2021), www.thelancet.com/journals/lanmic/article/PIIS2666-5247 (21)00123-3.

5. "Oxygen Concentrators during COVID-19," UNICEF China, August 3, 2021, www.unicef.cn/en/stories/oxygen -concentrators-during-covid-19.

6. "Facts about Gastroschisis," Centers for Disease Control and Prevention, www.cdc.gov/ncbddd/birthdefects/gastroschisis .html, accessed April 10, 2023.

7. See Katherine H. Campbell and Joshua A. Copel, "Chapter 20 - Gastroschisis," in *Obstetric Imaging: Fetal Diagnosis and Care*, 2nd ed., Joshua A. Copel et al., ed. (Philadelphia, PA: Elsevier, 2018), www.sciencedirect.com/science/article/pii/B 9780323445481000206.

8. See Naomi J. Wright, Augusto Zani, and Niyi Ade-Ajayi, "Epidemiology, Management and Outcome of Gastroschisis in Sub-Saharan Africa: Results of an International Survey," *African Journal of Paediatric Surgery* 12, no. 1 (January–March 2015): 1–6, www.ncbi.nlm.nih.gov/pmc/articles/PMC 4955493.

9. Cited in Muthukurisil Arivoli et al., "Multidisciplinary Development of a Low-Cost Gastroschisis Silo for Use

in Sub-Saharan Africa," *Journal of Surgical Research* 255 (November 2020): 565–74, www.sciencedirect.com/science /article/abs/pii/S0022480420303103.

10. "PIH's Five S's: Essential Elements for Strong Health Systems," Partners in Health, June 30, 2021, www.pih .org/article/pihs-five-ss-essential-elements-strong-health -systems.

11. See Arivoli, "Multidisciplinary Development."

12. Arivoli, "Multidisciplinary Development."

13. See "Drs. Hotez and Bottazzi Nominated for 2022 Nobel Peace Prize," Texas Children's, https://www.texaschildrens people.org/hotez-bottazzi-nominated-2022-nobel-peace -prize, accessed April 10, 2023.

Chapter 18: How Do We Measure the Worth of a Life?

1. See Elizabeth Ogunbamowo, "Uganda Loses First Medical Doctor in Ebola Outbreak," *The Cable*, October 1, 2022, www.thecable.ng/uganda-loses-first-medical-doctor-in-ebola -outbreak.

2. See "Ebola Disease," World Health Organization: African Region, www.afro.who.int/health-topics/ebola-disease, accessed January 23, 2023.

3. See "2014–2016 Ebola Outbreak in West Africa," Centers for Disease Control and Prevention, www.cdc.gov/vhf/ebola /history/2014-2016-outbreak/index.html, accessed April 10, 2023.

4. See "Ebola Outbreak 2014–2016 - West Africa," World Health Organization, www.who.int/emergencies/situations /ebola-outbreak-2014-2016-West-Africa, accessed April 10, 2023.

5. See J. Sylvester Squire et al., "The Ebola Outbreak and

Staffing in Public Health Facilities in Rural Sierra Leone: Who Is Left to Do the Job?" *Public Health Action* 7, no. 1 (June 2017): S47–S54, www.ncbi.nlm.nih.gov/pmc/articles /PMC5515564; see also "National Ebola Recovery Strategy for Sierra Leone: 2015–2017," Government of Sierra Leone, http://ebolaresponse.un.org/sites/default/files/sierra_leone _recovery_strategy_en.pdf.

6. See Andrew Green, "Obituary: Sheik Humarr Khan," *Lancet* 384, no. 9945, August 30, 2014, www.thelancet.com/journals /lancet/article/PIIS0140-6736(14)61428-8/fulltext.

7. Paul Farmer, *Fevers, Feuds, and Diamonds: Ebola and the Ravages of History* (New York: Farrar, Straus and Giroux, 2020), 481.

8. Joshua Hammer, "My Nurses Are Dead, and I Don't Know If I'm Already Infected," in *The 2016 Best American Magazine Writing*, ed. Sid Holt (New York: Columbia University Press, 2016); see also https://doctorsheikhumarrkhanfoundation.org /dr-khan-article-by-matter-p215-90.htm.

9. Farmer, *Fever, Feuds, and Diamonds*, 481.

10. "The Ebola Epidemic: The Keys to Success for the International Response: Hearing before the Subcommittee on African Affairs" (Washington, D.C.: U.S. Government Publishing Office, December 10, 2014), www.foreign.senate .gov/imo/media/doc/121014_Transcript_The%20Ebola%20 Epidemic%20the%20Keys%20to%20Success%20for%20the %20International%20Response.pdf

11. See Helen Branswell, "Ebola Experimental Vaccine Trial May Begin Soon in Uganda," STAT, September 29, 2022, www.statnews.com/2022/09/29/ebola-experimental-vaccine -trial-may-begin-soon-in-uganda.

12. Farmer, *Fevers, Feuds, and Diamonds*, 485.

13. See Andrew Pollack, "Opting Against Ebola Drug for Ill African Doctor," *New York Times*, August 12, 2014, www.ny times.com/2014/08/13/world/africa/ebola.html.

14. See Hammer, "My Nurses Are Dead."

15. See Sanjay Gupta and Danielle Dellorto, "Experimental Drug Likely Saved Ebola Patients," CNN Health, August 5, 2014, www.cnn.com/2014/08/04/health/experimental-ebola-serum; Linda Mobula, "When Potentially Lifesaving Drugs Are Both Experimental and in Very Short Supply: A Clinician's Story from the Front Lines of the Battle against Ebola," *American Journal of Tropical Medicine and Hygiene* 93, no. 2 (August 2015): 210–11, www.ncbi.nlm.nih.gov/pmc/articles /PMC4530735/.

16. Farmer, *Fevers, Feuds, and Diamonds*, 486.

17. Cited in Ramat Toyin Kamorudeen, Kamoru Ademola Adedokun, and Ayodeji Oluwadare Olarinmoye, "Ebola Outbreak in West Africa, 2014–2016: Epidemic Timeline, Differential Diagnoses, Determining Factors, and Lessons for Future Response," *Journal of Infection and Public Health* 13, no 7 (July 2020): 956–62, https://pubmed.ncbi.nlm.nih.gov/32475805.

18. See "2014–2016 Ebola Outbreak in West Africa," Centers for Disease Control and Prevention, www.cdc.gov/vhf/ebola /history/2014-2016-outbreak/index.html#, accessed March 1, 2023.

19. See Exodus 33:12–21.

Chapter 19: Wisdom, Worship, and Olaf

1. See 2 Timothy 2:14, 16, 23.

2. See Matthew 10:16; Luke 4:28–30.

3. Nehemiah 6:3 NRSVue.

4. See Nehemiah 5.

Chapter 21: A New Table

1. See "Golden Rule 1961," Norman Rockwell Museum, www
   .nrm.org/images/mobile-app/gr/gr.html, accessed April 10,
   2023.

Appendix

1. I also recommend curating your social media follows to reflect
   who you want to become. Who you follow and listen to on
   social media can profoundly affect your heart posture toward
   your neighbors, even when you don't want it to. I curated
   my feeds to see only certain people and then followed a lot
   of people of races, upbringings, and religions different from
   mine. And it changed me deeply toward solidarity. Social
   media exerts tremendous power over us. Pay attention to
   what you read or allow on your feed. I recommend following
   Drs. Madhu Pai and Catherine Kyobutungi (Twitter) for
   decolonizing global health conversations, Drs. Malcolm Foley
   and Jemar Tisby (Twitter) for American evangelical antiracist
   conversations, and Jasmine Holmes (Instagram) for great
   book recommendations from Black authors, including her
   own powerful books.